TURKEY

SYRIA

ANON

IRAQ   IRAN

YP   PAKISTAN

                              INDIA   BANGLADESH   HONG KONG   TAIWAN

                                                    THAILAND

ETHIOPIA

UGANDA

RWANDA   KENYA   MALAYSIA
URUNDI   SINGAPORE

TANZANIA

AMBIA   INDONESIA

SIA

KOREA

JAPAN

PHILIPPINES

AUSTRALIA

NEW ZEAL

45 YEARS
WITH PHILIPS

An industrialist's life

45 YEARS WITH PHILIPS

An industrialist's life

by

Frederik Philips

BLANDFORD PRESS
Poole   Dorset

First published in the English language in 1978 by
Blandford Press, Link House, West Street, Poole,
Dorset BH15 1LL.

Originally published in the Dutch edition
45 Jaar Met Philips
by Uitgeversmaatschappij Ad. Donker BV

World Copyright © Dr. Ir. F. J. Philips
Eindhoven 1976

ISBN 0 7137 0931 6

Photographs taken from Philips Central Photo Archive
Endpaper map shows world-wide outreach of Philips

Set in Monophoto Ehrhardt by Oliver Burridge
Filmsetting Ltd., Crawley
Printed and bound by Biddles of Guildford

Contents

How It Came About

It was only after a long internal debate that I decided to write this book of memoirs. Two considerations finally tipped the balance.

First of all, I realized that the years covered by this book, from 1930 to the present day, have been eventful ones for all businesses. Certainly, those in charge of Philips, with its world-wide ramifications, have had to face many difficulties. I have tried to describe how we responded to them and what measures we took to overcome them. The leadership of a large concern is always a matter of team-work, even if some carry more weight in decision-making than others. It is not easy to assess one's own share in this process, but my personal aim has always been that Philips should be a constructive force—a part of the cure, not the disease, of the world.

My second reason for deciding to write is my hope that this book may encourage young people to use their talents in some business—perhaps, even, a multi-national one—based on the conviction that the free enterprise system is the best available and is a source of strength to society. Such enterprises are not always in favour with young people today, but I believe that their energy and imagination would find ample scope in one of them, whether at home or abroad. Working with a great variety of people to spread prosperity all over the world is a healthy challenge for anyone.

Naturally, my life has been continuously interwoven with the Concern which bears my name. So I have tried to give some idea of what happens inside Philips. The conduct of any enterprise, whether large or small, is determined by people of flesh and blood, with all their faults and virtues.

My vantage point, as I write, is that of one man, myself. I am very aware that an enterprise only really exists by grace of the common thought and action of many, and our Board of Management, which has ten members, seems to me to have been a good example of such teamwork. But this book is primarily concerned with my own life in Philips. I have never kept a diary, nor did I make notes through the years, so I have had to rely on my memory. As it is in man's nature to forget or repress the disagreeable more easily than the pleasant, it is quite possible that the total picture has become somewhat rosier than it really was. But then I never intended this to be a strictly factual account. Wherever I could I have checked dates and details, and I am grateful to those who provided me with information, particularly our Records Office. But my aim has been merely to give my personal impression of events, and this does not deny others the right to have a totally different idea of what happened. I am also grateful to my friend Leo Ott, who worked with me on the Dutch edition, and to Peter Hintzen, Garth Lean and Ailsa Hamilton, who have worked on this English version.

It has been a great privilege to be involved for so many years in such an intensely interesting and unique concern, and I am grateful for the friendship which I have received from so many in the course of that work. I thank God for His help, and not least for giving me the seemingly indestructible health which the task requires. A harmonious family have been a great support—and above all my wife, who has stood by my side in good times and ill for over fifty years. That is why I dedicate this book to her.

Eindhoven
April 1974–March 1977

Chapter 1

On My Way to 'The Factory'

One beautiful day in September 1923 I walked along the Old Delft Canal. I was on my way to the barber to get my head shaved. This unusual step filled me with insecurity. I was enrolling at the Delft Technical University, and the student initiation for freshmen demanded it. I knew that I would lose, along with my hair, some of the protection which had surrounded me up till then.

After the barber, I presented myself at the main building of the University. I scribbled the required signatures and handed in the necessary documents. But immediately after these formalities, I was taken with some of my fellow victims into another hall. 'Taken' is putting it mildly. It was hard to tell whether you were kicked or beaten to your destination. The moment the door was slammed behind you, you were at the mercy of the mob, and in the club building where we went next it became even worse. I had arrived in a world completely different from the one I was accustomed to, a world apparently without shelter or compassion.

In my native town of Eindhoven, in the province of Brabant, things had been very different. There, I was the only son of the manufacturer Anton Frederik Philips. He had one passion, the factory: a passion conceived when he started helping his brother Gerard to make lamps in 1894. After his marriage he had to share his life with his family as well, but the firm, which expanded with tremendous force, absorbed his attention so totally that from my earliest childhood I heard him talking about 'The Factory'. He had always talked about it with Mother, who shared his interest with all her heart, and as soon as we could understand he talked with his three children—my elder sister Annetje, myself, and my younger sister Jetty.

In those years it was regarded as self-evident that I too would later be involved in 'The Factory'. But my father was not the kind of man to hand me privileges easily on a plate. I would have to earn my place at Philips. He wanted me to be an engineer like his brother, so my road to the business would lead via Delft. But it had, of course, to start in Eindhoven, with primary school and then the local high school.

You can imagine the kind of town Eindhoven was in those years if you realize that our high school was only a recent creation. Until then an Eindhoven boy who wanted a secondary education had had to go to the neighbouring town of Helmond. But now our new high school—a pleasant municipal institution, where boys of all backgrounds mingled in small classes—could offer the complete course!

My parents felt it was far from ideal that I had seen little more than my small home town. They encouraged me when, at the age of fourteen, through friendship with the two Visser 't Hooft boys—Wim, who later was Secretary General of the World Council of Churches, and Hans, who became a medical doctor—I went to one of the boys' camps of the Netherlands Christian Student Association, which were then popular. For several consecutive years I took part in these camps, and there a new world opened up for me. I liked the atmosphere enormously, and people I met there contributed to the growth of faith in me and in many other boys. At Delft, I met many friends from these camps.

My engineering studies had once been briefly in doubt. When my parents were making a trip abroad, I stayed with Herman van Walsem, one of my father's close colleagues and a lawyer *pur sang*. He told me such fascinating stories about his profession that I talked with my father about it. This upset him. He called Van Walsem in: 'What the devil are you doing meddling in my son's future? That boy has got to become an engineer!' So to Delft I went.

At that time very few industrialists sent their sons to college. Most of the students were from families with academic or military backgrounds. For in the last century it had been the successful merchants who had started manufacturing industries, and such parents thought it more important for their sons and successors to learn the trade in day-to-day practice. So I was a rare specimen. Also, 'Brabanders', men from the South like me, were few and far between in Delft.

I had already got to know the city before my enrolment as a student, and had even enjoyed a foretaste of student life, in the period of fine weather after my final school exams. I cannot imagine more wonderful days than those after you have received the final school diploma. It is as though a heavy load has fallen off. Full of illusions, you march into the future. And your immediate future consists of a long, care-free holiday.

During this holiday I was unexpectedly offered tickets for the Student Corps celebrations at Delft, which take place every five years. That year a play was staged, *The Assailants of the Tower* by Herman Teirlinck, which left an indelible impression on me. It was enacted on a beautiful summer afternoon in the flag-bedecked Market Square, with the impressive tower as background. The theme was the struggle between spirit and matter. Each time the Spirit got the upper hand, he climbed one battlement higher up the tower. This leading role was taken by an old friend who, however, was not exactly a mountaineer, so when he had to climb up the tower by rope ladder, a sailor—employed for the occasion—impersonated him. In those days microphones and amplifiers were not yet in use, so there were plenty of musicians and singers instead.

As I walked through the city, where people still moved about mainly on foot, by bicycle or by the steam train, I dreamed of my future as a student there. The canals reflected the sun, and were lined by lime trees and elms adorned with the fresh green of the young summer, setting off the beautiful old homes and buildings. And what a festive sight were the student body officials riding in open carriages, the horses decorated with plumes, slowing down their trot to cross the picturesque bridges!

Among the third-year students I discovered a friend from Helmond who was escorting his sister. That was not much fun for him, so I took care of her, and joined their group on various occasions. I did not miss a single item in the celebrations. We danced until the early morning; and the weather could not have been better. It was an ideal week.

When I entered student life in September things were very different.

Mechanical Engineering

On that day, when I walked from the barber to the Technical University, I was half-way on my road to 'The Factory'. Enrolling in the department of mechanical engineering was the result of a choice I had made long before.

It is difficult to believe today that at that time the Philips factories were making little else than light bulbs. After World War I they had just started making radio valves, and it was not until later that they went into radio parts such as loudspeakers and trickle chargers, and finally radio sets. So in the twenties physicists, chemists and electrical engineers were involved in the laboratory, but although mechanical engineers were required for the construction of lamp-producing machines, very few were employed in actual production.

However, in choosing my speciality I had had to take into account both my opportunities within Philips and my own abilities. I am strongly inclined toward the visual. Everything translates itself immediately into a picture in my mind. My gift is for the interplay of lines and the construction of things rather than for solving theoretical and mathematical problems. With this bent, it would have been hard for me to equal the exceptionally able electrical engineers and physicists in Philips. But in design I felt strong; and whatever you design has eventually to be built. So I had chosen mechanical engineering.

A freshman is always wrong. Because I soon accepted this as a matter of course, I got through this freshman period without any traumas, even though some of the older students made it plain to me that my presence at the Corps celebrations in the summer had been highly irregular. My own year elected me president of our student executive, which I considered a distinction for a Brabander.

In the Delft Student Corps the executive offices were taken seriously and the ordinary members took part with zest. A strict check was kept on proper administration, as I found out myself. In my second year I was nominated treasurer of the Alpine Club. My predecessor fumbled into my hands a tiny notebook, in which was recorded who was to pay and how much. I concluded that this was the way to do it, so my accounts became a mess, for which I was severely taken to task. Yet I was subsequently made Secretary; possibly the members thought that this time I would do better. In 1924 I also became an executive member of the student dramatic society. For two years I belonged as well to the first editorial board of De Spiegel, the student paper, which survives to this day. This was of permanent value to me, as was my part in editing the Year Book of 1928. The work on this paper—the board meetings and the selection and editing of the copy—are among my best memories of those student days. I had to wrestle with the scarcity of good contributions and go through all the pressures of press work. As a result I later became greatly interested in the Philips publications, and I still follow De Philipskoerier and Philips News with close attention.

Looking back, I realize that friendships born in student days are among the best of your life. You make friends without any ulterior motives. If you like someone, you act accordingly. Such friendships last, whether people are successful in later life or not.

As students we were completely uninterested in politics. The only exception was when, in 1925, the proposed treaty between Holland and Belgium concerning the Moerdijk Canal was being debated. This issue caused turmoil, even in Delft. Otherwise politics were taboo, and this fact filled us with pride. Politics were a matter for the hostile world outside;

later we would have to pay attention to them, but in our university years we refused to get involved—a contrast to today.

I did not work very hard in the first year—that would have been contrary to custom! The idea was that this year should be spent adapting to new surroundings and to a different way of studying. So I did not attend many lectures, though I did work at the drawing board and in the laboratory. Nor did I sit for any exams at the end of that year.

The atmosphere in the town of Delft felt to me different from Brabant, where everything was sunnier and more easy-going. In Delft the streets seemed dark and the cobbles perpetually wet in the frequent rain and fog. There was also a difference in mentality. If you bumped by accident into someone on a street corner in Delft the usual remark was, 'Hey, look out!' In Brabant it would have been, 'What's the matter, old boy, had a bad night?'

It was in Delft that I began to realize how much Brabant meant to me. Although my parents had not originally come from there, I felt strong ties with Eindhoven and Brabant. At primary school, where I was with children from all social backgrounds, and through our gardeners and others, I learned to speak the Brabant dialect. And I began to understand how the people of Brabant had been neglected through the centuries in comparison with those in the United Provinces in the north of the Netherlands, which dominated the country. In my Delft years I used to go home for the weekend once every three weeks. As the train crossed the Moerdijk Bridge I felt happier. There Brabant was awaiting me. I was going home. And I have felt like that all my life.

Engaged and Married

During my second university year I got engaged to 'the woman of my life'. I met her at some regular dancing evenings which student friends of mine had started in The Hague. At one of these I saw Sylvia van Lennep for the first time. She was not without admirers; I had my rivals. But, after meeting her a few times, I was convinced she was meant to be my life's companion, and nothing made me doubt for a second that she would become my wife.

At Christmas 1924 this conviction was put to the test. Some of us went to Brussels to attend a traditional student occasion. It became a memorable party, and we got into such a happy mood that three of us decided to go on to Paris. My reasons were special. My sister Jetty was at boarding school there, and Sylvia van Lennep was also in Paris. Besides, I knew my father had to be in Paris on business. From the Gare du Nord I went straight to his hotel, and found him at breakfast. I told him that I had just arrived with two friends and that we wanted to stay a few days. 'Dad,' I concluded, 'can I have some money?' My request met with a satisfactory response, so we spent some happy days there.

After a *thé dansant* I proposed to Sylvia, somewhere on a bridge in the middle of Paris. This did not go as well as I had imagined. It was so unexpected, she said. The possibility of our getting married had never crossed her mind! She was very upset. Curiously, this brush-off did not greatly affect me. Together we walked to the Rue de Bourgogne. We stood still somewhere in front of a window, until someone began to knock violently against the glass, shouting, 'Circulez, s'il vous plaît!' We walked on. We parted. 'Don't worry,' I said, 'we'll see later . . .'

I was so sure that it would work out all right that I went that evening with my friends to the Place Pigalle, where we had a splendid time. Even when a fortune teller told me, 'You will not marry before 32!', I was not disturbed. I was firmly convinced that Sylvia van Lennep was meant for me.

Then came Carnival time. I took her with me to Breda and 's Hertogenbosch, and we had some wonderful walks in the woods near Eindhoven. But she, with her northerner's caution, refused to commit herself for fear she might be swayed by the spell of Carnival and the beauty of the woods.

Some months later our Delft dramatic society put on a play. I had a minor part, so I invited her. Sleep was in short supply before these performances. We did everything ourselves. The set had to be made, the props had to be found, and you had to rehearse. You would hardly catch sight of your bed for days. A ball followed the performance. Down below you danced. On the balcony you could talk peacefully with a girl. While we were discussing the play, I heard Sylvia say, 'If you were to ask me again now, I believe I would say yes.' But I did not respond. I was too tired to take it in.

Late that night seven of us bundled our girls into a big hired car and took them back to their homes in The Hague. We were longing for sleep. I went to my lodgings. At last I could get a decent rest! The next day I woke up at about noon. Thinking back over the talk with Sylvia, the key sentence came back to my mind and I suddenly realized that she had said yes! I jumped out of bed and wrote a note saying I would come and see her on the next Sunday. Sylvia replied that I must find a suitable pretext to visit her parents' home. Luck was with me. That Sunday our national eleven won the big football match against Belgium. I entered her parents' sitting room shouting at the top of my voice, 'Have you heard? Holland has won 5—o!' This broke the ice, and that same day we got engaged.

It was, however, an 'unofficial' engagement. I was just twenty and she was even younger. Our respective parents considered us very young. All right, then, an 'unofficial' engagement, but everyone in Delft knew about it. We were engaged for more than four years—much too long. But one advantage of an early engagement is that you get to know each other's friends well. Sylvia took part wholeheartedly in my Delft life, and at times acted in our dramatic society's plays.

After her final school examinations, Sylvia did not want to go to university, but chose social work instead. For some years she worked during the mornings in what was then called a 'babies' refuge', an institute for unmarried mothers and their children. There she looked after the babies, which she enjoyed and which was a splendid preparation for married life. My parents, who had initially had some reservations towards 'the Hague girl', appreciated her involvement in this work.

But all the travelling began to worry me. My fiancée lived in The Hague, eighteen kilometres away, and I used to go there by bicycle. Some of my friends had motor cars or rumbled around on heavy motor-cycles. I had long ago promised my father that I would never ride pillion on such a bike, and I kept that promise strictly. But I began to exercise a bit of pressure: 'Dad, so far I've kept my promise, but I can't go on like this much longer. Please let me have a vehicle of my own.' So I was allowed to buy a small four-seater Renault. A two-seater seemed to Father less than adequate. His view was that I should have a car, however small, in which I could take friends.

Fortunately, I never looked on wealth as a right. My student friends used to say, 'Look, Frits, if I had an old man with as much cash as yours, I would throw masses of parties!' But I never felt any desire to be lavish with money or to give extravagant parties. I enjoyed joining in when we were in the mood, but I never became a real 'club fanatic', perhaps because of my early engagement.

We were married in The Hague on 4 July 1929, after delightful celebrations. In Eindhoven we had organized an informal garden party in the woods, which was drowned out by a cloudburst but ended up cheerfully in a local hall. We had a cherry feast in Zaltbommel, and were invited to dinner parties by uncles, aunts and cousins in The Hague. Like the rest of the world, Holland was experiencing the full glory of an economic boom. Nobody was aware that the Great Depression would, in the following autumn, start in America and spread all over the world. I whole-heartedly enjoyed those days, as did my bride, whom I thought the prettiest girl in the world.

My Studies Completed

Engagement and marriage meant very much more than a mere inter-mezzo in my university days. All the same, my studies had to be finished. Just at the time of my 'unofficial engagement' I sat my second-year exam and failed—a fact which has sometimes been an encouragement to my sons! But at the time it was a heavy blow for the two of us, as it meant losing a year. Luckily, I was able to catch up most of the loss, and I finally won my engineer's diploma in 1929, after six years, which is not bad going even today.

As part of our studies, we had to do at least six months' practical work as mechanics in a factory. I went first to a machine factory in Breda, and later worked at a lathe at Alfred Herbert's machine tool factory in Coventry. Every morning at 7.30 I started work with the rest of the men, and I made the same product as them, although not as quickly. There I found out for myself how wonderful it is, when you have to do mono-tonous work, to hear the 5.30 whistle. I also worked for six weeks with Citroën in Paris, where I learned to understand mass production.

At Delft, those who gave a lot of time to the various student associations, and so did not follow lectures regularly, had to have recourse to *repetitors*, or private tutors. I came into that category, and I vividly recall the person-ality of Dr. E. H. M. Beekman, who was in his day 'the' *repetitor*. He had organized his one-man business perfectly. He gave private tuition until late in the evening, and students could leave their work in a kind of pantry, where the door stood open all night. Our papers were left on a pillar of the staircase, and from this derived the special Delft verb 'to pillar': 'I still have to pillar my drawing pad.' Beekman used to correct this work, with admirable speed, while teaching mathematics at a secondary school. Dur-ing the sessions at Beekman's there were sometimes twenty of us. It may not have been an ideal way to learn a subject, but most of us who turned to him got through our exams.

At Delft, too, I became interested in architecture. It was in my blood, and if I had not been linked with Philips I would probably have studied it full-time. My mother's father, G. J. de Jongh, had been the great builder of the Rotterdam harbours, and my father too had been very interested in building projects. I followed two years' lectures in utility architecture, mostly wood and steel construction, and made a drawing for a factory building. Later this love of architecture stood me in good stead. It would be hard to find a concern which has built as much as Philips, and it has been an asset to know something about it when preparing and judging new factory construction plans in various parts of the world.

I took my Master's exam in June 1929, and my engineering degree was to be obtained in December. Our wedding came in between. This made possible a wonderful honeymoon, driving through Italy, Switzerland and Austria—a journey which remains a source of marvellous memories for us.

In Military Service

We settled in Bloemendaal, near Haarlem, as this was convenient for the military service which was still ahead of me. Most of my fellow students preferred to get this over as soon as possible by serving as ordinary soldiers, but I thought an officer's training would be excellent preparation for anyone expected to lead men later on. One could draw lots on where to serve, or volunteer for a particular section. I had applied for special service as an engineer, and been posted to the Artillery Ordnance Factory at Hembrug near Bloemendaal. This had many advantages. I could continue in my own profession and gain experience in it. Also I was not required to live in barracks and had only to keep normal working hours. These were most satisfactory, starting at 7.30 a.m. and ending at 4 p.m., with half an hour's lunch break.

I was posted to the cartridge factory, and given sufficient responsibility to interest me without having to carry an inordinately heavy load. The manager, I. L. E. Ornstein, was an excellent man. He was strict, which I thought an advantage, and I learned a lot. Soon I was made assistant to the head of the tool making section, and after some time I succeeded him. This gave me insight into planning, as the tools had to be absolutely on schedule if the factory was to keep working. We made dies for the manufacture of machine gun cartridges, which were mass-produced in enormous quantities. I learned there to make time studies, and saw how different people are from each other. One person might produce 125 units with the greatest possible ease, whereas another managed only 95 in the same time in spite of great effort.

It was also my first experience of handling men. At Hembrug the workers were a very mixed lot. People with strict religious convictions operated lathes next to others whose views were deep red. Then there were the regional differences. People from different country neighbour-hoods had little liking for each other or for Amsterdam folk, and others would never willingly live outside the centre of Amsterdam. So I was dealing with all sorts of people. I began, when I arrived on the job, by saying 'good morning' to everyone, which had not been the custom up till then.

Part of my job was to achieve adequate production. But the piece rate system then in use offered people little incentive. Whenever people ex-ceeded their assigned target, the rates were adapted to the improved achievement, a practice called 'levelling up'. Naturally no one troubled to produce too much. In order to get better production, it was essential that the rates be guaranteed for a certain period, however much people pro-duced. I was able to persuade the management that this was necessary, and that they should let me work it out in practice, on the clear condition that the rates would be left unaltered for a year. This meant, of course, that the rates had to be calculated accurately and honestly in the first place.

The introduction of the new system was an invaluable experience. At first people did not trust it, but when it became clear that there was to be no more 'levelling up', production began to soar continuously until some workers produced forty per cent more. This meant considerable extra earnings. Besides, people began to enjoy their work more. They began to think out faster ways of working while retaining quality, and took all kinds of initiative. It was an interesting time for the employees and for me. But after I had left there were questions in Parliament, alleging that the Ordnance Factory workers were being forced to increase production, and the piece rate system was again modified in such a way that it offered no challenge to anyone.

As might have been expected, the Communists branded me 'the factory boss's son'. A sheet called *The Ordnance Worker*, which said that the lamp king's son was busy exploiting the Ordnance Factory workers, was sold at the factory gates. But the workers took such statements with a pinch of salt, as the following incident shows.

May 1, 1930, Labour Day, on which people did not work, was coming up, and we suddenly got a big order from the Navy. Two destroyers were leaving for the Netherlands East Indies and had to take supplies of am-munition with them. Our tool making section was given a rush order for punches for four-inch cartridge cases. These punches could only be made on our two biggest lathes, which were operated by very skilled workers who both happened to be convinced Communists. The head of the cartridge factory predicted that these two men would not be willing to work on May 1st. I replied, 'Anyway, I'm going to put it up to them. The only thing I risk is a no.' So I went to them, and what was their answer? 'Well, Lieutenant Philips, if you think it's necessary, we'll come. Granted, it will be the first of May. But there will be another May Day next year.'

At Hembrug I also learned to understand something of the official mind. As I was a government servant myself on this job, I later found it easier to follow the thought processes of government officials. I tried in Hembrug to carry out my duties with exactness, but sometimes I made mistakes. We put out a lot of work to small suppliers, and how I squeezed them at times! I tried to force their prices down to the last cent, using the usual method: 'Sir, you are working for the Government. Your price must be the lowest possible. If you do not accept my offer, you won't get the order!' I have since realized that this was not the best way. Subcontractors often only had one customer: us. Even though I calculated accurately what our own cost would be for the same process, I sometimes arrived at prices which did not allow for a penny of profit, and I thought I was clever if I managed to get work done by subcontractors for those prices. When you are twenty-five, you tend to think too easily that you know too much. I was sufficiently punished for this youthful enthusiasm when it was my turn, some years later, to submit tenders to the big Government Posts and Telegraph Company.

During this time I also got to know the mentality of the Defence Ministry and of military men, whose approach is very different from that of business people. They see different priorities. They are not interested in keeping this or that company going. In the Ordnance Factory we sometimes had great difficulties because the military authorities felt absolutely no responsibility for what was, after all, a state-owned enterprise. Their basic philosophy was that an order must be placed with the lowest bidder.

I enjoyed my job there and made good friends, among the officers, engineers and others. I also won Ornstein's confidence, and since I had got my degree by specializing in tools and machine tools, I became his adviser for the procurement of such equipment. When this period was over, I was sure that both by selecting mechanical engineering as my subject and by doing my military service in the Ordnance Factory, I had made a good choice.

After I was 'demobbed' Sylvia and I moved to Eindhoven, where on 1 December 1930, I was to start in the Philite factory. So I was summoned by my father to discuss my annual salary. He opened the negotiations:

'Well, Frits, what do you think?'

'I think I should get 3,500 guilders.'

'Come on! All young engineers who start here begin with 2,400 guilders. Why should I pay you more?'

'Well, you should take into account that I have had a full year's practical experience—not just any experience, but experience in line with the job I am to do here. I believe I'm worth 3,500 guilders. Besides, other men who have been with me at Hembrug are getting that much elsewhere. Those fellows don't know their job any better than I do.'

'Yes . . . yes . . . perhaps you're right.'

'It might look odd if I applied for a job somewhere else, mightn't it?' He grinned a bit.

'All right, then let's start at 3,500 guilders.'

So our first talk of this kind ended. I had the feeling that my father appreciated my salesmanship. I had not sold myself too cheaply. And that was how I arrived in 'The Factory'.

Chapter 2

At the Philite Factory

The manager of the Philite factory was a chemist—the right man in the right place, as Philite, our brand name for a then common type of synthetic material, was a chemical product. But it was now vital to have an uninterrupted flow of parts for our increasing production of radio sets, so there was a need for someone who would co-ordinate production and see that delivery deadlines were kept; and this became my responsibility.

I tackled my new job with energy. The plant had just been considerably extended, and Philips generally was expanding fast, with the Dutch factories already employing 28,000 people. The Philite factory had its own atmosphere, as it still has today. It worked round the clock, as the hydraulic moulding equipment and other expensive tools had to earn their keep, and continuous production was needed to reduce waiting times and meet delivery dates.

We produced both for domestic and construction needs, radio parts being our main product. We made the fronts and backs of sets, and then complete cases, as well as loudspeakers. Plastic was then unknown. Philite was a type of Bakelite and used a process invented by the Belgian chemist Baekeland at the beginning of this century. The raw materials were phenol and cresol, both derivatives of coal. These were put into the mould in powder form, sometimes pre-pressed into pastilles which contained standard quantities, to save powder and reduce the amount of dust. A corresponding counter-mould was pressed against the mould, and the material was melted by heat and a pressure of two hundred atmospheres. Then the result had to be 'baked' for some minutes in order to harden. After this, the press could be opened and the product taken out to be polished and finished. The only noise in this otherwise quiet process was the cleaning of the moulds by blasts of compressed air.

Our press operators had to be extremely skilled and precise because of the varied requirements of our customers. Philite products for the X-ray factory had to be made with special care, to withstand very high voltages. This meant that they had to be pressed very tightly and evenly so that there would be no cracks or bubbles.

This work put me among machines, but especially among people. I got on well with the manager, Roelof Houwink, and with the other engineers and department heads, the foremen and press operators. Together we tried to establish systematically which problems were most apt to occur, and to search out the causes of waste. But, above all, I concentrated on getting the work better organized so that we could deliver our products to the radio factory on time, for if any one of our parts was late, it stopped the assembly line of the set concerned. Here my experience at the Ordnance Factory was a great help.

One aspect of continuous production was that I often had to be on the job at night, especially when we were starting to make some new product. This gave me a chance to pay special attention to certain processes, which was often impossible in the rush of the day. The nightly trial runs also provided an opportunity for closer contact with the workers, and more time for talking. To walk through a department when it was not fully working had other advantages as well. I could see clearly whether order and cleanliness were being maintained, where there were leaks and where the press powder, costly even then, was being wasted.

During these first years with Philips I also got to know some of the non-technical aspects of the company. I began to notice how work was done within a department, and the relationships between departmental chiefs, foremen and production workers. I became familiar with piece rates and how they were calculated. I had to find out where unfairness arose and how to remedy it. I had to hire, assess and promote employees, and some-times unfortunately to dismiss them. As we were supplying other fac-tories and departments, I got to know them, too, and the people in them. Every newcomer to the Philips management, even today, goes through this type of training.

As I became familiar with the system of payment in the Philite factory I ran into some trouble—for the first time, but not the last, in my career. The director in charge of the company's social and personnel policy, Z. T. Fetter, was a man of impeccable fairness who dealt with me not as the boss's son but as any other Philips engineer. When a worker made a special effort I wanted to give him a reward, in money or time off. Fetter was absolutely against this. I insisted, but he did not budge. 'You have to consider the rules of the company, and they do not allow this kind of thing. You can't get around that,' he said. Of course he was right. But at times I found it difficult.

After six months I got the Philite factory production properly organized.

Delivery deadlines were kept, provided we received the moulds on time, which did not always happen. Making moulds is not simple. They are of very hard steel, because of the heavy pressures they have to stand, and a lot of craftsmanship is involved. They were made in the tool making section of the machine works, so both the Philite and radio factories depended on this section for meeting their schedules.

So I went to see the Assistant Managing Director responsible for this operation, P. F. S. Otten. Otten was married to my elder sister Annetje, so I knew him as Frans. I suggested to him that he should entrust my job in the Philite factory to someone else so that I could try and reorganize the tool-making section according to a modern system. The man I suggested was my own immediate subordinate. But Otten knew that a good second-in-command is not always the best leader, and he appointed instead a man who had been doing good work in another department.

In the new section, too, my Hembrug experiences were useful. I had learned there to work with planning boards, a system which I now introduced in Eindhoven, so I knew at a glance where we stood with the various orders. It was evident that delays were occurring through lack of co-ordination and this, in turn, was causing trouble in other departments. As a result, departmental heads and foremen were taking superficial measures which alleviated difficulties momentarily, but which really shifted them from one area to another without solving them.

Planning schedules were not the complete answer. In one case, a toolmaker had worked all weekend on a stamping tool which was said to be urgently needed. This meant extra pay for him, but inconvenience as well. Some days later he noticed that his piece of work was still in the storeroom. When I heard of this I was furious. Naturally, his work had to be checked, hardened and finished, but if it had been so urgent that a man had to spend his Sunday on it, it should have been dealt with by 10 a.m. on Monday. To maintain a closer check on work planning I introduced red riders on the planning board for urgent jobs, indicating that deviation from the schedule was not allowed without consulting me. The plant manager, a hard worker and able engineer, had to get accustomed to the fact that a young pip-squeak had arrived with a new system. The result was that production in the toolroom, after half a year, was functioning excellently.

I was next sent to the machine works proper. There, among other things, machines were made for the automatic manufacture of lamps and radio valves, and production went up fast. My job there took much longer than six months.

Meanwhile I was confronted with a very difficult set of problems. The Great Depression, which began on that notorious Black Tuesday of October 1929 in Wall Street, hit Eindhoven mercilessly. In the first half of 1930 we did not feel the effects too much, but in the second half, things changed. Growth was arrested. Sales were reduced, even though in some departments there was still plenty of work. In my own section I soon felt the adverse winds with full impact.

In this rather difficult period when I was getting broken in at Philips my wife was a great help, because of her genuine interest in my work. This was all the more remarkable because her background was so entirely non-industrial. But she felt immediately at home in the Philips community and was also greatly interested in everything to do with her new surroundings, so I could discuss my problems with her. During my forty-five years with Philips her interest has never flagged. In that respect the history of the Philips family has repeated itself.

In 1930 our eldest child, Digna, was born, a delightful little girl who made us very happy. We had moved to Eindhoven, to one of the houses recently completed for engineers. A secondary school occupied two houses in the same block, and added to the friendly atmosphere of the neighbourhood. When our second child, Anton Frederik, was born in 1932, we treated the entire school to biscuits and sweets, a traditional Dutch way of including other people in the joy of a new arrival.

To be back in the town of my birth had many attractions. I met old friends with whom I had been scouting years before, and in the bowling club I found many Delft friends who were now employed by Philips. But my greatest delight was my young family, and I enjoyed seeing Digna grow up in the Brabant surroundings which were so familiar to me.

Trip to America

In 1931 my day-to-day work was interrupted by a trip to the United States. Today such a journey is a commonplace, but in those years it was the dream of every young engineer. In the preceding decade the USA had overtaken Europe in manufacturing methods. I think the Americans owed this extraordinary advance mainly to their success in training the young.

The young American nation, fused together from all the peoples of Europe, was filled with an indomitable urge to get ahead. Most immigrants had had few prospects in Europe. In 'God's own country', however, they were accepted as citizens at once. Their children were taught at school that America was the land of the future, where anybody could have a fair chance provided he was willing to work hard. They showed great energy and endurance, and realized that if they wanted to succeed, they had to learn their trades well.

American industry, too, had received a powerful stimulus during World War I when an enormous war production had to be achieved in a short space of time, forcing it to master mass production even more perfectly. Mass production had flourished before that in two fields particularly—the armaments industry and the manufacture of sewing machines. Singer had been 'the' sewing machine manufacturer for the entire world. A high standard of precision had to be maintained. Buyers demanded absolute certainty that these machines would work perfectly, even in the remotest villages of the least advanced countries, and that spare parts would fit. Later, automobiles became a mass product. In the twenties the automobile industry became the engine of all industrial development in America. It pulled in its wake affiliated industries such as steel, upholstering, painting and many others.

As young engineers at Eindhoven we had read a lot about this, particularly since the Americans produced much scientific and technological literature. In my own line of machine tool making, the Americans had overtaken us in Europe in many respects. They built their machines with a more liberal hand, daring to use materials abundantly, unlike the Germans, who calculated everything so minutely that their end products tended to be rather sparse.

So when in 1931 my father went to America and asked me to go too, I naturally seized the opportunity. He was accompanied by Herman van Walsem and Emil Hijmans, our leading patents expert. Their programme consisted of a series of negotiations. As I was not involved, I was able to make my own schedule, and I visited machine tool plants with such famous names as Warner & Swasy, Cincinnati, and Gould & Eberhard, as well as other great companies like General Electric and the Radio Corporation of America.

It was a shock to see the effects of the Great Depression in America. I saw factories in which only one in three machines was working. On the street corners people were selling apples in order to earn at least something. In that hard country, where social benefits such as unemployment relief were unknown, people were thrown into abject poverty. I had dark forebodings that the Depression would soon have similar effects in Holland, even if they would be mitigated a little by our social policy.

The well-known aeronautics factory of Pratt & Whitney at Hartford was a frightening example. This factory had been considerably expanded just before the Depression had set in. So the space available was about eight times larger than necessary. Nonetheless the plant made a deep impression on me because of its enormous size. In the end Pratt & Whitney managed to survive and when, years later, I visited this plant again, I found a strange thing had happened. Its size no longer impressed me, although it was the same factory, for in the meantime, the scale had been enlarged everywhere.

I was also struck by the difference in size between the American giants of those days, like General Electric and Westinghouse Electric, and Philips, which was working only with low voltage electricity. Today these firms are much the same size.

In this connection, I think of a conversation which my father had in 1934 with David Sarnoff, President of the Radio Corporation of America. Sarnoff came to Eindhoven, where he visited our factories and particularly the laboratory. My father introduced him to some of his associates. 'Well, Anton, I think your staff is a staff of babes,' said Sarnoff. My father's reply was immediate: 'Yes, David, and that's just what I'm so proud of.'

During my visit to America I was interested in plants manufacturing the kind of machinery which we were using ourselves, and I was impressed by the openness of the Americans. I could never detect any tendency to conceal experience or knowledge. So I soon discovered that American industry relied more on working experience than on complex calculations. One example of this relates to some work I had done during my Delft studies. As a graduation assignment I had designed a shaper— a well-known subject in machine construction. My calculations had soon convinced me that a very high surface pressure would occur in an important part of the machine. I concluded that the part concerned must be made three times bigger if it was to meet the requirements the professor had listed. As far as I then knew, such an implement did not yet exist, and I had doubted whether its construction was practicable. In Cleveland in 1929 there had been an exhibition of machine tools, which one of the Philips managers visited. I had asked him to send me all available catalogues and folders about this type of machine. When these papers reached me, I had seen with surprise—and satisfaction—that people in America had started to make that particular part as large as possible. After careful study of the diagrams, I was convinced that I was on the right track, and, in fact, my professor was quite happy with it.

My trip to America was two years later, and I visited a well-known shaper factory. I asked the manufacturer why he had only in recent years resorted to the heavier construction, and told him that my first calculations had pointed in the same direction. To my astonishment he remarked that they never spent much time on calculations. 'We have made these machines for years, and noticed that this particular part wore out quickest. That's why we decided to make it as large as possible.' It was a strange feeling when this manufacturer introduced me to his son with these words, 'This is Mr. Philips from Holland. He knows more about the construction of shapers than we do.' Americans are very polite, especially when meeting a potential buyer of their machines!

My father's negotiations were finished, and it was time to go home. Again we went by ship, something strange to remember in this age of air travel. The departure of the old *Statendam* for Rotterdam was quite an event, for we had got to know a lot of people, and they came to see us off. Champagne flowed and our section of the ship became a veritable party. It was a merry affair, such a departure, with presents coming in from all sides. In those days it was still a big thing to travel from continent to continent.

The *Statendam* was slower than the Cunard and Hamburg-American Lines ships, but the atmosphere on board was all the more pleasant for that. We met many interesting people, and the ship's cuisine enjoyed a high reputation. My father enjoyed dining well and taking a lot of time deciding the next day's menu.

If such journeys were expensive, they were worth it, and were as a rule only made for pressing business or family reasons. Our fellow passengers looked rather different from those with whom you travel by air today— no sweaters or blue-jeans!

The Storm Breaks

In 1931 the Great Depression broke over Philips. Sales diminished. Orders ceased. The drop in the sterling exchange rate caused big losses which were only partially covered by forward sales. This was the beginning of dark years for my father. If he wanted Philips to survive and to give employment to thousands in the future, small measures—like leaving vacancies unfilled—were not adequate. Philips had to dismiss large numbers of workers at a distressingly rapid rate. I had joined the Concern when it employed 28,000. In 1933 the total had fallen to 16,000. Only about 450 were working in the Philite factory, instead of 750, and the staff had to be pruned as well as the workers.

In those years unemployment benefit was still administered by the trades unions and was very meagre. That was bad enough, but the unemployed man had also to struggle against the terrible feeling that he was useless. The basis of his existence was threatened. Many were uncertain whether they could go on living in their own homes. Anyone who owned one had first to consume that part of his possessions before being eligible for relief.

No one knew how long it would last. Nobody—whether he had operated a lathe, or worked as an engineer or in the laboratory—could look forward to a date on which he could begin work again. For me personally there was another difficulty. When a man was given notice, he naturally did everything he could to keep his job. If all his endeavours failed, he wanted to see the manager, and at the Philite factory that was me. So he would request an interview with 'Mr. Frits', so that he could then tell his wife that he had not left anything undone. But I was as powerless as anybody else. I could only sympathize, which was small consolation to him.

The situation was aggravated because current ideas of how to combat depression all came down to one rigid rule—to cut all possible expenses and reduce labour costs to the bone. All inflation was considered evil. So the guilder was sacrosanct. Only in 1936 did Holland reluctantly leave the Gold Standard—one of the last of the so-called Gold Bloc to do so. We at Philips had been urging this for a long time and, when it happened, it helped us to re-employ many people.

Later I came to realize what a deep scar this long depression left in the United States and Europe. At the assemblies of Moral Re-Armament I made friends with workers from many countries. From them I heard what workers think about employers in clearer terms than I had ever heard in our own factories. In Eindhoven I was always the boss, and so people did not express their feelings about the managing class to me as quickly and as candidly as they might have. What they would say at times was, 'Our boss isn't all that bad, but in general they're a bunch of dictators who don't care.'

If you study history, it is clear that it is usually the ordinary man who is the one to suffer. Whether in times of starvation or war, from the Middle Ages to the Napoleonic wars, the little man has always borne the brunt. In times of pestilence it was the poor who were first affected, as they were unable to move and there was hardly any room for them in the hospitals. In times of recession they got kicked out first, and when harvests were bad, they were the first victims. When in the 19th century the Industrial Revolution started, people dared to hope for more work for hundreds of thousands, with new opportunities for all. But even that did not turn out quite so well, with repellent practices like child labour.

It was natural for the workers to organize themselves to try and force an improvement in conditions. But it is sometimes overlooked that in Holland the first social laws, including the Law on Child Labour, were initiated by Liberals, and that in Britain the improvements in the workers' lot were sometimes stimulated by enlightened employers. There, too, the first unions were started on a Christian, rather than a Marxist, basis. It is also easily forgotten that a man like Frederick Taylor, the pioneer of time and motion studies, did not intend to exploit the workers. His first concern was to see how the work could be done with the least possible effort. The fact that his principles have been wrongly applied and that the system has sometimes degenerated into checking up on people with a stop watch should not be blamed on Taylor.

I believe that many who work in industry and who feel at home there have found not only material security, but also the pleasure and satisfaction of achieving something together. And for them it is a tremendous blow to be made redundant. After the Depression of the thirties, I felt that we as industrialists must do everything in our power to avoid a recurrence of that kind of misery.

New Products

After some years, my work with Philips changed. I had started like any other engineer, but it appeared that I had some commercial talent—which was not surprising, perhaps, in Anton Philips' son. So I was put in charge of overseeing new products. Production at Philips had at first followed two main lines, lamps and radios, but gradually all sorts of new products were being introduced. The variety was soon so great that it was hard to see how they were connected with the original ones, but almost all, like the radio valve, had in fact been developed from the original light bulb. The connection with amplifiers and installations for addressing large crowds was clear. The 'Voice of the Giant', as we called it, was heard on many squares and meeting places far beyond Holland, as, for instance, a combination of microphones and unusually powerful amplifiers which was used in St. Peter's Square in Rome.

Other new articles, like mercury switches and rectifiers for charging batteries, were also being produced. It was discovered as well that direct current was particularly suitable for welding thin sheets. So we began to get involved in the welding industry, and manufactured welding rods. We also made something very different, the power-factor correction capacitors which improve the efficiency of electric circuits. By way of the talking film, for which we originally produced loudspeakers, amplifiers and sound heads, we ended up making film projectors. There were many such products, some with interesting possibilities, but in their diversity they all had one thing in common: they were produced on a relatively small scale which did not yield large profits. Nor was anybody in top management keeping an eye on them. Otten and his colleague O. M. E. Loupart, who were in charge of policy, had, during the Depression, had their hands full keeping the main products going. So it was decided that I should oversee these new ones.

I soon discovered that marketing these products was even harder than producing them. In matters of light and radio we were well equipped. We had a good sales organization of people who knew their subject thoroughly. But this was nearly worthless when it came to selling new products in a suspicious market which knew little or nothing about Philips. One problem was the lack of adequate documentation. We had no appealing folders, no catalogues or price lists suitable for our normal sales channels. So we engaged people to produce new material, put others to work to sell our amplifiers and projectors, and our activities expanded steadily.

One product which at first gave us a lot of trouble, but from which my father and Dr. Gilles Holst, the head of our laboratories, had great expectations, was the sodium lamp—a type of lighting especially suitable for roads. This project was also entrusted to me. When you pass the countless rows of sodium lights along the roads today, you have to admit that my father and Holst were right.

The sodium light, a gas-discharge lamp like the mercury lamp, was a result of our own research. Yet I discovered that our old, dyed-in-the-wool lamp hands, in contrast to Holst, were relatively sceptical about it. So its road to success was strewn with many obstacles, although the scientific basis of the product was sound. The light only contained one colour, yellow, the colour to which the human eye is most sensitive. If you shine yellow light on a road, all traffic is easy to see, even if the light is less strong than that of traditional lamps.

Getting the sodium lamp introduced as street lighting was a very difficult job, in which we were given a great deal of help by Professor Cees Gelissen, Managing Director of the Limburg Provincial Power Station, a man of unusual foresight. My father agreed with him that an extensive test should be made. Philips would furnish the lamps and fittings free of charge, the power station would provide current and install cables and poles. So in 1932, Limburg had the first road in Europe lit with these modern lamps. It was the best show room imaginable. Prospective buyers could see for themselves what the sodium lamp had to offer.

Orders began to come in, at first from other countries. In Britain, Purley Way near Croydon Airport was lit with sodium lamps. One spectacular order was the lighting of the Antwerp-Scheldt tunnel in Belgium, where no less than 1,100 of our lamps were installed. The opening of the tunnel in November 1933 was an important national event. Public enthusiasm was so great that the crowds began to walk through the tunnel before there was a chance for any ceremonial. As the man from Philips, I was one of the official party which could not return through the tunnel because it was entirely blocked by enthusiastic people. So our return trip was by ferry!

Our lamps gave light, it is true, but their span of life was lamentable. We had to replace so many defective lamps that a department was established at Eindhoven for that purpose alone. However, we learned from our mistakes, and the quality of the lamps improved strikingly. We also simplified the initially complicated manufacturing process.

My father was always intensely involved in 'the new lamp'. He believed that all roads should be lit in this modern way, and a lawyer employed in our secretariat, who had good connections with the Ministry of Public Works, was instructed to go into the question. But my father's relentless initiative also had its disadvantages. At one point nearly everybody was involved in this drive to get the sodium lamp established. People were working on it in the laboratory, in the pilot plant and in the sales department. Others were keeping in touch with the Public Works Department. Still others were studying the fittings and road surfaces. And my father would give the same problem to different people to solve, which caused trouble and misunderstanding. In the end, he had to admit that things could not continue like that, and asked me to co-ordinate the various efforts.

So I began to give exact instructions about who was to continue on the project and what each man should do, and kept trying with all the tact I could muster to dissuade my father, whenever he had new ideas about 'the lamp', from getting people working on it. Nevertheless it must be admitted that he did manage to focus a maximum of attention on the project.

The Trades School

Through my work in the machine tool plant I became involved in the Trades School, which I consider one of the most important of the Philips institutions in Eindhoven. It was started by my father in 1928, when he saw the need for a technical training course of our own.

Some form of technical education was in existence in Holland through crafts schools, of which we had one in Eindhoven. There boys were trained as carpenters, blacksmiths, plumbers and fitters, and in many other trades. But that was not what was needed in the Philips factories. We needed machine tool makers, men who were able to make moulds, and such people were extremely rare in Holland at that time. In the south they were simply non-existent. As a result, our mould-makers came from Germany, Czechoslovakia and Hungary. So my father wanted to train our own boys in this craft. He foresaw that, as we made an ever increasing range of products, the demands for such skills would also increase. He refused to believe that Dutch workers were less capable than foreigners.

We already had a training course for foremen, for which trainees were selected from our own personnel. A worker with good brains could get additional training with us, and would often qualify for a more skilled job.

The Trades School had a different aim—to train youngsters in such skills that they would be able to find their way inside the company without undue difficulties. Both theory and practice were consciously directed towards this aim.

As I had the supervision of the machine plants and various workshops, I was particularly interested in this training. For years I attended the deliberations of the examination committee, on which sat representatives from the metal workers' unions and other Eindhoven industries, but no one from Philips. I have also attended for years the occasions when diplomas were handed out to the boys.

The results of this education were excellent. Very few boys failed. The teachers worked hard, giving private lessons to the weaker trainees. The school was so popular that the number of applications greatly exceeded the places available, so we could select. It was possible for trainees to follow up their four-year course with a two-year supplementary one, after which they received diplomas as fully-fledged craftsmen. After that they could follow a draughtsman's course. A great many of the trainees rose far above being skilled workers. Some became designers, others became departmental chiefs, others continued their technical education, and a few became engineers. One became a university professor. Later, travelling abroad, I was delighted to meet former boys from the School in responsible posts in many countries. But, from our point of view, the finest aspect of the venture was that the level of craftsmanship in our own factories improved considerably.

The Trades School left people free. After completing their course the boys were free to work wherever they wanted, and we were not obliged to employ them. The school therefore qualified for state subsidies. Its diploma was valid everywhere. Other industrialists in and around Eindhoven employed the trainees, and if they did well there we were delighted.

The Metals Circle

An institution useful to Philips and active in a rather limited field was the so-called Metals Circle. It came into existence when I started to work on sales. I had to market all sorts of products and we could not afford to ask high prices, so we had to work efficiently and economically. I discovered that there was hardly any contact between the various machine shops within the Philips organization. It seemed to me imperative that the men managing the machine works and the other metal processing departments should meet regularly to exchange experiences, working methods and so on. So in 1932 the Philips Metals Circle was started.

Initially only a few people were involved. Apart from the management of the machine works at Eindhoven, only the managers of two or three of our other Dutch factories, and a man from the laboratory who was especially interested in metals, took part. I was chairman until the late fifties, a job I enjoyed. It was not long before managers from Britain, Germany and Belgium joined us, and then designers were also added. The Circle was primarily intended to enhance our collective technical knowledge, but, in fact, it yielded its best fruits in the field of human relationships. The various manufacturers got to know each other personally, which facilitated business contacts later on. And during the meetings everyone was keen to put something new on the table. The heads of the various workshops, who had worked in isolation until then, were proud to demonstrate to the Metals Circle how they had invented a press which would cause less waste or how their workers had developed a new machine.

One step forward was the standardization of machine tools. Previously the Philips factories had bought equipment at random. Now we tried to establish centrally what were the best machines for various jobs. The

Eindhoven machine works helped in this by testing everything. So it was agreed, for instance, that the clamp presses would henceforth be bought from Raskin in Belgium, and turret lathes from Herberts in Coventry. For ordinary lathes we chose Kaerger in Berlin and later Cazeneuve, a French plant. Milling machines were bought from America.

The Metals Circle did splendid work, and continues to do so. Even though there are frequent changes in membership, we sometimes have meetings with former members. I attended such a meeting in 1973, when we visited the Twente School of Technology. There we were received by Professor Dick van Hasselt who, as a young engineer, had been the Circle's secretary. At our request he continued his membership of this Circle after he became a professor. In the same way other university professors are also members. This has proved a good means of strengthening the ties between higher education and industry. For Philips this is easier than for others, because in the field of metallurgy we have no secrets. We find that the more we inform others about what we are doing, the more this advances the level of technical know-how in Holland. In the long run, this is to the advantage of us all.

Chapter 3

My Father and his Colleagues

I got an entirely new idea of my father through working at Philips. At home he had been Dad. In the Concern he was the leader, the entrepreneur who took decisions, who pushed and stimulated. As such he influenced me greatly. This story would be incomplete if I did not write at some length about him, not least because I am learning to see him more clearly as time passes. He was obviously an industrial genius, but in addition he had some special qualities. What struck everybody was his inexhaustible energy to initiate new ventures. He did not only think, he acted, and acted immediately. If he heard, for instance, that one of his staff had fallen ill, he would lift the phone at once and arrange that a bottle of red wine or something similar was taken to him. When he heard that someone in the company was having difficulties he would instruct his office to go into it and report within twenty-four hours. A reply like, 'I will have a look at him one of these days, Mr. Philips,' did not satisfy him. No question of that! I was inclined to see things a bit differently, especially if I felt the matter was not urgent. But as far as he was concerned, everything had to be done *now*.

'Yes, my boy,' he would say, 'you must see to it that you have as few preoccupations as possible. If you plan something, carry it out immediately. Then you can strike it off your list.'

A second principle which he propagated to all and sundry was, 'Check whether what has been agreed upon or ordered is carried out.' 'Follow it!' was his slogan, and each day he gave the example himself.

My father always wanted the firm to expand. Something new had to be starting all the time. New products had to be finding their way from the factory into the wide world. He was deeply interested in our laboratory, where scientists were continuously searching for answers. He would follow the progress of a project with keen interest, until a prototype or a final product landed on his desk—if, in fact, the thing was small enough for that. He did not like big objects. Once during a general discussion a staff member suggested that Philips might go into heavy electrical engineering, like General Electric. My father said curtly, 'That we should definitely not do. Don't ever raise this subject again. Any time spent discussing it is time wasted.'

He believed firmly in consumer goods. And he had a sharp eye for that kind of business. Whenever he was confronted with a new idea for a product, he would either say, 'That's going to be something!' and talk of it with great enthusiasm, or he would say, hesitatingly, 'I don't know . . .'. Almost always he was right.

He was particularly interested in those fields where we had been pioneers. Thus, he exerted himself to make the short-wave transmitter to the Netherlands Indies a success. The same was true of the X-ray equipment, which has never been a big earner for us, but whose usefulness for public health he recognized. And he was tremendously enthusiastic about our newly developed electric razor. When the first discussions about production took place, 50,000 was considered adequate for that year. My father said, 'What? Do you fellows think 50,000 is going to be enough? We're going to make 5,000 a day!' Everybody thought this was nonsense. Today we manufacture seven million a year, which is 23,000 each working day. He also had high hopes regarding television long before the Dutch people had any idea what it was all about.

My father's methods were both practical and simple. Of course he often had to negotiate, and often at high levels. For these occasions he prepared himself carefully. He knew exactly what points he wanted to discuss and always stuck to his main lines.

If he had an interview with a cabinet minister he was always ten minutes early, and used that time to talk to the doorman or secretary. Though he was not an easy man, he always had immediate and excellent contact with people of varying backgrounds. He was helped by his marvellous memory, a gift I would gladly have inherited from him. If my father had talked with a doorman about his family, he would still remember years afterwards that the man had told him about his eldest son having some difficulty with maths at school. He would immediately ask how the boy was getting on now at maths—and his interest was genuine.

His memory was, in a word, formidable. He found reading long reports boring and superfluous, so he would ask the writer to come and see him. Immediately he would say, 'You have written this report. I have heard about it and I readily believe that it is excellent. But please sum up its main points for me.' After listening he would perhaps ask for some explanations. Then the main points would be inscribed so sharply in his memory that six months later he could, if necessary, talk intelligently about them.

With increasing admiration I saw how accurately he judged people. After World War I he realized that Philips should take more care of its employees. He had got to know Fetter, who was then a government factory inspector, and asked him to join Philips to organize factory safety. 'Fetter, from now on you are my conscience as far as caring for our men is concerned,' he said. Fetter accepted, and did a splendid job. Later he was put in charge of the department of social and personnel affairs, along with G. F. Evelein. Fetter was to become, in 1946, Holland's Director General of Labour.

I remember another example from 1937. In that year there was a Colonial Exhibition in Paris. The botanical decorations in the Dutch exhibit were created by J. R. Koning, head of the parks and gardens department of the City of Amsterdam. He had praised to my father the work of his young assistant who, he said, was not only a good man but had done a first-class job. My father asked him,

'When the exhibition is over, do you have work for a young fellow like that?'

'Unfortunately not. I wouldn't know what to do with him.'

'Please send him along to me!'

The young man came to Eindhoven and made an excellent impression on my father. At the end of the interview my father said, 'Do you know something? You're going to sell diamonds for me!'

The young man was not to sell diamonds to jewellers, but diamond dies to camp factories, and he became a renowned expert in this field.

I always liked to observe the way my father dealt with people. At times he had to give people hell. The offender was summoned and would have a difficult half-hour, but he would never leave 'Mr. Ton's' room a defeated man. When he closed the door behind him, he would be determined to do better in future. My father never destroyed his associates. He built them up. People who felt that they did not get enough opportunities in their work under him may have seen this differently. Yet, on the whole, my father was right in his assessment of people's possibilities. He was slow to praise and did not hand out easy compliments. But people appreciated his word of recognition all the more when a big success was achieved. When, for instance, one of our men came back with an order for a new road lighting system, my father was enthusiastic and did not hide it. He also had his black sheep among the Philips flock, people who could do nothing right in his eyes and who naturally felt nervous when they were summoned. In the twenties a certain purchasing agent was always in hot water; but this did not prevent him from purchasing for us for many years.

Towards me, my father was definitely critical and deliberately sparse with praise. He wanted nothing more than that I, his only son, should find a place in the top management, but I had to earn that place myself. I sometimes felt that he wished that I had my sister Jetty's character. She was not the studying type, but was decisive, intelligent and quick-witted. At any rate, he realized that he had to teach me a great deal in order to make me into a good industrialist. One day, an engineer who had just returned from the States had to report to him. My father asked me to be present. I decided beforehand to be very attentive so as to learn how he would tackle such an interview and what questions he would put. The result was that I hardly opened my mouth. The visitor had not yet left the room when Father complained,

'Darn it, Frits, why didn't *you* ask that man anything?'

'I wanted to see how you handle a situation like this and what questions you ask such a man.'

'All right, but next time you must take part.'

A practical habit of his was to tip a hotel porter upon arrival and not wait until he left. He knew then that the man would do his best for him. He got on well with sleeping car attendants and always got the best berth. But being an impulsive man, he could fly off the handle if things were not as he wanted them. A *maître d' hôtel* would catch hell from him if the soup was cold. He would be angry with hotel porters if the car he had ordered did not arrive on time. On such occasions he could raise Cain. Nonetheless, he managed to leave such an impression that waiters and hotel porters have told me years later how warmly they remembered him.

When we children saw him in one of his rages, we loathed it. I swore to myself that I would never be like that. And yet . . . Before the war, I was in London where I had to catch a plane at Croydon Airport. I was told at the desk that the plane had already left, but when I went to the restaurant I saw it still standing on the tarmac. Furious, I went back to the desk. I told them in a voice which was far from low that if they had given my seat away to someone else, it would have been better to tell me straight. I really blew my top. And what did I see later in the gossip column of the British paper *Aeroplane*? 'Some continental foreigner—obviously myself —had made a terrible fuss in the reception hall.

My father had all sorts of hobbies. He farmed. He raised all kinds of animals, even a special breed of pigs. He kept ducks. He tried his hand at forestry. But his great love was art collecting. As he grew older this absorbed him more and more, and gave him ever greater satisfaction. He was always on the look-out for additions to his collections. Often I heard him say, 'Oh, shares? But you can't look at them! I would rather put my money into things I can hang on the walls. You can enjoy them every day.' He really did not buy so much to invest as to enjoy. With hindsight one can say, however, that putting his money into these things was a lot better than any alternative investment he could have made.

He did not concentrate solely on large objects. He collected in various fields according to his own method. Often he had to go to Paris for talks. He would arrive the evening before; negotiations would start early and be finished by 4 p.m. He would return by the 8 p.m. night train, and meanwhile visit a few antique shops on the left bank of the Seine. After the war, I went with him several times. Delft plates were cheaper there than in Holland, and we were very pleased with ourselves when we found something to our liking.

He liked to follow the important auctions. If he detected something he wanted, he wrote the sum he was ready to pay for it in the margin of the catalogue. He had unlimited confidence in the Eindhoven antiquarian, Frans Jeschar, who would buy for him. After such an expedition Jeschar would display the objects he had acquired in the conference room next to my father's office. My father would then call me in and say, 'Frits, come and have a look. Jeschar has bought a few things.'

Uncle Gerard

My father's earliest colleague was, of course, his brother Gerard, the founder of the firm. In my boyhood, Uncle Gerard and Aunt Joh had been familiar figures. They had no family, which may have been why they were a bit shy with us children. We, on our side, looked on them with a certain reserve, as when we visited them our clothes and finger-nails were specially checked to stand up to Aunt Joh's critical inspection. On the other hand, Aunt Joh loved sweets. As a result she was far from slim, but our visits were a success from the eating point of view.

Uncle Gerard studied mechanical engineering at Delft and chemistry at Leiden. He was a real, old-fashioned engineer. He regarded mathematics—a subject about which he knew a great deal—as the true basis of all engineering, and he loved to test our knowledge. He had a broad field of interest and liked travelling to inform himself about all sorts of things.

His knowledge was astonishing and he loved to talk about it, a fact from which I benefitted a great deal. If you went for a walk with Uncle Gerard he told you precisely how the landscape had been formed, what had brought about hills, forests, farms and lands. His driver, who received a daily dose, became a truly well-educated man.

Uncle Gerard's characteristics—he was precise, persistent and knowledgeable about the scientific basis of factory work—were of great importance to Philips. At first he used to tackle the technological problems in the manufacturing process himself, but in 1909 he employed our first engineer, J. C. Lokker. In addition he employed a number of first-class designers—something unusual for a light bulb factory—thus enabling Philips to build its own machines. The light bulb machines for our factories around the world are still made in our own workshops.

Uncle Gerard and my father differed greatly in character. I was always struck how these two opposites appreciated each other, although this did not stop them sometimes getting in each other's hair. When, as an adolescent, I had serious talks with Uncle Gerard, he often praised my father abundantly. 'Frits,' he would say, 'you don't realize what a terrific father you have! The way Ton works, the way he sees a thing through, deserves the greatest respect.' And my father would also express admiration for his brother: 'Uncle Gerard is terribly clever. And the way he goes at it until a problem is solved is remarkable!' He sometimes felt that people did not sufficiently evaluate Uncle Gerard's achievements. Fortunately they were recognized among those best qualified to judge. In 1917 the School of Technology at Delft made him an honorary Doctor in Technical Sciences.

When Uncle Gerard retired in 1921, he withdrew completely. First he went on a long journey, and then he settled in The Hague. He never spent another day in the factory. That was his way, though, of course, he remained a member of the Supervisory Board.

Other Colleagues

In 1932, during the Depression, Philips' nominal capital had to be reduced by 25 per cent. This was an awkward operation, inevitable because the original capital could no longer yield returns. In the end this capital reduction contributed towards restoring profit margins, and shareholders were later compensated for what had been taken from them, but at the time it was very unpopular at the Stock Exchange.

This operation did not affect me personally. I was just an engineer with a job of my own and not much concerned with the financial condition of the Concern as a whole. For my father it was different. He was a man who liked expansion and stimulating people. He hated large-scale dismissals. Even before the Depression, if anyone had to be fired, he had left it to others. Now thousands had to go. It was a painful operation, even worse than the capital reduction. The very existence of people was at stake. In all this a man with determination was required. The man who fought with most distinction on this front—for a battle it was—was Frans Otten. I had first got to know Otten when he was still a student. It was he who delivered to us as very fresh freshmen the traditional 'thunder speech'. And he made a good job of it—he really thundered! As president of the first year, I had had to reply. That was no small task considering the harassment you underwent. Your shoe-laces were tied together. People spilled beer over your clothes. Yet you had to continue your speech without batting an eyelid.

Frans Otten had acquired an excellent reputation among his fellow students. He was a daring man, with many gifts. When I heard that he was considering applying for a job with Philips, I told my father that he should try to get him.

Otten came to make our acquaintance. It was then that he first met my sister Annetje. Later, when he had joined Philips and was living in Eindhoven, he got engaged to her and, in 1925, they were married. Otten started as an engineer in the pilot plant, where the first models of new products are made. Later he went to the radio valve plant where he made an important contribution to its reorganization. Soon he was put in charge of the production of radio sets. His star rose so fast that after only a few years he had become an Assistant Managing Director. Suggestions were made that he had got the job because he was the boss's son-in-law, but informed people knew better. Otten had started off with a handicap. Because of military service during World War I he had begun his studies late. Nor had he had the customary spell in a lamp factory. So he was considered an outsider. But his leadership qualities could not be doubted.

He showed his real worth during the difficult years of the Great Depression. With a strong sense of justice and with colossal courage he restored the company to viability. In this task he won the full support of my father and of other senior staff members, but it was he who bore the final responsibility. And he did not take it lightly. Interminable meetings were necessary far into the nights and all through Saturdays. I watched this struggle against the Depression at close quarters and it filled me with admiration. In all this, nobody was more grateful to Otten than my father, and he never concealed his appreciation.

Another most valuable man in those years of crisis was Professor J. Goudriaan. He had taught business economics at the Netherlands School of Economics in Rotterdam and at the Technical University in Delft. When, in 1932, Otten heard Goudriaan lecture to our staff, he was so impressed that he suggested that my father invite him to work for us. Goudriaan accepted our offer and in 1933 became an Assistant Managing Director. At that time the Board of Management consisted of my father as Managing Director, and Loupart, J. H. Gaarenstroom, Lokker, Otten, P. N. L. Staal and Van Walsem as Assistant Managing Directors. After Goudriaan joined the board, Otten became Chairman of the Assistant Managing Directors' Council, with Van Walsem as Vice-Chairman.

Goudriaan's nomination was, as may be realized, quite exceptional in the Philips community. He was entrusted with the reorganization of the accounting department and the processing of data and statistics. In the years when we only produced lamps and radios, cost calculation had been somewhat neglected. The production cost of a lamp had always been relatively easy to calculate, as we knew what glass and wire cost. But when we started on radios, calculations became more difficult. Initially it was not all that important. From 1927 to 1930 enough sets were sold to leave a generous credit balance at the end of the year and nobody worried too much about precise cost calculations. But Otten had a sharp eye for such things. He knew the value of accurate figures. And when, after 1930, we had dipped into the red, he was trying to find out what caused our losses and what could be done about them. Goudriaan gave the answer.

To begin with, he introduced budgeting. This was done rather rigorously. It was agreed with each departmental chief what energy, wage and repair costs he was allowed for the coming year. Thus, everybody was confronted with what went wrong in his own department. It took a while to get accustomed to this, but in the end the system worked. Today budgeting is common practice and Philips is inconceivable without it. We also began to pay attention to internal pricing. It was decided that profit should be made only in one place: when the final product was sold to the customer.

In 1938 Goudriaan became General Manager of the Dutch Railways. There, too, he achieved remarkable results.

Two men who worked closely with my father deserve special mention —Herman van Walsem and Othon Loupart. Van Walsem, a Leiden-trained lawyer, joined my father in 1919. With his able legal mind, he was a splendid negotiator. He was not only sharp and to the point, but also a pleasant man with a great sense of humour. With him my father, in 1924, founded Phoebus, a lamp manufacturers' organization, consisting of the German, French, British and Hungarian industries and including Philips. It took tremendous tact to get it going, and the organization yielded good results for all concerned, including the consumers. Later, Van Walsem showed his considerable talents in patent negotiations with the Radio Corporation of America and other international concerns.

Loupart was another accomplished negotiator. He came from that curious region of Moresnet, formerly part of the Dutch province of Limburg and subsequently a bone of contention between Belgium and Germany. During World War I the Germans hermetically sealed off this region, together with Belgium, from Holland, by erecting high electric fences, called the 'deadly wire'. But, with the aid of a barrel, young Loupart managed to creep through this fence. He studied at the Rotterdam School of Economics, and when he started as one of my father's young assistants was put in charge of commercial negotiations. Through his tremendous energy, his discernment and his astonishing productivity, he rose more rapidly than anybody else at the time when we were moving into radios. He travelled widely, and it was through his work that our world-wide sales organization was created.

In many ways he was an original. He would talk in long and hopelessly involved sentences in which he was capable of making the most astonishing jumps, and which seldom ended grammatically. When negotiating he would start his wonderful exposés with a firework of words. We in Philips were used to this, but the other side had one of two reactions. Some would think, 'What a brilliant man, saying all those things that I don't understand!' Others would get nervous. Loupart used to ventilate ideas which were ten or twenty years ahead of his time and which sounded fantastic. He was also able to present our efforts in a most impressive light. Sometimes this led to contracts which we were unable to fulfil. This was then regrettable, or sometimes worse. For instance, we concluded a contract with the French to furnish X-ray equipment which was away beyond what we could handle.

I learned my lesson as far as Loupart was concerned early on. Telecommunications—at the time almost virgin territory for us—was his domain. We had talks with people from the International Telephone and Telegraph Company. During the talks Loupart made such claims about what we were capable of doing in telecommunications that even we, who should have known better, came under his spell. The ITT men were, I could see, deeply impressed. In reality, we had very little to offer, and fortunately the negotiations came to nothing. Much later we had a good laugh with Loupart about these talks. By that time Philips had become one of the larger companies in telecommunications, and Loupart, through his skill in international negotiations, had contributed to this in no small way.

His strength in negotiating was that he was wise—and sometimes generous. In this respect he was my father's pupil. His view was that the trading partner should always benefit as well. My father was against deals which the other party would regret within a year—he wanted both parties to be happy in the long term too. Sometimes Loupart was so generous that I thought he had gone too far, but in the end he was usually proved right.

Of course, we had our quarrels too. At times he got on my nerves with his long-winded thought processes, and I doubtless often irritated him. Nevertheless we were real friends. After his retirement in 1956 I enjoyed going to his home for an evening's chat about all sorts of ideas which occupied my mind. It was a delight to get his view on them, as he was a man of experience and vision.

Loupart and Van Walsem as well as Otten were men who, along with my father, left their mark on Philips' pre-war development. They also gave stimulating leadership to the reconstruction and expansion after 1945. But, before 1940, it was those four who determined what Philips was and became.

Chapter 4

Research and Result

I have always been keenly interested in the applied research in physics which is done by our company. Such research is a real Philips tradition. Uncle Gerard was our first researcher. In his tiny laboratory he himself discovered the best way to make light bulbs. My father, too, understood the importance of industrial research. They both learnt from experience how dependent you can become on patents held by other people. For instance, lamps made of drawn wire, and the spiral wire variety—half-watt bulbs filled with argon—were based on patents held by competitors. To become independent we had to build up an arsenal of patents of our own. This made fundamental research necessary, something entirely separate from the actual manufacturing. The man put in charge of this was Dr. Gilles Holst.

Holst began by trying to establish what happens inside an ordinary light bulb. His papers on this were published by the Royal Netherlands Academy of Sciences, and he also wrote a booklet which summed up briefly and accurately what was then known about light bulbs. The curious thing is that even today research is still being done to establish what happens when the tungsten thread pulverizes and when evaporation leaves sediments inside the glass bulb, the objective being to find out what temperature the spiral reaches at various stages and how this temperature can be spread evenly over the entire length of the thread.

Holst laid the foundations of research in Holland, and also left an imprint on methods employed both to solve problems and to inspire researchers. He gathered round him a group of top-class scientists,* and was highly esteemed both among his industrial colleagues outside Holland and in academic circles. In 1930 he was appointed to a Chair at Leiden University.

Like many people of rare talent, Holst was remarkably modest, but

*Names like Oosterhuis, Van der Pol, Hertz, Bouwers, Tellegen, Van Arkel, De Boer, Penning, Reerink and Van Wijk have become known far beyond the confines of Philips, and this list is by no means exhaustive.

that did not prevent him from fighting for his convictions. Needless to say, the first-class scientists working for us did not always see eye to eye. Often they evaluated new ideas in diametrically opposite ways. Thus Dr. van der Pol, well-known in our company for the elegant way in which he applied mathematics to his problems, demonstrated long before 1940 a radio broadcast using frequency modulation. The experiment succeeded marvellously. Reception was noticeably better than that obtained by the usual amplitude modulation. But Holst saw no future in the idea. He thought it would be too expensive. Today, of course, FM has become common.

Holst encouraged his staff to try completely new ways in order to find original solutions. He had his own methods for this. Once he took on a young physicist from the University of Utrecht whose doctoral thesis on light had been exceptionally well received. This young Ph.D. arrived in our laboratory full of self-confidence, expecting to shed his 'light' there. But Holst said to him, 'Here you will be working on acoustics.' He felt that a person would be more original and inventive working in a field completely new to him than if he merely continued in that covered by his studies. For, in his own line, Holst thought, he would rely too much on the experience of his professor, who was not always completely up-to-date.

New Products

The regular flow of new products played a predominant part in the expansion of Philips, both before and after the war. Indeed, half of our turn-over has usually consisted of products which we were not manufacturing, or which had not even been thought of, ten years before. Keen research is the life-blood of the company. For years we were spending an average of seven per cent of our turn-over on research and development.

In the twenties, Philips research was particularly concerned with electrical discharge in rarefied gases, sodium and mercury vapours. In the next decade, Holst and his colleagues had the conviction that we should study solid state physics. As a result, we went deeply into magnetics and began to manufacture new magnetic materials needed, for example, for loudspeaker components. Among them was 'ticonal', then the most powerful magnetic material available, in which a Japanese patent was also involved. One of the results of this research was a new metal strip material of which we made Pupin coils of exceptionally high quality. Later this development produced ceramic materials with magnetic characteristics, like 'ferroxcube' and 'ferroxdure'.

We were experimenting with television as early as 1935, although it reached the general public in Holland only in 1950. We also devoted our attention, quite early on, to research in nuclear physics, a field in which we had bought patents from the Italian physicist, Professor Fermi. Holst knew how to smell out in advance what was going to be important and he thought that Fermi's inventions might one day be useful. When years later the Americans, in developing their nuclear weapon, entered the field covered by these patents, Philips claimed its fee. After prolonged litigation, our rights were recognized, but the sum paid us was in no proportion to the subsequent applications. We ourselves achieved successes in nuclear physics when we developed high voltage generators, the cyclotron and special measuring equipment.

Other research, closer to daily industrial life, was connected with welding techniques. Here our activities were concerned with the new products of which I had been put in charge, so I was deeply interested. In the first place, our researchers wanted to know exactly what was actually happening in the welding process. With a so-called high-speed film camera, which at that time had a capacity of 3,000 frames per second, films of the welding process were made, including photographs of melting and flowing metal drops. This led to a thorough analysis of the process. As a result all sorts of interesting discoveries were made and, in due course, found a first expression in the quality of our welding rods. Later this research led to entirely new welding processes, so that Philips today not only furnishes a large percentage of welding rods, but also has a considerable share in the professional welding equipment market.

One real Philips invention, with which I have had a lot to do, is the dry-shaver—the Philishave. This product was mainly developed in our radio laboratory. My father had confidence in it, even though he had difficulty in keeping his beard clipped with the first primitive models. But I do not think that any of the men who experimented with it had any idea that it would become a world-wide hit. For me, it was a favourite project because mechanical problems always appealed to me. Our dry-shaver was introduced on to the market in 1938, with only one shaver head. To improve its performance and achieve a better adaptation to the hand, a two-headed model was developed during the war. I was enthusiastic about it, but our people dared not go through with it for fear of its becoming too expensive. I refused to accept this. My estimate was that it would lead to a price difference of two and a half guilders at the most. A few two-headed shavers were made in a new and better shape. When the Germans imprisoned me, I took an experimental model with me and so was able to keep myself neatly shaven. After liberation we started selling the two-headed shavers. It turned out that the increase in product cost was slightly less than two and a half guilders!

The Philishave is a typical example of development work orientated towards daily use. In addition, Philips was continuously working in specialist fields, like X-ray lung examination. My father was particularly interested in this, and was thinking about X-raying the entire population to prevent the spread of tuberculosis long before anybody else had thought in those terms. In this line of research we were helped by two able doctors in our own medical service. One of them, Professor A. Bouwers, was a gifted scientist, a man full of creative ideas, with a sharp eye for the practical application of discoveries. One of his first great inventions was the radiation-safe X-ray tube, which largely reduced the risks of radiation for the operating personnel. The traditional tubes had had to be masked with lead sheets. Radiologists must still protect themselves against radiation, but Bouwers' invention meant a tremendous improvement. His second pioneering invention was a portable set which made possible the taking of X-ray photos in the patient's home, using a high-tension cable insulated in a special way. The set could be carried in a case and connected to the ordinary mains.

Later, Philips made the so-called rotalix, an X-ray tube which is now in general use. An ingenious construction, which included a disc revolving very rapidly in a vacuum, made it possible to produce X-ray pictures of hitherto unattainable clarity. The practical execution involved many problems, both in maintaining the vacuum and in the construction of ball bearings permitting very high velocity which would, in addition, stand up to vacuum conditions. But the answer to all these problems was found.

Making our own X-ray tubes involved the technology of soldering lead glass to chrome iron which we were casting and rolling ourselves. As a result of this and of further development, we have for several decades enjoyed a world-wide reputation in X-ray equipment.

The Hot-Air Engine

Another very special project was the hot-air engine, now also referred to as the hot-gas engine. The principle is not new. As early as 1817 Robert Stirling designed this engine and actually built it. Ever since 1938 when we started our work upon it, I have been keenly interested, and am convinced, in spite of many set-backs, that we should not give it up, because of its great promise for the future. If I had not had continuous faith in the project, we would have abandoned it long ago.

Long before World War II we were already making battery-fed receivers which were particularly designed for use in the tropics and for countries where electric power was not universally available. But in the tropics batteries are not an ideal source of power. In those early years, their span of life was relatively short, and they did not survive long storage. The result was that these battery sets caused endless trouble. For in those days only radio valves were known and they consumed a great deal of power. So our laboratory began to tackle the problem.

The idea was to produce a cheap source of energy which would have to provide no more than 6 watts, a gadget running on petrol or spirits. Dr. Harre Rinia investigated simple machines capable of generating electricity and ended up looking at toys. In a toy shop he found such a hot-air engine. He studied it. He found that it worked, but very inefficiently. As the hot air was continuously moved from the heated to the cold section, a lot of heat was lost, so its useful effect was nearly zero. He then thought of installing a regenerator in the tube between the cold and hot sections. It was a tiny tube, filled with copper chips which could preserve the heat. He built a machine on this basis, took measurements and saw to his astonishment that the effectiveness of this primitive gadget was exceptionally high. A new model was built, and Rinia observed that, in fact, a large proportion of the heat was preserved by the regenerator so that less heat, that is less fuel, was needed. This made the tiny machine a great deal more attractive. Later our laboratory improved the machine further, first by installing an extra cooling system, and then by moving the entire apparatus into a closed system under high pressure. This enhanced its efficiency again. So it became an engine with such an interesting performance that people saw in it possibilities for uses other than just generating a few watts of electricity.

During the war, further work was done. It was inevitable that the Germans, who roamed our laboratory with keen curiosity, should notice the hot-air engine. They wanted to know what it was. Explanations were given. But the Germans decided without further thought that it was ridiculous to expect it to work.

After the liberation of the south of Holland in September 1944 an interesting thing happened. Shortly before their withdrawal, the Germans had, in panic, abducted quite a lot of materials and models, including the Stirling engine model. Only a few days after the liberation of Eindhoven a committee headed by Sir Robert Watson-Watt, the English scientist to whose work the British owed the invention of radar, visited us on behalf of the Allies. When we told our guests that the Germans had taken the Stirling model with them, it provoked their interest. Six months later a five-man team went to America, carrying with them a model of the hot-air engine. As a result our laboratory in the United States got an order from the US Navy to develop a certain type of engine on the basis of that model. People in America worked intensively on this project, while research was also continued in Eindhoven. Some engines were actually made in America, but as a result of a change of command in the Navy, the work was abandoned there, although we continued to make progress in Holland.

Relevance of Research

During his visit Sir Robert gave a lecture to our scientific staff about the discovery and development of radar—an exposition so crystal-clear that it left a lasting impression. He also emphasized the importance of Philips' contribution to the British war effort. In 1939 and 1940 we had transferred all our designs and scientific data on our newest radio valve to our factories in Britain. During the war years, our Mullard factories manufactured forty per cent of all Britain's radio valves, and this newest receiver valve, the EF50, had been an essential part of the radar installed in British aircraft. According to Sir Robert it had, with its exceptionally high performance, contributed greatly to victory in the Battle of Britain.

Meanwhile my father had had similar experiences in America. On his insistence, factories were started there to support the Allied war effort. We began with manufacturing very thin wire from tungsten and molybdenum, which was much in demand. For this purpose, we managed to smuggle out of Europe diamonds for wire-drawing dies. In another place we cut quartz crystals for transmitters in aircraft, while yet another factory made radar valves for the armed forces. For these activities Philips was twice given the 'Army-Navy Production Award for High Achievements in War Productions', which particularly pleased our American employees.

But peace production is our main aim. Our laboratories now constitute a source of patents which are essential for our industrial life in Holland. The main task of our patents department is to enable us to undertake new products and working methods without being impeded by other people's patents. For sometimes you see an excellent solution to a problem but cannot use it because another concern owns the patent. If there are agreements between the principal suppliers of new inventions, that is the various research laboratories, permitting each to utilize the other's patents, everyone can work more efficiently. Fortunately we were able even before the war to make such agreements with RCA, General Electric and others as a result of our own strong patent position.

It is impossible to assess the importance of having been able to keep our research organization intact, even in critical times. The first difficulty occurred during the Great Depression. The temptation then to economize on research, which did not appear the most urgent need, was strong, and momentarily we reduced our onward speed. Some recently employed engineers were dismissed. But in 1934 we began to employ able researchers again, and went full speed ahead. As protectionism was strongly increasing, we were forced to expand our factories considerably in most European countries.

This required a great deal of attention and money. Yet we persisted in our belief that we must maintain the pace of our research work.

The second period which might have been fatal to our research was the German occupation of Holland from 1940 to 1945. But because the Germans believed in their own superiority and speedy victory, they left us in relative peace. We were even able to continue with our television tests. Probably the Germans hoped to reap the fruits of our efforts for their 'Millennium'. But the efficiency of our work was hampered by a variety of factors: the abduction of young laboratory workers; the need for a number of leading people to go into hiding; and the tensions caused by resistance work which was carried on at all levels of our company, as, for example, when an entire radio transmitter was secretly built. All these factors did not make the work of Holst and his colleagues any easier.

Yet in spite of every difficulty we did succeed in keeping our physics research organization in good trim. If we had been forced to re-create an internally cohesive apparatus of this potential from scratch after the war, it would have taken a long time before we could have done anything with it. As it was, we had a large staff of first-class workers who were very keen to get going again. And this was true for our organizations outside Holland as well.

During the war, we had already done a lot of development work on radio valves through our daughter enterprise Mullard in the United Kingdom. After the war we built a new laboratory in Britain. A similar laboratory is now in operation near Paris. In Germany, Philips possesses two laboratories; the one in Hamburg is specially geared towards practical application, while that in Aachen concentrates on scientific research. The North American Philips organization has a laboratory north of New York, which was headed by the American physicist Dr. Duffendack.

I did a lot to encourage this international expansion, especially after Holst retired from the Board of Management, when part of this work was entrusted to me. I felt that we must not limit ourselves to Holland in our search for clever brains. When we began this in 1948-49 we were naturally not looking towards Germany with too much enthusiasm. But I wanted to move ahead regardless. After all, a new Europe could not be built without Germany. I engaged a few promising German researchers and brought them to Eindhoven, so that they could acclimatize themselves to our mode of working, which was less rigid than in Germany. As the director responsible for research, I also convened annual meetings of all heads of Philips laboratories, which helped to create extremely good team-work. International committees were formed which defined the various objectives for research, so that the work could proceed without overlapping. In the committee meetings Belgians, Germans, French, British and Dutch confer in a fraternal spirit. Once a year we organize an exhibition at which the contributions of all laboratories, covering very diverse fields, can be seen. Such an exhibition may have as many as fifty stands, and provides a bird's eye view of current Philips research. Not long ago two of our research workers won the Veder Prize for the video long-playing record which they developed. It contains both sound and vision, and can be played back through a special apparatus into an ordinary TV set.

Team Work

Inventions rarely come ready-made out of one human brain. Most new products which Philips markets are the result of teamwork as, for instance, one of our great post-war inventions, the cassette. Of course, one man had the basic thought, but before something existed which customers could put into a tape recorder, a team experimented with many models until at last the right product was reached.

In practice, a patent is usually the fruit of teamwork, although the initial discovery is often one man's idea. So when an invention is developed in a research laboratory, the question often arises to whom it belongs. In

Germany, the person who has the first idea retains what might be called the intellectual ownership, but we in Philips consider this wrong. The danger is that he may hold back part of his invention, which might be advantageous for him personally but harmful for the final results of the research. We argue that the researcher has been engaged by us to invent or develop original things. This is what is expected of him. His salary is based on the assumption that he will be inventive regardless of whether his work yields results or not.

In addition, different scientific disciplines are represented in a research laboratory. Physicists, chemists, electrical engineers, mechanical engineers and mathematicians work together. And inventions are like other intellectual activities: only a small percentage is inspiration, the rest perspiration. In every laboratory people are working year in, year out on difficult, sober and systematic work which will never produce a patent, but which requires dedication, knowledge and enthusiasm. There are, as well, the people working with equal commitment on some project which does hold out the promise of a patent, but the lucky one who finally produces it will never be able to do a proper job if the way has not been prepared by the patient colleague with his measuring gear. So we think that patents produced by our research should be considered as the fruit of common effort. They are a collective intellectual property which is owned by Philips.

Scientists are, as a rule, keener on publishing their findings than receiving money for them. Their real reward and satisfaction is the recognition of their fellow scientists. If a person invents something very interesting and it is not published, then it is no good to anyone, least of all to the inventor. Scientific publications determine people's standing. In this respect Philips has a great tradition. Holst always encouraged his collaborators to publish. Many have had ample opportunity to do so, not least through our own scientific journals. In 1936, I personally took the initiative in launching the *Philips Technisch Tijdschrift*. After the war the Philips Research Bulletins were started. Also, scientists working with us are given great freedom to attend international congresses in which they can make their own contributions, where they can discuss their work with others or follow the latest developments in their profession. At such meetings Philips is generally represented by several scientists.

Our international research network, with our physics laboratory as the centre, is to me one of the most inspiring features of our world-wide Concern. New discoveries are continually made at a most encouraging rate, resulting in new processes, new systems and new products which in

turn provide employment for thousands. All this is the result of teamwork between able and enthusiastic men.

In this age when science has become so complicated that no researcher
is capable of doing anything significant without the help of others, I
cannot wish anything better for our research staff than the satisfaction of
achieving a valuable result together, through their united knowledge and
experience.

Chapter 5

New Conviction;
New House; New Work

Time after time Sylvia and I had been invited by friends to discuss with them something which had given them an entirely new vision not only for their own lives, but also for the situation in the world. We did not really feel we needed this. We were happily married, I had a good future before me, and we were blessed with three healthy children—Digna, Anton Frederik and Annejet. We had understood that it had something to do with faith. But, then, we had a faith. We had been married in church, and of course we had had our children baptized.

Our friends persisted, but on the dates they suggested we were always occupied. At last, they asked us to name a date. Since we had no free weekend, we chose Sunday 27 and Monday 28 August 1934, straight after the annual flight of amateur pilots over Holland. As we stepped out of our car in front of the home of our friends, the Sillems, we agreed that we would above all try to keep our sense of humour, to survive what we feared would be two terribly serious days.

This pact turned out to be superfluous. We met there a number of extraordinarily cheerful and warm-hearted people, and there was plenty of laughter. They were part of an international group of people known as the Oxford Group, people who had banded together to try and live the Christian life without compromise. They did not aspire to be a new church or denomination, but to bring a new spirit to all the churches and into every sphere of everyday life. They owed their name to the fact that their ideas had first taken hold in any large way among students and dons at Oxford.

What these friends had to offer was very simple: 'Praying is not just talking, but above all listening. God is ready to guide our thoughts if we give Him time to do it. The only condition is that we are prepared to carry out what He shows us. We should check the thoughts we get against

standards which Jesus has shown us in the Sermon on the Mount—
honesty, purity, unselfishness and love.'

We were deeply impressed. Could what our friends said really be true?
If our Creator could speak in our hearts in this twentieth century as He
did to people in the stories in the Old and New Testaments, this would not
only make people a lot happier, but could alter the world.

Sylvia and I tried to assess what these standards would mean for us
personally. Our friends had told us, 'You can't build a new house on the
ruins of an old one. You have to start by clearing the rubble.' Sylvia
believed that it would make very little difference in her case. She says she
considered herself quite honest, very pure, and enormously unselfish, but
not all that loving. She was aware of her sharp tongue, with which she
sometimes hurt people badly. That, she felt, must change. She saw
another thing. After the divorce of her parents, her relationship with her
father and stepmother had grown cool and then cold until finally her
father had completely broken with her. The first time that she listened to
the voice in her heart, it became clear to her that only right relationships
could fit into this new world, and that she had to rebuild this relationship.

My first thought was about honesty. Honesty and openness are
indispensable to build up mutual trust in business, but to be absolutely
honest at home, I discovered, was more difficult. Still, I decided to clear
the decks as far as the past was concerned and to start afresh. This took
moral courage, but it made a lot of difference in the relationship between
Sylvia and me, and it has proved a blessing for us and for our children.

As we arrived back home in Eindhoven that Monday in 1934 we were
hit by a shattering piece of news. That same day, Sylvia's eldest brother,
Warner van Lennep, had been killed in an accident. After completing his
theology studies at Utrecht, he had that summer discovered the adventure
of mountaineering. In the Mont Blanc region, he was fatally hit by an
avalanche. He was twenty-nine years old. To all of us this was a terrible
blow. That same night we met Sylvia's father on the train for Switzerland.
Of course, the great common grief made it easier to restore the relationship. What had been a bad relationship, based on our assumption that it
was impossible to get on with him, changed in time into a warm friendship
which lasted until both parents' deaths. This change filled us all with
lasting joy.

My resolve to try and walk God's road had an influence on my relationships with all my fellow men, including my father. We were linked by
many bonds of common interest, such as love of art and nature, and our
devotion to the company. But like most sons, I had my points of criticism

against him. I felt, for instance, that he lost his temper too often about things which were not worth it. On the other hand, I was a bit of an artist and would let my imagination wander, and sometimes, if he wanted a thing done immediately, I would forget. Then I would always have a good excuse ready. So I decided to stop this. I told myself, 'If you have forgotten, say so!' As a result he began to trust me more, because, of course, he had seen through my excuses. All in all, my new attitude to life created a warm and lasting friendship between us.

Listening to God also brought some deep changes to Sylvia. For example, she had always been fearful that her loved ones would meet with some accident. During the war years the likelihood of this was not diminished. When in 1942 Eindhoven was terribly smashed up by bombs, she realised how deeply eight years of listening had affected her. She remained strangely calm as, from the outskirts, she saw bombs dropping on the centre of the city where our six children were. When she tried to explain this to herself, she thought of Jesus's words in the Sermon on the Mount, 'Seek ye first the Kingdom of Heaven and everything else shall be added unto you.' She had sincerely attempted, stumbling and getting up again, to walk God's road, and He had freed her from fear.

We discovered that listening to God is quite natural for children. Usually Sylvia read a piece from the Bible to the children before they went to bed. Then, after some minutes' silence, each of them told what he or she had thought. This had often to do with very simple occurrences. One was grateful for something. The other said sorry for some wrong thing he had done. Again another was ready to give something up, or wanted to do something for our guests. They were things which can come up in an adult's heart as well as in a child's. It created great unity in our family, and we would not have known how to bring up our seven children without these times of listening together.

Family life has always had a high priority for us. To play games or to read to our children on Saturday nights was more important than any social engagement. I always took the holidays to which I was entitled, and we have wonderful memories of those weeks together in various parts of Holland. As the children grew older we also took them abroad. One high point was the annual winter sports vacation which the whole family enjoyed from the time when our eldest daughter was five—except of course during the war.

As our children grew up I devoted a lot of attention to their development. Our eldest son, Ton, was too young to study at Delft immediately after passing his final school exams, so he went for a year to Dartmouth

College in the United States. Our second son, Warner, who wanted to go to the Rotterdam School of Economics, chose a ranch school in Arizona, where he took up riding seriously. I was able to make trips through America with both of them. With my third son, Frits, I travelled for some weeks through Switzerland, and that too was an unforgettable experience.

Men who, in the world's opinion, make brilliant careers—cabinet ministers and presidents of large corporations, for example, often have no time left for their families. In our company, too, I have known people driven by their desire to get ahead, or because they are sincerely doing their duty, to work through entire nights. When they do this year after year, it becomes a habit. And even if they succeed, what is the cost? Their family may end up in ruins, and the education of their children is often a disaster.

I believe that a fully rounded personality works most efficiently. A man with the right balance between the various elements of his life is closest to the Creator's design. The man who takes time for his family and for sport is also naturally efficient at his job. If he can relax at home in the evenings, this benefits not only his family but also his work next morning. We industrialists can check up on ourselves. If the letters we dictate become longer and our exposés at business meetings become more extensive and involved, if we begin to avoid making decisions, in other words if we are working less efficiently, the balance has gone wrong.

Of course I have sometimes found it necessary during certain periods to put aside everything else to get some work done, but I have been able to avoid its becoming a habit.

Sylvia and I have often wondered what would have become of our marriage without God's guidance and the conscious challenge of high moral standards. Any marriage, however smooth from the outside, has its troubles, and ours is no exception. We are very different in character, and if we have succeeded in keeping united, any couple can. It is a consolation that even the mistakes we make—and with God's help restore for—can be of use to help others to make the right choices. One important factor for us has been to have a purpose bigger than building our family, the purpose of playing our part in building a world as it is meant to be.

When we met the Oxford Group in 1934 we discovered the personal experience that men can change and so better relationships can be created in the world. In the years since then I have seen countless examples of the birth of unity and teamwork, in families which had been divided and between races, classes and countries which did not naturally work together.

Of course I have also had less positive experiences. For if people decide to let God guide them, they expose themselves to criticism. This criticism may often be specially strong from those close to one. In spite of the changes which had come in our family relationships, neither Sylvia nor I managed to convince my parents or sisters of the importance of the Oxford Group's work. Their attitude remained sceptical. My father went further. When he heard that I had booked a hall for an Oxford Group meeting in Eindhoven, he demanded that I should cancel the meeting. I refused point blank, whereupon he said, 'Then I shall cancel the hall!' My reply was, 'Dad, if you do that I will go to America.' That was the end of it.

Later, a moment came when my brother-in-law Frans Otten felt he had to face me with a choice. He discussed this first with my wife, for whom he had a great regard.

'Sylvia,' he said, 'the moment has come when Frits will have to choose: either Philips or the Oxford Group!'

'Frans,' she replied, 'I know which he will choose. But you should realise that the choice you are really putting to him is: Philips or God. Is that what you mean to do?'

'No, Sylvia, if that's the way you see it, I won't force a choice.'

In the years after 1934 we saw at first hand how the ideas of Frank Buchman, the initiator of the Oxford Group, took root in Europe. At large meetings in Scandinavia he faced the world with a challenge to go God's way instead of the way of materialism, a challenge which is still relevant today. At the British Industries Fair at Birmingham in 1936 we attended an impressive meeting to which thirty-five special trains had carried participants from all parts of Britain. A year later, a week of meetings took place in the Vegetable Hall of Utrecht. A commercial artist from Philips had designed a most appealing poster, representing a ship going down the slips with the phrase, 'The new Netherlands is being launched'. That week I had promised to be available to help in Utrecht. Because some colleagues, including Otten, had to be abroad, I could not keep my promise, but I was present during the weekend. On Sunday morning Frank Buchman asked me to lead the meeting. I did not want to refuse, though my father had urged me not to take any prominent part. It was an impressive meeting and I felt I had not done too badly. But when my father read the morning paper next day he was much annoyed . . .

In 1938, Buchman, sensing the world's need and the imminent threat of war, launched a programme of Moral and Spiritual Re-Armament from the East End of London. Almost simultaneously, but independently,

Queen Wilhelmina spoke in our country about the need for a moral and spiritual re-armament of nations.

De Wielewaal

We had been happy in our first home at Bloemendaal and then in the engineer's house at Eindhoven. But in 1934 we moved into our new home, De Wielewaal. This was the end of a story which really began back in 1912 when my parents bought a property on the outskirts of Eindhoven. It was a forest of firs, traversed by rather monotonous avenues of oak. As the years went by, my parents changed it until it became a paradise, with a beautiful pine grove and fine rhododendrons.

The story of the actual house De Wielewaal—the Golden Oriole—began a lot later, on the day soon after our engagement when Sylvia and I saw a house under construction which appealed to us both so much that I wrote to the contractor asking for the name of the architect. Some weeks later a man rang my doorbell in Delft and introduced himself as Frans Stam, the architect of that house. He wanted to know whether I intended to have a house built. I told him that I was not yet even married.

'But after you are married, wouldn't you consider building a house?'

'Consider, yes, Mr. Stam. But how long it will remain in the considering stage I don't know!'

'Haven't you got any ideas? You seem to be interested in my work, and I haven't got a job on at the moment. So I suggest you allow me to make a sketch of a home for you.'

I told him that I did not want to enter into any commitment and would not dream of incurring expense. But he insisted.

'Tell me what sort of rooms you would like to have in your house,' he said.

I thought aloud: 'A living room, a hall, a dining room, a study, a nursery . . .'

'And how many bedrooms?'

'That depends on the number of children.'

'How many do you hope for?'

My fiancée and I had discussed this subject several times. Our expectations were large. So I replied without hesitation, 'Six.'

'That would mean three double bedrooms for the children,' he concluded.

After some to and fro, he left. Some months later he again stood at my front door, a cylinder under his arm. It contained a plan of the home of our dreams. Sylvia and I liked it, and we carefully stored it away. We also started to pay more attention to houses and to details in the homes of friends and acquaintances. We noticed things we definitely did not want in a home of our own as well as things which we found attractive.

After a while Stam came back for a talk, and this time Sylvia was there. I had begun to feel that one day he would be our architect. I mentioned the kind of bricks I wanted in case we should build, and that I wanted an open fire-place decorated with the Delft tiles which I was passionately collecting. We also discussed the roofing. The house we had seen had had a thatched roof, but when I had talked to my father he had warned me, 'You should never have a roof like that. You'll always be afraid of fire.' So I told the architect that I did not want a thatched roof.

'All right, then I suggest Limburg slate.'

In high spirits we continued letting our imaginations roam about our possible future house. What would the drains be like? What kind of windows would be most suitable?

Stam again turned up with new drawings, but even just before our marriage we felt no urgency about this house. We invited him to Bloemendaal, and later he came to see us about once a year in Eindhoven. Each time the drawings were improved, mostly on the initiative of Sylvia who copied the plans on to graph paper so that she knew her house intimately before anything had been built. She knew which way the doors would swing, where the wash basins would be and where the different pieces of furniture would be placed. Meanwhile I worked on the designs of the fire-places.

My parents had followed all these activities with interest, and one day in 1934 my father said, 'Frits, I don't see this Depression passing soon, but building prices are low now. Why don't we make a start on that house of yours? You have three children now, so you need a larger home.'

So our home, De Wielewaal, came into being. It was built on my parents' property according to Stam's design, adapted to our wishes and ideas. He created an ideal home for us, in which we have lived very happily with our family ever since.

More Responsibility

At the Annual General Meeting in 1935 I was nominated an Assistant Managing Director. This enlarged my responsibilities. A year later Frans

Otten was made Managing Director—the only one—while my father became President. Then in 1939 my father became Chairman of the Supervisory Board and Otten was made President, with Van Walsem, Loupart and I as Managing Directors alongside him. In a few years there were more changes at the top than in many years before, for my father had been sole President for seventeen years.

I believe that this process began with the death of my brother-in-law Sandberg in an air crash in 1935. This shocked my father into fresh thought about the continuity of Philips and the need to broaden the base of top management. Then in 1936 my father contracted food poisoning. At first it did not seem serious, but he was ill in bed for some months and his kidneys were affected. He was sixty-two and he suddenly realised that even he was mortal. He felt he must prepare for all eventualities. The most important outcome was that, in the years leading up to the war, Otten was increasingly charged with the day-to-day leadership of the Concern. My father liked him and appreciated his honesty, decisiveness and tremendous capacity for work, together with his ability to penetrate to the heart of problems.

Meanwhile, even before I became an Assistant Managing Director, I had been attending the weekly meetings of the Board of Management. There, each member reported the developments in his field. Loupart, freshly back from one of his trips, would tell about his talks with our overseas managers. Van Walsem would report on negotiations with various partners and competitors. Otten would talk about financial matters and our investments abroad. I would make a modest contribution concerning new products for which I was responsible. My father would listen attentively, ask questions and draw conclusions. I learned a lot from those occasions.

As a result of the Great Depression, every country was trying to protect its industry against outside competition by increasing import duties and imposing quotas. To maintain our share of the market, we often had to start new factories or expand existing ones. When, for example, we could no longer import radios into a country which had been one of our traditional markets, we had to start producing inside that country. This could easily have conveyed the impression within Holland that we were transferring production and employment to other countries, but it was not so. Experience had taught us that when we had a factory of our own in a certain country, the total volume of our exports to that country actually increased. For when local production starts, an increasing volume of parts is required from Eindhoven, as are machines and measuring equipment.

As we become more prominent in that market we also receive more orders in Eindhoven for special products of which too few are required for local manufacture.

Our existing factories in Czechoslovakia, Yugoslavia, Roumania, Hungary and Poland were expanded enormously in that period, so that we became the biggest radio manufacturer in those countries. But it took a lot of work, and we had to send many of our best people there. Fortunately, our managements there soon succeeded in finding good people locally.

I often had to travel to Poland in connection with large orders from the Polish Posts and Telegraph Department, in particular for Pupin loading coils, which were used to improve the performance of telephone cables. Poland agreed to buy these coils from us provided they were made locally. We succeeded in setting up production there and supplied thousands of coils. It was plain to me, in those years, that the Poles saw that war was coming. The army wanted special transmitters and receivers, and our Polish factory developed its own sets. Our radio factory in Czechoslovakia enjoyed an excellent reputation, and the same was true for our plants in Hungary, Yugoslavia and Roumania.

In Germany the situation was different. Towards the end of the twenties we had taken over the Lorenz factory. As a result of losing a patent case, Philips was only allowed to manufacture 30,000 radio sets a year there—a ridiculously small number. So we sold the Lorenz factory to ITT. During the boom period of 1928 we had acquired the lathe factory of Kaerger in Berlin. At that time we so urgently needed all sorts of machine tools and parts that Kaerger started producing them for us, until the Depression in 1931 when we no longer needed them. Then the factory concentrated on lathes again. It had some very good designers and for years Kaerger lathes were the best in Europe. When, after 1932, the Russians increased the pace of their industrialization, they placed large orders with Kaerger and always paid for them promptly. But after the war Kaerger was in what became the Russian-occupied sector. So this firm went on the list of the well-known enterprises which have been taken from Philips without a cent of compensation.

During this period our laboratories provided us with many patents which made it possible to diversify into all sorts of new products. A large number of these came under the professional division, including the Pupin loading coils. Our sole customer in Holland for these coils was the Posts and Telegraph Department. Selling the first of these Pupin coils to that Department in The Hague caused me a lot of trouble! Philips had not yet been accepted as a reliable manufacturer in this field. I had to sit through endless talks with the patience of a saint and to reduce our price to the point where I doubted whether we would make anything out of it. It was then that I was reminded of my own haggling with suppliers when I was with the Ordnance Factory. The chickens had come home to roost!

Our sodium road lighting was also making headway. In 1935 I went with my father to France to attend the inauguration of the new road lighting system at Nevers, where a trial stretch of several kilometres of the so-called 'route bleue' from Paris to Nice was lit this way, as was the Amsterdam–Haarlem road in Holland.

We were also first in the field with television and invested a great deal of money in it. We realized that we would not make anything out of it for the time being, but felt it might become the successor to radio. We were already selling our first TV sets in Britain in 1937, for it was there that television first got under way. In 1937, too, David Sarnoff, by then President of NBC as well as of RCA, asked me, 'Well, Frits, when do you reckon TV will really start in America?' We were not thinking in terms of a world war, so my estimate was 1942.

Meanwhile we made some demonstration sets in Eindhoven. At the annual Utrecht Fair we exhibited a portable television installation mounted on a trailer, which attracted great attention. Later, this trailer visited Belgium, Hungary and Roumania. The experts agreed that our sets were among the best, but commercial development remained in the future.

I have already mentioned the film projectors which started yielding profits before the war. Soon after the introduction of the 'talking film' in 1928 we began to work on equipment for it. The first sound films were shown with the help of gramophone records, for which Philips provided the amplifiers and loudspeakers. Then the sound was recorded on the film itself. So we started manufacturing recording heads through which the light track on the film was transferred into sound vibrations. It was not long before we specialized in supplying and installing complete projection equipment, using the projectors of the German firm of Nietzsche. Our machine factory had little to do in this Depression period, so I suggested that we should start making projectors ourselves. We started by producing equipment which looked very much like the usual machines, but we got into great difficulties. We made a number for British Gaumont which were not adequate, as we had trouble in making an essential part called the 'Maltese Cross', so that order was a complete failure. Incidentally, we later managed to make this same part so superlatively well that our 'Maltese Crosses' became the world's best.

After Hitler's seizure of power in Germany in 1933, a senior employee of the firm of Bauer, one of our main competitors in this field, came to Holland because, being a Jew, he could no longer work in Germany. He suggested we should start a new series of projectors, as he thought the existing machines were out of date. We christened this new machine the Family Projector, in the trade FP for short, and it became a great success. At the time carbon rods were still used in the lamp, but one of our research people, Cornelius Bol, developed a remarkable small, very high-pressure mercury lamp, the construction of which was also a great achievement. At first this lamp had too brief a life-span, but this difficulty was soon eliminated, and our Bol bulbs would last for hundreds of hours. They were mounted in pairs, so that if one failed, the second could be switched on immediately. Later other lamps were designed for cinema projection. So we began to sell hundreds of film projection installations each year.

An organization for sales and service had to be built up. At first we had to work with salesmen who did not understand the niceties of the trade, but were keen that we get involved in the financing of all sorts of cinemas. This later led to painful losses. In the end, we learnt our lessons, and we now know the trade thoroughly.

Today film projecting has been automated to an extent unthinkable before the war, when there had to be an operator behind every single projector. Interestingly enough, research played only a small part in all this. The film projector was essentially a mechanical product. In those years, unlike today, our researchers had little interest in mechanical problems. Today we know a lot about lubrication and all sorts of modern ball bearings because we need them. But the early problems with those film projectors were solved by our designers and specialists in the machine works. Problems like that are more easily eliminated by experience than by science.

As a result of getting involved in sound recording through film projectors, we made the acquaintance of the American Fred Miller, who had created a system of his own. In the usual photographic light track on the film at that time the emulsion grain prevented perfect sound quality. Miller had invented a system consisting of a minute cutter making a sound track in the gelatine layer, which made perfect sound recording possible. A machine had to be designed which could translate this idea into a working reality. Jan Hardenberg, who had acquired expert knowledge as a designer and builder in our glass factory, succeeded in making an excellent recording machine. The Philips-Miller system was then used when top quality sound was required, for example on Radio Luxembourg. This commercial station had a studio in London where sound recordings were made on a series of Philips-Miller machines. During the war the speeches of King George VI and Winston Churchill were recorded on these tapes and broadcast by the BBC. After the war we had hoped for a more universal use for these machines, but soon the magnetic tape recorder came into use and was perfected so rapidly that the Philips-Miller system became obsolete.

The severing of the link between gold and the guilder in 1936 had a very positive effect on Philips. The number of people we employed in Holland again increased, until, in 1939, our total in Europe was 45,000, more than ever before. In those years it was very difficult to assess the future economic situation reliably. In periods of boom every industrialist is inclined to start creating new plants, while it takes a tremendous effort during a slump to undertake new construction which may be essential in some years' time. It is a bit like weather-forecasting, when, if you are in the midst of fog, it is hard to imagine that there may be bright sunshine fifty miles away. You have to have the courage to make decisions without a timetable which tells you when booms and slumps will arrive and depart.

In 1938 our senior man responsible for personnel policy retired. This responsibility was entrusted to me, and I was glad to undertake it, as men had always interested me much more than machines. Looking back now, it seems odd that our annual reports in those days only used to talk about financial and business information. These reports were meant exclusively for the shareholders, and the social aspects and our policy regarding our employees were thought irrelevant to them. At that time I, too, thought this natural. It would be unfair to criticize the management of those years for this, for they were only following the prevailing custom, but our present practice of paying more attention to human relations is, of course, right from every angle.

Trip to Russia

In 1939, Holst and I, accompanied by our wives and our chief engineer Van Dobbenburg, made a trip to Russia. This visit was motivated by the interest shown by the Russians in our manufacture of radio valves and medical X-ray equipment. We wanted to know how serious their interest was and what they were doing in these fields themselves.

We flew via Berlin, Koenigsberg and the border town of Brest-Litovsk to Moscow. For 'security reasons' our slow Junker aircraft was not allowed to fly higher than 3,000 feet. Our progress was not very rapid, and because of the low altitude the flight was bumpy. But it was beautiful weather, with bright sunshine and white clouds. That part of Russia is full of forests and lakes.

Our trip lasted three weeks, and took us to Moscow and Leningrad. Even though none of us spoke Russian it was full of interesting experiences.

We were immediately struck by the strong trust in the future which prevailed in the Soviet Union. At that time we in Western Europe were less confident. After World War I we had passed through many difficulties, followed by a big boom which had suddenly come to a halt in 1929. Since then we had experienced so much adversity that optimism was rare. In Russia we saw huge charts everywhere, installed in all possible places, on which sharply rising lines portrayed rising production. Last year the number of shoes manufactured was so many; this year it would be so many more. This seemed to be true for most products. Belief in a rosy future was drummed into people's minds.

So it was important to remind oneself that, up till 1917, Russia had not lagged behind industrially in comparison with other European countries. At that time the Russians made the best railway equipment, the largest aircraft, the finest ships, and excellent telephones. They were the biggest producers of galoshes. Russia used to be the granary of Europe. Because of the Revolution, all this had collapsed, so everything had had to be rebuilt from scratch. That is why the lines on the graphs could show such steep rises. Russia urgently needed West European technology to get back on her feet.

The State was managing everything. We had many talks with officials who invariably showed themselves delighted by our visit, but the Intourist people guarded our every step to such an extent that it was hardly possible even to walk by ourselves on the streets or to visit a museum. We did attend a soccer match, which was one of our most amusing experiences. At that time the Russians did not know how to play football and the teams looked more like twenty-two schoolboys running after the ball in a playground. Whenever anyone fell or stumbled, resounding laughter broke out on the stands. In fact, at that time Russian spectators went to football matches to have a good laugh. Today they go to see first-class play.

I admired the large parks where people could enjoy themselves with their children, as well as the grannies so necessary for looking after the children while the parents worked. The early attempts of the Soviet authorities to undercut family life seemed to have had little result.

A curious feature was towers from which people jumped attached to a sort of parachute. After climbing the tower they stepped into a kind of harness which was linked to a parachute on a cable, and then jumped into the void. The towers were not tall enough for the parachute always to open completely, but the cable prevented people from landing too hard on the ground. To me it seemed an odd exercise, and I have never seen it anywhere else. We also attended an enormous air show with perhaps 100,000 spectators, where we saw for the first time a large number of parachutists jumping simultaneously. Apparently the authorities wanted to popularise parachute jumping, hardly with peaceful purposes in mind.

The housing situation was deplorable, with several families sometimes living in a single room. The Government was attempting to alleviate some of the misery by providing social centres to give people at least some elbow-room. There were also some arrangements for children—for instance, there were special rooms in which children from five upwards were taught ballet.

Sarah Holst and Sylvia went out to look around during the day, but their enthusiasm about what they saw was dampened at night by what we told them about the endless talks resulting in nothing. In addition to the gentlemen taking part in these talks, there were always some silent persons present who obviously had to report on the others. Later it became clear to us that some of these silent men understood Dutch perfectly. Apparently secret microphones had not yet been developed.

At the universities and schools which we visited I noticed buildings only five or six years old were already falling to pieces. Here and there cement would fall off the walls. It was also a depressing sight to see so many women dressed in sacks, sweeping the streets. Men's suits never really fitted, and sometimes people looked as if they were going about in one another's clothes. People seemed to try to express their individuality with caps, which took little material. There were caps of many colours and kinds: green with marble-like yellow, old-fashioned caps with a huge peak worn at a slight angle, caps with lacquered peaks, some turned upwards. We called the wearers of these last the optimists. The pessimists would wear the peak downwards. Very few wore hats, but it was evidently no longer a sign of capitalist mentality if a Russian was wearing a hat.

The factories we saw looked all right. In a radio factory, valves of a type which had been in use eight years previously in Holland were being manufactured, but the very best of that period had been selected, those which were least complicated and most suitable for mass production. Factories were always run by two managers—one a worker who had climbed through the ranks in the Party and the other a man who knew something about the manufacturing process. The latter was often a German.

We had no chance to meet the factory workers, but the girls looked fresh and neat. They might live in crowded conditions, but they were strikingly clean, something which one also notices in Asia. As far as I could see, people worked hard in the factories, and sophisticated experiments were carried out in the laboratories which we visited. But it was our impression that if something was developed it would take a very long time to reach the production stage, and might never reach it. It is, I believe, a characteristic of Russian intellectuals that they are keen on research but that after they have discovered something worthwhile their interest often flags. They find turning it into a standardized product less interesting. For example, we saw sodium and mercury lamps, but they had not managed to find ways to mass produce them.

We had several talks with the commercial authorities and with officials of the light bulb industries' trust. They became quite cordial when they heard that Karl Marx had worked on *Das Kapital* in my grandfather's home at Zaltbommel, and countless glasses of vodka were then drained in honour of the Philips family. As a matter of fact, we never had the feeling that we were considered despicable capitalists. They respected technological and industrial abilities.

It was of course impossible to talk to the man in the street. In Moscow a girl from the State Travel Agency was detailed to accompany us. She was a typical Party member with crude stockings free from any bourgeois taint, but in Leningrad we were given a guide with silk stockings, whose father was a leading engineer in a diesel engineering factory. This girl turned out to be much less doctrinaire.

We were staying in old-fashioned hotels where the towels were worn thread-bare, but where we got a clean one every day, however full of holes. A lady with keys was posted on every floor, and this did not give us a sense of freedom.

On our return trip we spent some days in Warsaw, a striking contrast. After Moscow, Warsaw looked like Paris. People were well-dressed. There were many cars in the streets. The drivers, too, had different habits from their Russian colleagues, who drove us around in their beautiful Intourist cars at great speed, loudly honking their horns while pedestrians jumped for their lives.

Later we received a return visit from a Russian delegation who were deeply impressed with our factories, especially with the conditions of our employees. For them the homes in which our workers lived were unbelievable.

We offered them an X-ray tube and equipment plant for thirty-five million guilders, including our know-how. But they did not accept it, and that was the end of our Russian adventure.

Family Occasions

In these years I was given a great deal by my wife and by our children, as they grew up with the normal joys and sorrows of a large family. We were also part of a larger family of which my father was the centre, and where by tradition he exercised authority in an almost patriarchal way. He was generous with advice, and followed with close attention the progress of his nephews and nieces and grandchildren. He enjoyed it intensely when the whole family turned up for birthdays and other festive occasions.

Then there were the delightful Sunday evenings in my parents' home, De Laak, where we generally went for dinner—Annejet and Frans, Jetty and Henk van Riemsdijk, Sylvia and I. After dinner we would talk about the situation in the world and in our own country, and usually in a highly critical manner—no government could fully please us. Then at a given moment my mother would give the signal to stop the discussion. The men would stay talking together for a little, and then join the ladies in the living room, where the table would be cleared for bridge or for another card game we could all play together.

We all enjoyed these times at De Laak. But as 1940 approached, they were overshadowed by increasing fears for the future.

Chapter 6

Philips Prepares

Years before World War II broke out, we made preparations as far as possible to protect Philips in case of war. It was Otten who first noticed the dark clouds in the political sky and initiated these preparations. Loupart, too, who remembered the German invasion of Belgium in World War I, insisted on them more and more. Meanwhile, our country showed a general lack of realism, although a few fortifications were built near bridges. However, we in Philips had for a long time been receiving disconcerting information from our factories all over Europe as well as warnings direct from Germany, and we were forced to think seriously of what would happen to the Concern if Holland was involved in war or even occupied.

Van Walsem used all his legal inventiveness to find the right answer to this question. First, the headquarters had to be moved outside Holland, to a part of the Kingdom of the Netherlands which could be expected to remain safe. Willemstad on the island of Curaçao seemed the best choice. The second step was to start two Trusts. The British Trust, created on 1 May 1939, was based in London and comprised all our companies in the British Commonwealth. The American Trust was formed in August of the same year, in Hartford, Connecticut, with the aim of safeguarding Philips' interests in North, Central and South America. This was done to prevent the Philips establishments abroad from being declared enemy property if Holland was occupied. Through these arrangements all our factories would be turned over to the two Trusts, which would run them on behalf of the rightful shareholders. The members of the senior management would, as far as possible, act as advisers and trustees. Thus the link between the various components outside the occupied territory would be preserved.

For this solution we needed the co-operation of the Netherlands Government. A law had to be passed enabling a limited stock company to move its registered office outside Holland. As our information became even more alarming we kept urging the authorities to make haste with this law, and when at long last it was passed on 26 April 1940, it turned out to be only just in time.

This meant that Philips outside the European part of the Kingdom of the Netherlands was safe. But what would happen to the business inside Holland in case of war? This, too, demanded attention, and it was not a small matter. But it was a long time before we could get the Dutch Government interested. Only after the Munich agreement in September 1938, when Neville Chamberlain and his French colleague Edouard Daladier left Czechoslovakia to Hitler's mercy, did our Government take any initiative.

We were faced with a number of practical tasks. We realized that our Concern possessed something of irreplaceable value in its research apparatus and that this would be important for our allies. So we decided to move the essential nucleus of our laboratories to Britain. We bought the Snowdenham Hall estate in Surrey, where the research staff could live. About two hundred people, including thirty of the senior management, were involved. Everyone had to move first behind the Water Defence Line in the western part of Holland. This was considered a last-ditch redoubt, as it was defended by the natural barriers of the big delta rivers and was to be reinforced by a number of inundations. In making these plans we were working on the assumption that the Dutch armed forces would be able to keep the enemy outside the Water Defence Line for several weeks. Preparations for this evacuation were made quite early on, and each member of this group obtained a passport and other necessary documents. In these arrangements we had the fullest co-operation of the British Government.

Plans had also to be made, in co-operation with the Departments of Defence and Economic Affairs, for the manufacture of military transmission valves, of various means of communications and of ammunition components in Holland. We agreed that this war material must be made behind the Water Defence Line, and so we bought a factory in The Hague for making transmission valves while, for the manufacture of cartridges, we were able to get the former Austrian cartridge plant at Dordrecht. We aimed in each case to start with a minimum of equipment to which additional machines could be transferred from Eindhoven. We also asked a retired army officer, Lt. Gen. H. G. Winkelman, to prepare an evacuation plan which would take all the military aspects into account.*

---

*It was this General who later, in February 1940, was unexpectedly nominated Commander-in-Chief of all our armed forces, and was then faced with the impossible task of bringing our defence into a state of preparedness.

Meanwhile some steps were taken for our defence—only it was too little, too late. Thus, two hundred 37 mm. anti-tank field guns were ordered from the Austrian firm of Boehler. Shells capable of piercing armoured plate had to be manufactured for them, so we began manufacturing these shells at Dordrecht. Our research department developed a new system for hardening the shell-heads with a special high-frequency technique which did not make the rest of the shell too brittle. After a short time our shells were noticeably better than Boehler's.

The deliveries of these guns stopped when Austria was annexed by Germany, and we were given an order for the anti-tank guns themselves. Suddenly we had become gun manufacturers! In order to co-ordinate this highly specialised work our people at Dordrecht literally had to work day and night and, within a year, we succeeded in delivering our first anti-tank gun. This was in April 1940, and within weeks that same gun was being fired at enemy armoured vehicles just outside our factory.

In January 1940, when we were working flat out to produce the anti-tank gun, I visited a lieutenant colonel who was a big wheel in army supplies procurement. This man had the nerve to tell me that he wanted to cancel the order. After the German victory in Poland, Boehler had informed him that it could again supply the guns previously ordered. Would I regard the order as cancelled?

I was livid, and said, 'Colonel, if the Germans invade us, people may be hanged from the trees of this square because they sabotaged our national cause in precisely the way you are intending to do now. This is treason!'

I regarded this message from Austria as a German ruse to make us stop our production. Meanwhile they would never supply us with the guns. My indignation was caused both by this man's naivety and by his cancelling an order on which people had worked day and night, work done not for profit, but to contribute our small bit to our national defences. In the end, the order was not cancelled.

Meanwhile we were also planning for the survival of our non-military plant in Holland, if the invasion we dreaded should materialize. Even if Philips' registered headquarters were transferred to Curaçao, there must be a legal framework for what would be left in Eindhoven. So an operating company was set up which rented factories and installations from Philips Gloeilampenfabrieken NV in Curaçao. This operating company was to be managed by some of our senior staff, who would stay behind and make the most of the current circumstances. Our primary duty was, of course, to look after our employees' interests. Nobody had the faintest notion what would happen to our factories in the event of a German occupation. Would all activity be stopped? Would the machines be taken to Germany? Or would everything be put under German management? The latter possibility appeared to us most likely, but nobody knew for sure.

It never crossed my mind that I would play a role in all this. I had been mobilized. Possibly I would continue working for the war effort inside the Water Defence Line, with the chance that I, too, would eventually leave for Britain. Perhaps I would be made a prisoner of war and either be taken outside Holland or condemned to inactivity inside Holland. These were only suppositions. The reality turned out to be different.

We took some very down-to-earth measures. For instance, we had many thousands of pay-packets prepared so that we could pay our employees even if confusion reigned, as it actually did in May 1940. We also, somewhat optimistically, set up a separate sales organisation in Bloemendaal to continue supplying Philips products to the west of the country.

False Alarm

On 8 and 9 April the Germans attacked Denmark and Norway, and our senior management decided not to take any chances. Many families moved to their wartime accommodation, behind the Water Defence Line. In my own family an additional condition was claiming our attention. Our sixth child was expected at any moment! Preparations had been made for Sylvia in the hospital in Eindhoven when the message came that wives and children had to be evacuated.

The birth of our previous children had always taken quite a long time. Even though the first birth pangs had started, we put the cradle in the back of our car, with all the other necessities, and left for The Hague. It was a critical situation. It was quite possible that the child would be born en route. Somewhere in a hospital in 's Hertogenbosch, in Utrecht, in Gouda? We did not know, and could only hope that we would make The Hague in time. In fact, it was a very peaceful drive, and we had the fullest confidence that God would let the child be born at the right moment. We arrived at the hospital in The Hague at about 11.30 p.m. and were received in the maternity ward of the hospital.

After this I went to the Department of Defence, to try to find out what was happening. German warships had been sighted in the North Sea, but it was hoped that they would not come to Holland. Possibly it was a diversionary move connected with the invasion of Scandinavia.

I went back to the hospital. As the situation was unaltered, I returned after midnight to the Defence Department. Nobody asked for my identification and I walked straight into the telephone exchange room, where civilians were on duty. It terrified me to think how easy it would be to overpower these unarmed men and take control of our defence communications. The officer in charge had a phone, so I contacted Otten in his office in Eindhoven.

Early the next afternoon our third son, Frits, was born. Sylvia stayed in hospital for ten days and then moved to a house in the city which we had rented for evacuation purposes. Nobody could say how long our stay inside the Water Defence Line redoubt would last, so our children joined us. My parents also moved into an apartment in a local hotel, and particularly valuable items of my father's collections were moved to safer places, as well as the silver and antiques from our own home.

As the situation then seemed static, I went back to Eindhoven, and later my family returned there too. We were very uncertain about the future, because intelligence from across the borders made us expect the worst. But while our minds told us that war was inevitable, we continued to hope all the same . . .

Chapter 7

War Breaks Out

Early in May the international situation was so tense that women and children were once more evacuated behind the Water Defence Line. Sylvia again left for The Hague, with six children, a cat and a canary, while I stayed on in Eindhoven. In the early evening of Thursday the ninth, I was playing a game of tennis with friends. Though we were worried, it seemed sensible to relax. At about seven a message reached me that I was urgently wanted on the telephone.

Immediately I had a hunch that this was it. Oddly, it was partly prompted by a book which I had read twenty years before, in which people in Belgium had been playing tennis when the news of the 1914 German invasion had come like a thunder-bolt from a clear sky.

On the phone I heard a well-known voice: 'It's Frans!'

'What's the matter?'

'I've just had a message from Germany that it's going to start tonight.' This message, though terrible, did not surprise me. What struck me was the similarity with the occurrence in the book. I put on my uniform and went to the head office.

At last the crisis had come. We would have to decide immediately whether to evacuate or not. The accuracy of the message was not in doubt, but in view of the mood prevailing in The Hague we were unlikely to get an official order. So we had to act on our own. We decided to evacuate.

Messages went out. General Winkelman's plan was put in motion. Though it was evening, Philips became a beehive of activity. Shifts of men started dismantling machines. The work was done with admirable decisiveness. Everybody knew his task. Trailers and trucks rolled in and, in the darkness of the night, the first columns were formed. Everything was running so smoothly that I dared to go home to take a two-hour rest. On my return the columns were still waiting. Then, at about 4.30 a.m., the signal was given to start for our positions behind the Water Defence Line, in which we had unshakeable confidence. We could hear the German fighter squadrons high above, and hoped their mission did not include obstructing us.

The operation started well. The different columns were composed according to plan. Mine, consisting of about sixty cars, transported employees needed inside the Water Defence Line. Among them were several officers, like Otten who was a captain in the Reserve. Some were in uniform, others in civilian clothes.

We soon met our first obstacle. The Moerdijk Bridge was occupied by parachutists! Part of the column was then diverted and our section crossed the estuary to Numansdorp. We did not get much further because the southern part of Rotterdam had also been taken by German parachutists.

In Numansdorp, we experienced our first air attack. Our column had evidently attracted the enemy's attention. The air-raid sirens howled. With some companions I sheltered in a house, and out of the window saw a plane drop four bombs in our direction. The plane's speed was such that the bombs could not hit us, but they were a terrifying sight, growing bigger and bigger as they fell. We ducked down as well as we could, and listened to the explosions some way behind the house.

We had to spend that night on farms on the island of Hoeksewaard. The six officers among us took turns keeping watch, naively hoping that we could defend ourselves with our service pistols against heavily-armed parachutists. Even so, we slept reasonably well, and kept our patriotic sense of humour. Nor did we neglect our outward appearance. While using our faithful electric shaver we thought up this jingle:

> Though the war goes ever so mean,
> Philishave will shave us clean.

The following day, our section managed to cross the Nieuwe Maas by ferry boat west of Rotterdam, and towards nightfall we arrived in The Hague. I at once went to the Ministry of Defence. According to reports, our army had managed, during the first day of the war, to stop the enemy advance at several points, but German air superiority was so overwhelming that our position was considered difficult. Fierce fighting was going on along the Grebbeberg defence line and the Dutch command was considering a counter-offensive from the south. This never materialized, nor did our plans for our factory evacuation succeed. The whole column got stranded and none of our machines reached their destination.

I was billeted in a house with other Reserve officers in The Hague, but there was nothing for us to do. This frustrated us greatly, and when we heard that men were needed to operate the anti-aircraft batteries near the Ordnance Factory, we volunteered at once. We left at 4.30 p.m. for Leiden, where we passed the Dutch batteries near Valkenburg firing at German paratroopers on the nearby airfield. But just as we arrived in Leiden, we heard on the radio that Holland had capitulated.

This was a terrible moment. Of course, we realized that capitulation meant avoiding further disasters. Our air defence had been knocked out and we could see black smoke from the terrible fires of Rotterdam miles away, a grim warning of what would befall other cities if we continued a battle that could no longer be won.

Once again we felt useless and aimless. So we went back to The Hague. The day before, my parents with Otten, Van Walsem and Loupart had left by British destroyer for England. It was a tremendous shock to hear that Max Vlielander Hein, Sylvia's youngest step-brother, had been killed in action during the last hours of hostilities. Commanding his section, he had courageously covered his company's retreat. After the liberation he was posthumously awarded a high decoration, which Sylvia's mother received from Queen Wilhelmina.

In The Hague I first tried to get an order from my commanding officer to escape to Britain, but he said he could not give such an order. Should I go without authorization, which at that point still seemed possible? I went to see Sylvia. The two of us had to do some deep thinking. I was a Reserve officer, with experience in production and organization. Would I, in Britain, be able to help the Allied war effort? Or should I stay in Holland to share the war-time fate of our Philips community, who might otherwise feel abandoned? With The Hague chaotic around us, we thought over these questions, ready to do whatever God required of us. Soon we felt a great certainty that we were meant to stay in Holland. And as we sat there on the edge of the bed, God said to us: 'Don't look on the task ahead of you as a heavy burden. You are chosen to bear this responsibility.'

The curious thing was that after this decision we felt completely at peace. We went to sleep, expecting the next step to be revealed to us. And next day, as if we were being shown what to do, one of our Eindhoven staff turned up out of the blue. He had hitch-hiked to The Hague and was delighted to find us. He urged me to return to Eindhoven to help to clear up the confusion there. One problem was that although an operating company for Holland had been set up, it had not been made clear who was to lead it. A sort of board had been formed, but it did not work, as none of its members had ever held responsible management positions.

All sorts of small difficulties had arisen—conflicts, for instance, about who was to sit in which room. We had foreseen many difficulties, but not those. Moreover, the Government had given no guide lines as to what to do in case of enemy occupation.

Naturally I agreed to start for Eindhoven immediately, but I did not know yet whether I was to be taken prisoner of war. So I went to see General Winkelman, and he arranged with the Germans that I should be given a leave pass for a week. I had no clothes except my uniform, so I had to drive across an occupied country dressed as a soldier, passing endless German columns on their way to the battle theatre in Zeeland and Belgium. However, they let me through. I even got into conversation with some German soldiers on my way, and always asked them: 'What have you come here for? There was no war going on here before you came!' They invariably replied that they had come because we were planning to let the British in via the Hook of Holland. This, of course, was nonsense.

Back at Eindhoven, I put on civilian clothes and went to our head office. After the first day I had succeeded in restoring peace and order in our ranks. After a week my leave was over; so I returned to The Hague. It was clear that my presence in Eindhoven was essential. The Secretary-General of the Trade, Industry and Navigation Ministry, Dr. H. M. Hirschfeld, was a highly capable civil servant, who despite his Jewish ancestry enjoyed the Germans' confidence. He managed to persuade them that they had to release me if they seriously intended to get the Dutch economy moving again. So I was demobilized and took up permanent residence in Eindhoven again.

My family also moved back to Eindhoven, and we had to decide where to live. De Wielewaal was some distance outside Eindhoven and there would soon be restrictions on civilian petrol. We could use our bicycles, but the distance would be a problem. My father's home, De Laak, was both empty and in the centre of the city. Both De Wielewaal and De Laak were the kind of houses the Germans would be likely to requisition, and we thought they would do less damage in De Wielewaal, whose interior was white-wash, than in wood-panelled De Laak. For the children, too, it was better to live in the middle of town. So we decided to go to De Laak. Soon afterwards, Luftwaffe officers moved into De Wielewaal.

One good thing about that bad period was that I was able to spend much more time with my family. Our eldest child was nine and the youngest only a few months old, and I was glad to be so much more at home. But the occupation also brought many bitter experiences. We were living in an atmosphere of uncertainty. Day in, day out, a deluge of lies descended upon us. In addition there was the constant threat of something terrible happening in our immediate surroundings. It was a situation which one has to live through to understand. People who managed to escape during the occupation told me later that even they found it difficult after a few months of liberty to imagine what this lack of freedom meant.

I now had to decide our attitude towards the occupying power. It was our job to keep the company together as well as we could and yet to avoid making any contribution to the German war effort. We also had to make the lives of our 19,000 employees and their families as bearable as possible. The first question to be decided was: Which products do we continue and which do we stop? One early decision we took was to start the factory holidays earlier, which gave us a breathing space in which to do some deeper thinking. We also decided to function as an exclusively Dutch firm.

In order to get a grip on Dutch industry, the Germans soon nominated so-called *Verwalters* (trustees) to the larger companies, which had to pay them. Philips was assigned two, Dr. O. Bormann and O. J. Merkel. Both of them were members of our Supervisory Board in Germany, which was some comfort. But they were placed in a difficult position, especially Bormann. He was Managing Director of the German firm of Pintsch, with which we had a know-how agreement, had had good relations with my father and had until recently been looked upon as a friend. Now we had to answer the agonizing question of how we were to deal with these supervisors who had been forced upon us. An outsider might say, 'It is wrong to shake the hand of any German,' but that is not so easy if you are dealing with a man who was so recently a friend, even though he had now become a watchdog. So I did not adopt this attitude. But when once in 1940 we invited Bormann and Merkel to dine with us, the experience was so difficult for my wife and myself that we never did it again.

The Germans considered Philips important enough to place it under the direct supervision of one of their ministries in Berlin. But different ministries began to quarrel about manufacturers, and radios were used for propaganda. So at first Dr. Joseph Goebbels' Propaganda Ministry wanted the job, the last thing we wanted. Other contenders were the army and the air force. Our *Verwalter* Merkel happened to be especially friendly with an important air force general. This appeared to be the least harmful connection and, in fact, the Reich Aviation Ministry succeeded in pulling Philips into its sphere of influence.

Dutch industrialists had to live in a continual state of uncertainty. None of us knew where we stood. Instructions about how much to cooperate with a possible occupying power had never been issued. The only clue was in the Land War Regulation, which stated that we were not to make arms, ammunition, military ships, vehicles or aircraft, but did not mention communication equipment. At first, the Germans' belief that they had already won the war was a help. Why should they bother about ordering communication equipment? Their lightning conquest had meant only small losses of equipment, and those losses could easily be replaced by their domestic manufacturers.

One plant in which we thought the Germans might show special interest was our arms and ammunition factory in Dordrecht. They came to have a look, and I conducted the talks with them. I was helped by their victorious mood and their sense of superiority. They thought that our attempts at arms manufacturing could not amount to much. What would a Dutch lamp and radio company know about manufacturing arms in comparison with the German arms industry? I did everything I could to strengthen this attitude. I explained to the gentlemen how amateurish we were and that we had not even really started production. About our shell-head hardening process I kept quiet.

Meanwhile I agreed with Frans den Hollander, Managing Director of the Ordnance Factory, that the big automatic lathes, our most important machines, should be transported quickly to Hembrug. To make this move plausible we made it appear that these machines did not belong to Philips but were on loan from the Ordnance Factory. Den Hollander had still to negotiate with the Germans about what to do with the Hembrug installations, so it did not matter to him whether he had a few more machines, but I was grateful to be rid of them. So immediately after the capitulation we succeeded, under the eyes of the Germans, in dismantling our arms factory.

We had to keep the Dordrecht plant running, but our local manager managed to delude the Germans into believing that lathes were in great demand in Holland. He then started producing simple lathes suitable for trades schools, where no costly precision lathes were needed.

In this early occupation period I also had dealings with some of the Dutch authorities. We had incurred considerable expenses in evacuating men and machines when the Germans invaded. Officially, the Dutch authorities owed us compensation, and, as a lot of money was invested, we could not afford to forgo it in those difficult times. I ran into objections from a certain Engineers' general. When I explained our claim at a small meeting in The Hague, he wanted to know precisely who had given the order to evacuate on that fateful night. Luckily, I knew that this general had been peacefully at his home in Wassenaar during the invasion, so I retorted, 'General, as our columns started moving from Eindhoven in the middle of the night in order to reach the Water Defence Line fortress—a move which had been agreed with the Department of Defence—you were sleeping in your bed.'

As I was only a first lieutenant, I did not like having to say this to a general, but I felt I had to speak up for Philips. The result? Our expenses were redeemed in accordance with regulations.

Meanwhile, there was much confusion in Holland. Many Dutch believed that our country would be for some time entirely under the German heel, and came to the conclusion that we must just make the best of it. The more optimistic thought that we were merely under military occupation and would be left in peace. There were also some 'fellow-travellers'—either partial or complete—who were willing to give Germany a chance. By them I was repeatedly advised, 'You ought to go to Berlin and talk with the big people there so that they will take you seriously.' Others on the contrary felt that I should not even receive a German in my room.

I also had to grapple with an incessant stream of rumours. One person would say, 'Telefunken is about to take you over.' Another would tell us, of course 'from the most reliable source', that another firm was interested. My concern about what would happen to Philips was understandably acute. One morning I received a clear answer to my prayers for strength: 'Frits, don't worry. Philips will either be preserved or destroyed. Your job is to do your work as well as you can each day. For the rest, you must trust.'

This thought not only filled me with a sense of peace that morning, but also kept me going during the entire war period. So although I was only thirty-five, I was able to help many of our people who were often faced with colossal problems. I was able to stay optimistic about the final outcome of the war and encourage many people, especially the men in the factory, who were only too eager to be contaminated by the optimism of 'Mr. Frits'.

Soon it transpired that the Germans considered me too young to be the head of the Philips Concern. In addition, they wanted a smaller directorate which they could manipulate better. That directorate was formed, but I managed to stay on. It consisted of five members: Holst, P. R. Dijksterhuis, J. C. de Vries, K. K. H. Spaens and myself. I acted as chairman of the directorate and was officially regarded as President of Philips. This team was a solid combination, which is not to say that I always had an easy time. Some, at times, talked with the *Verwalters* without consulting me, and I was ready to assume that they hoped to serve the interest of Philips in that way. But this came to an end when the students of Leiden and Delft started resisting the Germans and two Delft students were executed. I had attempted, through our *Verwalters*, to warn the German authorities in Berlin of the far-reaching effects these executions would have, but in vain. This tragic event was a turning point for many Dutch who had believed that some accommodation with the Germans was possible.

Contacts Across the Borders

All the international links and contacts to which we in Philips were accustomed had of course been broken, but in Eindhoven we were still deeply interested in all Philips companies in other European countries, whether they were already under German control or not. In August 1940 we heard that our company in Czechoslovakia wanted to purchase a glass factory. Our factory manager was still in charge, and he sought our opinion. I succeeded in getting a *Marschbefehl* (marching order), so that some of my colleagues and I were able to go there. It was an interesting trip to a beautiful country. In the countryside the shops were still well supplied. And during a picnic on a drive to a glass factory outside Prague, we were able to talk freely with our Czech friends, and soon discovered that the Czechs felt exactly the same as we did about German domination. The glass factory was never bought.

We had to go back to Holland via Berlin, where we had talks with the Germans. It appeared to be true that Telefunken was trying to get some hold over Philips. We resisted this, but the scheme actually failed because of the intervention of the Aviation Ministry, which wanted to keep Philips under its own supervision.

In the Hotel Eden we were delighted to experience an air-raid alert— due, it later appeared, to one British plane flying over the city. Goering had proclaimed only a short while before that this could never happen, but now all the hotel guests were assembled in the cellar. We Dutch sat there smiling happily amid gloomy German faces.

Our own organization in Germany, which we contacted at that point, did everything possible to assist us in Holland. Only a few of the management turned out to be real Nazis, and after the war they disappeared. The majority understood our predicament.

The Germans permitted us to export to neutral countries in Europe, such as Spain, Sweden and Switzerland, so we were able to keep our sales organizations going there. The same was true for Hungary and the Balkan countries, which had been a significant market for Philips from the earliest days and were still outside the German sphere of influence. We owned several valuable factories in that region, and I convinced the Germans that it made sense to co-ordinate our business in the Balkans. I got another *Marschbefehl*, and in November 1940 I made a trip to Budapest with two other Philips men. We invited our managers in the different Balkan countries to meet us there, and it became a conference on future policies. As these managers were receiving instructions both from New York and from Eindhoven, it was very useful to agree on basic policy and so prevent conflicts. We agreed that we should try to continue supplying them from Eindhoven. We also saw how important it was to give these men support and encouragement, and I told them that they enjoyed our fullest confidence, whatever the circumstances might be. Troubles were coming all too soon, as the Germans and Italians overran these countries shortly afterwards.

From Budapest I managed to telephone Otten in New York. The connection was made via Portugal, and we were sure our conversation was being tapped by various agencies, so we were cautious, but tried to cover the essential points. We agreed to avoid conflict over our factories in the Balkans, and to settle any differences after the war was over. I also said that in Holland we would do all we could to keep Philips alive—a statement any eavesdropper was welcome to hear.

In Budapest, where abundance still prevailed, I bought Sylvia some warm dresses and a sheepskin coat, which I tied around my suitcase as if it were a rug. At Vienna station an aged customs official objected, then I said to him, 'Remember what we in Holland have done for the Austrian children!' He made a gesture and whispered, 'All right, move on!' That coat has given good service to our family for over thirty years.

Even though Philips could no longer work on the large scale to which we had been accustomed, the Germans had their own big ideas for us. They felt that the 19,000 we were employing in Holland were too few, and should become 30,000. I told them this was impossible because of space. So then they wanted us to start building. I had always enjoyed building, so I liked this idea, and I tried to figure out how we could build without enlarging our productive plant. For years we had felt the need of a big warehouse, and here was our chance. I went to the Germans and said to them, 'You want us to build, don't you? Well, the thing we most need is a warehouse.' The gentlemen nodded. So I immediately took the matter up with the Government Commissioner for Reconstruction, to whom I also told our real reasons. He at once promised us the necessary permits for building materials. So we were able to invite tenders. It was to be a building in three parts, separated by fire proof doors and covered by an enormous flat roof.

This experience might have given us the impression that the occupation authorities wanted us to continue our own programme of producing consumer goods. But there were the military hobbyists to reckon with. Germany was full of inventive military men thinking up clever gadgets which might be useful in the war. But to invent such things was not sufficient; they also had to be made, and that was often the bottleneck. German industries like Siemens, Telefunken and Lorenz did not like getting involved in these military brain-children. They knew how much effort went into making a prototype, and that if, miraculously, a useable object resulted, it would not be profitable. So they kept these amateurs at a safe distance.

But some of them had heard about us. They would turn up in Eindhoven, penetrate to one of the *Verwalters* and so find their way into our research and development department. If such a man succeeded in getting the *Rüstungsinspektion* (Armaments Inspection) on his side it sometimes happened that we were invited to develop the gadget. This was not so serious as it sounds, because such an order meant a colossal amount of drawing work, while the chances that a useable apparatus would result were next to zero.

So we did take on some of these jobs, but never without pointing out a few basic facts to the Germans. They had to understand that we lacked experience in the military field. We were simple people who could only manufacture lamps and radios so it was unwise to expect us to do anything else. Of course, they then pointed to our research laboratory. So I would explain to them that the people there were working on things which would only reach the market in ten years' time at the earliest. Usually I would add: 'Gentlemen, you should never count on too much help from our people. We consider ourselves at war with you, because your armies have overrun us for no valid reason. Perhaps it is impossible to force someone to be terribly stupid, but it is certainly impossible to compel people to be very intelligent. If you give us orders involving our research and development divisions, and our people there have no enthusiasm for what you ask of them, the chances are that it will come to nothing. So you could land yourselves in big trouble.'

For I knew that they, like the *Verwalters*, were regularly checked up on and asked what had become of the initiatives they had taken. All in all, we succeeded relatively well in avoiding military contracts. Our only factory making communications equipment for the Germans was our transmitter plant, the NSF, at Hilversum. The manager, however, was very clever in deceiving the German customers, so what he supplied was strictly limited.

Woltersom Organization

Towards the end of 1940 it became clear that the occupation authorities wanted to remodel the Dutch economy on German lines. The committee charged with this task was chaired by H. L. Woltersom, which made him a controversial figure.

Woltersom was also a member of the Supervisory Board of Philips, and at one point was a real help to me. One of the German hobby horses was the so-called Winter Help Scheme which had replaced all private charities, and with which no Dutchman except collaborators wanted to have anything to do. The Germans did everything in their power to induce Dutch companies to participate in this strange form of welfare, which was liberally intermixed with propaganda for their 'New Order'. Philips, being the biggest firm in Holland, was selected to make a contribution to this Scheme—to wit, a generous gift from the management and a collection among the factory workers. All of us in Philips rejected this. Our *Verwalter* Merkel did not give up hope and went to see Woltersom in his capacity as a member of the Philips Supervisory Board. He was worried he said, about something which he could not discuss so easily with 'that fellow Philips'.

'What do you want Philips to do?' asked Woltersom.

'I should like to have a big collection organized in all the Philips factories,' replied Merkel.

Woltersom looked worried. 'If you force a collection like this on Philips, you'll be so hated in Eindhoven that you may wake up one morning with a knife in your back,' he said. 'I would not be able to guarantee your safety. These southerners can be impulsive.' Merkel dropped the idea and Philips was able to keep this kind of forced collection outside its gates.

The Woltersom Organization worried us, but was not enforced strongly by the occupation authorities because of FOEGIN, a pre-war electronics manufacturers' federation, consisting of people accustomed to work together. FOEGIN was moved *in toto* into the newly formed industrial organization, with the result that very little changed. We worked with about forty industrialists and the urgent item on the agenda was always the distribution of the diminishing supplies of raw materials.

As our co-operation was so smooth, we managed to keep the Germans out of our affairs. Of all the FOEGIN people there was only one we did not fully trust. One of the positive aspects in that grim episode was that my Philips colleagues and I got to know our fellow manufacturers well and we were able to help each other.

The first winter of the war was not all frustration and misery. As everything was scarce, sales were no problem. And as foreign travel was less possible I spent a lot of time with my family at De Laak. So we were happy together as far as occupation conditions permitted. Our Sunday mornings in particular had their own character. I used to read the children's Bible to my children and often to some of their friends. Accompanied on a small house organ which Sylvia and I had given to each other on a wedding anniversary, we sang hymns, especially those which had particular relevance to the situation, like the sixteenth century hymn written during the war against the Spanish:

> Fortunate the land protected by the Lord,
> If the enemy is all around
> With murder and arson
> And if it's thought he will conquer
> Then he's doomed to fall.

This was a comfort to us. Then one of the family would say a short prayer. And, so strengthened, we could face the difficulties of the coming week.

We had no illusions that conditions would improve. More and more articles were rationed and, despite assurances to the contrary by the occupation authorities, we knew that it would get worse. Everybody who could made his own arrangements. I agreed with a local farmer that he would supply us with milk. I bought him a good pedigree cow on condition that he would send us one gallon of milk a day even in the period when the cow was not producing. We also agreed that he would buy any calves from me at normal market prices. This worked splendidly and we were able to help many mothers with babies throughout the occupation years.

We also acquired a tandem bicycle. Sylvia had to get accustomed to leaving the steering of the thing completely in my hands, but the extra bell gave her plenty of compensation. This means of conveyance, which also gave us exercise, came in very handy. We were able to see many parts of the country, and in those difficult days it became all the dearer to us.

Chapter 8
A Risky Jubilee

23 May 1941 was one of the most astonishing days in my life. The occupation, with its constant pressures, had lasted for over a year. We had gone on working and hoping; but when we realized that Philips' fiftieth anniversary was approaching, we did not feel like celebrating. We agreed to mark the day in a simple and modest fashion. The only thing we planned was an occasion for our senior staff—on Monday morning at about 11.30 some forty of us, Dutch men and women, would raise our glasses to a better future.

Our thoughts naturally went to Uncle Gerard, for it had been he who in 1891 had gone to the notary public to get the foundation documents for our company made out. He had started the company and was now living in The Hague, while my father, who had made it great, was in America.

In The Hague, I bought a fine silver cup which I had suitably inscribed. A few days before the anniversary, Lokker and I went to see Uncle Gerard in his flat to present him with it. He was very pleased. Then we drank cups of real coffee, a rare luxury. On that day in May, both Uncle Gerard and Aunt Joh were hale and hearty, and I was struck by the lucidity of their minds, even though they had both passed eighty. Little did I realize that eight months later both would die within a few days of each other.

Lokker and I thought that this little presentation would be almost all that we would do to celebrate our 'silent jubilee'. But the whole thing turned out quite differently. At nine o'clock on the Monday morning the phone in De Laak rang. A voice from the head office expressing both fear and joy spoke to me:

'Mr. Philips, flowers are being brought in here by the car-load!'

'What? Flowers?'

'Yes, it seems that the news has spread that Philips is fifty years old today. The hall here is full of flowers. You ought to come and have a look.'

When you look at flowers, of course you take your wife. So at about ten, Sylvia and I arrived at the office. We were amazed. Every firm with which we had done business for half a century, as well as an overwhelming number of private people who wanted to show solidarity in those days, had sent flowers in such quantity and variety that we were overwhelmed.

That was only the beginning. Hardly had we entered the building than resounding applause started from all floors. We looked up and saw landing after landing filled with people, the entire head office personnel, staff members, department heads, secretaries, correspondents, accountants, all hanging over the banisters, hundreds and hundreds of people who clapped and cheered in order to express—yes, what were they trying to express? At that moment, one of the most moving in our lives, my wife and I realized the powerful feeling behind it. People were thinking: 'We are all under the heel of the occupying power, but today we can let go. For we are all Dutch, and we are also Philips people!'

It was a combination of patriotism and a feeling of belonging together. Because my name was Philips and because I was then the only member of the Philips family present, those feelings concentrated on me with a strength which would have normally never been possible. It was completely genuine and overwhelmingly spontaneous, and I have never felt as strongly as at that moment that this company bearing my name is in fact something more than a series of factories making products.

After the cheering had at last ceased we thought that the celebration was over apart from the glass of sherry in the Philips Recreation Centre. Around 11.30 the senior staff members walked there. Our manager from Brussels had come for the occasion, and there was a homely atmosphere in the small hall. The *Verwalters* had had the tact not to turn up, so we were by ourselves. It was planned that work would start again in the afternoon, at least we thought so. . .

At twelve o'clock, when the lunch break had just started, we heard a noise in the streets. Suddenly a large crowd of Philips workers began to gather. Some were on electric lorries, others on foot. They came from the glass factory and the machine plant a little beyond it. A full-fledged demonstration began, with hastily prepared banners reading '50 years Philips'. Some people had put on costumes, for which the carnival-minded Brabanders have a special talent. Soon we were standing on the steps of the Recreation Centre taking the salute at a parade. It was a parade without end. When the people in the adjacent factory saw what was going on, they too joined the demonstration.

That afternoon I was scheduled to attend a luncheon at the municipal school. I had not even sat down there before a call summoned me back to the head office. There I was met by a colossal mass demonstration. A big portrait of my father was carried around. Group after group marched through the gate, and I was lifted shoulder-high. People were waving and cheering incessantly. I started to wonder how the Germans would react. I took a radical decision: 'I am giving you the afternoon off!' I called at the top of my voice. This meant that the Germans would not be able to say that there had been a strike, which was against their regulations. Word soon spread to the other factories.

I went at once to the *Verwalters* and explained that under the circumstances it had been best to give people a holiday so there would be no trouble for them or me. They could see no alternative, and approved.

But the afternoon off fanned the festive spirit to greater flame. The factories emptied and the decoration shops filled. Soon they were sold out. Everywhere people put on all the national colours they could get hold of. Countless paper caps in red-white-and-blue and in orange appeared. Some people had dummy trumpets. People danced in the streets. Everybody marched past the head office where my wife and my sister Jetty had arrived to see the festivities. When we heard that some parts of the cortège were moving to De Laak, Sylvia and Jetty let to 'take the salute' at this traditional place.

The Quisling police chief feared that his reputation with the Germans would be impaired by these events and tried to disperse the crowds, without success. Someone heard him mutter, 'They should turn the machine-guns on these people!' Meanwhile we stood with a great number of the staff in the windows of the head office. There were shouts of, 'Hello, Frits!' I was worried. My instinct told me that this would not end well. We had little to fear from the guards at the factory gates, who were elderly men of the German police guard. They did not understand much, and often did not even notice when someone stuck our national colours in the barrels of their guns. But there were rumours that the so-called *Grüne Polizei* (special police) were coming from Tilburg. Elsewhere other incidents were taking place. Some people danced around a German car at a railway crossing, singing a patriotic song. There is even a story that a train full of German soldiers passing through Eindhoven started cheering like mad, seeing the festivities, because they thought the war was over. Then the *Grüne Polizei* arrived and began to sweep the streets clean. But at 3.30 p.m. heaven effectively intervened. Torrential rain started to fall, and people dispersed.

The aftermath of the jubilee day was less cheerful. The Germans imposed a curfew. Nobody was allowed on the streets after eight. We had planned to spend the night with Jetty and her husband, the Van Riemsdijks, who lived across the street from De Laak. There we were going to listen to the speech my father was to make over the radio from the United States.

Just around eight o'clock I saw some boys, pursued by Germans, running through the Van Riemsdijk garden. I had had enough experience to know that intimidation was the best way of handling the Germans. I opened the window and shouted at them in German that they had no business in that garden. When they replied that there were people in the garden I cut in, 'There is no one here. If there have been any, they have already left.' We thought this was the end of it.

But more German visitors were to come. First there was a phone call summoning me to the *Ortskommandantur* (garrison commander's office). I told them that I was dining, and if they wanted to see me they should come to the Van Riemsdijk home. Meanwhile I made contact with Willem de Graaff, our advisor for external relations. After a short while he arrived, followed by two Germans who wanted to have a talk with me. I at once went on the offensive:

'Gentlemen, you are behaving stupidly. After all, we do have the Philips jubilee today, and what is more natural than that the people in this city should act accordingly? There is no question of a popular uprising. Yet you force people to stay at home from eight o'clock onwards. Why do you always react to things in such a stupid way?'

'Yes, but Mr. Philips, how do you explain the flag on your house over there?'

It was true, we had raised the Dutch flag for the occasion. I said, 'But isn't that what we do on an anniversary? You can't expect me to hoist the German flag. We have only one flag in Holland, the Dutch one. So if we are celebrating, that's the one we raise.'

'And what about all those demonstrations and the display of orange and all that?'

'Look here, if we put on festive colours we always use red–white–and–blue or orange. We haven't got any others. Nobody should read any wrong intentions into it. It's only natural.'

'But it is against regulations, just like that flag of yours.'

'If people celebrate spontaneously, nobody should be thinking of regulations.'

'But it was very objectionable to have people dancing around one of our cars, and with orange flags at that!'

'Do you know what I think would have been a tactful way for you to respond? You should have clapped and cheered too. That would have been much more intelligent than to be so touchy and always to conclude that people are doing something against you, when they are just enjoying themselves. Aren't people entitled to a bit of fun once in a while?'

The gentlemen departed. Later we were able to tune in on the radio, and in fact heard my father's voice—a very fitting end to that day. Apart from a few small incidents it had all gone unexpectedly well. Even so, we got quite a fright when we discovered that a *Grüne Polizei* man had been hiding in the rhododendron bushes below the window where the radio stood. For it was absolutely forbidden to listen to broadcasts from Allied countries. Fortunately, the policeman had not heard a thing.

So the fiftieth anniversary of Philips lives on in our memories as a powerful demonstration of unity, mutual loyalty and enthusiasm in the midst of the occupation. It gave us a powerful, positive stimulus. And soon stories about it, usually greatly exaggerated, were circulating all over Holland.

One humorous side-light was the reaction of the military commander of Belgium, General von Falkenhausen, who happened to be visiting his friend, our *Verwalter* Dr. Bormann, that day. Of course, the two men had noticed the festivities and next day Bormann told me that his guest had been deeply impressed by the 'marvellous team spirit' prevailing in the Philips factories in Eindhoven. It had not penetrated to him that he had witnessed an outburst of patriotic sentiment; nor that he had been driving around with a Dutch flag stuck on his spare tyre.

Chapter 9

A Turning Point?

Less than a month after our unusual jubilee, Hitler invaded Russia. Even though the Germans in Holland continued hourly announcing new victories 'on all fronts', I was convinced that this would bring the eventual German defeat at least a year nearer. It was hard to assess the consequences for Philips. Meanwhile, we were still busy building our new warehouse.

The construction progressed steadily. One question was the enormous flat roof. It seemed a pity to leave such a vast surface unused, so we made a list of possible uses. At the top of it was an acoustic studio. A second item was a laboratory in which Dr. van der Pol could make short-wave tests. The third was a gymnasium. The acoustic studio would be placed in the centre of the roof, to avoid interference from the vibrations of the lifts at each side of the building. For sound insulation, double walls were required. These plans could only be carried out after approval by the *Verwalters* who in turn were held accountable by the Germans. In practice these men had no staff or know-how adequate to go into the decisions thoroughly. So we were able to continue without much interference. Even so, we had to buy a lot of material on the black market. The tower was to be so high that it could not be built during the war, and the wood ear-marked for this purpose lay for years in a timber yard in Deventer waiting for the liberation.

That liberation might now come earlier. So I decided that our warehouse should be completed six months ahead of schedule.

I discussed this with our construction engineers.

'We must speed up construction of the warehouse by six months.'

'In that case, we must pour the concrete earlier.'

'Do you have enough people?'

'We have enough building workers, because there are a lot unemployed, but we haven't got enough wood for scaffolding and shuttering.'

'Then you must buy extra wood from contractors who have no work. How much will it cost?'

'We would guess between twenty-five and thirty thousand guilders.'

'It's worth it. Can you see it happens?'

So the building was completed ahead of schedule. It was the only new building which went up in Eindhoven during the war. This gave me real satisfaction, not least because the great quantity of building materials which it consumed could not be used for more harmful projects. The extra expense did not worry me. We preferred putting money into plant to keeping it as cash, which we expected the Germans would take with them when they withdrew.

Initially, however, the Russian campaign provided Hitler with successes which made many of us fear the worst. The Germans penetrated rapidly and deeply into Russian territory. But after a few months, the promised victories, such as the seizure of Moscow and Leningrad, did not materialize, nor did the Russian armies collapse as totally as had been predicted. The thundering propaganda, always accompanied by impressive fanfares, managed to conceal the 'non-victory' from the German population, but German industry had to face up to reality. It had to be geared increasingly to war production only. This included communication equipment, and so German industry could no longer manufacture radios for their own people. Consequently we had to make radio sets for Telefunken, Siemens and other companies. Our Philips products had to be sold in Germany under these other brand names, but we were thereby able to keep our own people employed without directly contributing to the German war effort.

The Germans by themselves could no longer carry out their own industrial schemes. We were asked to develop equipment resistant to desert conditions, mainly for the Afrika Korps, which initially managed to conquer large tracts of the Mediterranean coastal region. However, it was increasingly difficult for us to get raw materials. The Germans possessed insufficient quantities of nickel, copper and other materials, and a distribution of these rare commodities was organized through a voucher rationing system. Our strategy was to get hold of as many vouchers as possible and then to deliver as few products as we could.

We became past masters at being involved in the development of highly sophisticated equipment without ever producing anything. The above-mentioned military hobbyists who had obtained high level sponsorship for their ideas provided us with the chance to do this. Every new product, small or large, requires a lot of drawing work. Each component has to be designed, and the whole thing has to be worked out on the drawing board. So the number of drawings needed can vary from several hundreds to more than a thousand. Experience has taught us that no drawing is without errors, and it is the job of the manufacturing department to spot these errors. That is where drawings are conscientiously studied and corrected, or at any rate faults are pointed out. Instead of checking a portfolio completely after which, perhaps, some seventy corrections would have been suggested, our production planning division would send the portfolio back to the Germans after about ten errors had been found. When this same portfolio was returned again from the drawing department, they would spot fifteen more errors and send it all back again. Sometimes, too, portfolios would get lost as a result of air raids. So progress was slow. It is impossible to make a man run who is dragging his heels, though our people had to be careful that no one could accuse them of sabotage.

The danger of ill-advised sabotage was always present. Resistance against the German occupation was increasing steadily. In Philips we had had, since 1932, a representative body of the employees called the Works Committee whom management consulted regularly. We agreed with the Committee members that we would fight the German plans systematically from the head office. They saw that if workers started cutting machine belts or doing things like that on their own, it would render us powerless to resist effectively from the top. It might have brought about a complete German take-over and the new management would then have dealt harshly with such practices. On the whole people respected this division of tasks. It did not prevent a steady deterioration in the quality of our products, but this we did not mind.

Of course many deliveries to the Germans failed completely, and this subtle game was in good hands with our Philips personnel at all levels. But our adversaries were not disposed just to accept things unchecked. Several times a year a committee arrived from Berlin to find out what deliveries had been made. We would carefully prepare for these talks. In actual fact our deliveries were limited, but the production charts we gave our visitors showed steeply rising lines which were adjusted every six months. The reports were co-ordinated so that the statements of different divisions would tally.

We would confer in the morning until lunch with the Berlin visitors. That *Mittagessen* was particularly important. Despite war-time scarcity we would manage to serve a sumptuous feast. When talks were resumed, the visitors were in no mood for deep scrutiny. We made sure that they departed convinced that everything would go better in the coming months. In this our charts did a useful job. Little did we think that those same figures would have such dramatic consequences one day in 1942 . . .

With my father in 1915.

My mother as I knew her in my youth.

4 July 1929.

More than a quarter of a century later.

Our 45th wedding anniversary.

With Dr. Frank Buchman (right) at the Moral Re-Armament Assembly
in the Vegetable Hall at Utrecht (May 1937).

On holiday with my friend and brother-in-law, Frans Otten.

My first plane, the Koolhoven FK 26, in 1935.

Forty years later, in the pilot seat of a Philips Air Service Mystère-20.

An outburst of enthusiasm at the 'risky jubilee' of May 1941 in the
middle of the German occupation.

Near the head office, lifted shoulder-high, May 1941.

The air raid, 6 December 1942.

Part of the Eindhoven factories today.

The Board of Management in the early fifties. From left to right: Tony Guépin, Herman van Walsem, Frans Otten, myself, Othon Loupart and Theo Tromp.

Meeting with workers engaged in building their own homes in the winter of 1945–46.

Our home, De Wielewaal.

Verwalters

How to deal with the *Verwalters?* This was a source of mounting difficulties. Their position was far from simple, and mine was even worse. They had been put there to see that things in Philips were done in accordance with German wishes and interests. But they knew they could not count on real co-operation from our side, and we realized that their bosses always wanted more from them than they could deliver.

Our first *Verwalters*, Bormann and Merkel, had been nominated at the beginning of July 1940. On 20 July 1942 they were dismissed by the 'Reich Marshal of Greater Germany'. Their superiors had found them too accommodating towards us. Presumably Bormann felt relieved. He had little respect for the Nazi regime, and had, I knew, personally regretted the invasion of Holland. He never tried to use his position with us to line his pockets or to seek any personal advantage. Initially he was not a party member. Later he was forced to join the National Socialist Party, but he wore the party badge on the inside of his lapel.

Merkel had friendly relations with some senior officers. Whenever he went on tour to Berlin or elsewhere he stuffed his car full of radios which he generously handed around to his military friends. He appeared initially to be more flexible than his colleague. He used to tell me that the Government in Berlin had preferred to put Austrians in charge of Holland because they would be less rigid. The German Governor, Dr. A. Seyss-Inquart, and his Finance and Economics Commissioner, Dr. H. Fischböck, were, in his view, examples of this and he expected that everything would go fabulously well.

In the second half of the summer of 1940 I had an odd conversation with this man. He asked me to come to his office and said, 'Mr. Philips, I would like to have a serious talk with you. I have just been in The Hague, and I was told there that the German authorities are not happy with the way the National Socialist Movement is being led here. It leaves a great deal to be desired. In this "New Era" it could be so important if some prominent Dutch leaders were to join this movement. Such people could do much good for their nation. An entirely new relationship between the occupation authorities and your people might follow.'

I replied, 'Mr. Merkel, when you talk to me like this I consider it an attempt to induce me to commit high treason.'

Undaunted he pursued his theme, and I repeated, 'Mr. Merkel, please realize that in my eyes this is a provocation to treason!'

For the third time he insinuated that I should back the Quisling movement, whereupon I said, 'Mr. Merkel, it might be better if I left the room, for I am not going to talk about this.'

Bormann would never have said a thing like that to me. In his heart he cursed the Nazi fellow-travellers as much as I did. But Merkel was different. In those days the Germans still believed that they would soon be ruling the whole of Europe, and if Merkel had achieved his aim, he would have risen steeply in Berlin's esteem.

Merkel's character showed itself clearly in the fate of the portraits of Luther and Melanchthon by Lucas Cranach the Elder, which belonged to my father's collection. Goering had great ambitions as an art collector, and my father's collection attracted his attention. Merkel did all he could to acquire interesting pieces for Goering. We told him that most of the collection was no longer in Holland, having been transferred to Scandinavia and from there, possibly, to America. The truth was that they were stored in the vaults of a Hague bank.

By this means we managed for the time being to stave off this raid on our art collection. Then a time came when Goering particularly wanted to get hold of more of Cranach's works. Again Merkel came to inquire after my father's two Cranachs. He did this with so much emphasis that at length we felt it better that these paintings should emerge from their hiding place so as to avoid the greater harm of a thorough search. So we hung them on the walls of our house. When he kept on enquiring we told him that both of them were in our house. He came at once to take a greedy look at them and said that he was ready to pay any price. I told him that they were not for sale.

When he saw that I remained firm, he tried a different tack. The supply of raw materials stagnated. Merkel hinted that if the Cranachs were not surrendered, Germany would no longer supply us with raw materials. That was a tough problem for our Board of Directors. For a long time we discussed whether we were justified in endangering the livelihood of thousands for the sake of a couple of paintings, however valuable. Merkel again turned up to have a look at the Cranachs. Finally Sylvia said, 'Mr. Merkel, if you want to steal them, go ahead. But you'll never be able to buy them!' Beforehand she had stuck the text of Luther's famous hymn 'A mighty fortress is our God' on the back of the Luther portrait. Merkel left with the two paintings under his arm.

After the liberation the Luther portrait was found in Germany, and returned to us with the text of the hymn still on its back. The Melanchthon portrait has never been found.

When Merkel died years later it was in obscurity and rather poor circumstances. Bormann was gaoled for some time after the war. When he was well over 80 I visited him in Locarno. We were able to discuss with light irony the difficulties which had existed between us during the occupation, and we were reconciled. I was much impressed by the way he helped his invalid wife.

Bormann's and Merkel's most important successor was Dr. L. W. Nolte, manager of the AEG branch in Nuremberg. He was a manufacturer through and through, a man whose sole aim was to push up production. Though he respected the Philips factories, he continued in the Merkel tradition to give away carloads of radios. After him there were a number of other *Verwalters*, who succeeded each other at an increasing pace. The pressures they applied became harder and harder, which meant more threats and difficulties for us personally.

The occupying authorities never succeeded in controlling our research department. We were working on a list of subjects which had previously been approved by the Germans. Every four or six months our progress on them was checked. The result was generally disappointing because many researchers were also working on other projects. Fortunately we always knew ahead of time when an inspection was to take place, so that the correct instruments and models could be found on the research desks. Nothing would be seen, for instance, of the complete 15 kw radio transmitter which was to start broadcasting from Eindhoven shortly after the liberation as the voice of the new radio station Radio Free Holland. A lot of transmitter equipment was also under construction for the underground. By tacit agreement I kept out of this. Our experiments with television continued because the Germans realized its importance for the post-war era and they knew that their own industry was unable to devote time and energy to it.

When a new *Verwalter* came, I thought it important to get to know him. As I had to deal with him, I wanted to be sure that he would not feel personal animosity towards me. The *Verwalters'* attitude towards me had to be, 'Even if he won't discuss our Nazi system with us, you can rely on his word. He says either yes or no.' I would go and meet a newcomer in the evening and explain to him what Philips was all about and how we worked. He would then feel that he had been received properly. If you left a man like that to rely exclusively on information supplied by Quislings telling him a pack of lies, or by contacts with the Germans, it only made the relationship even more difficult. So I also made it my business to spend a few hours once every two months talking with these people. I preferred to do this in their homes rather than in the office. The homes requisitioned for the *Verwalters* were houses of Philips people who had managed to escape in time to reinforce our staff abroad.

At times these contacts with the *Verwalters* were very difficult for me personally. One day, for instance, I was going to have a difficult talk with the *Verwalters*, and my heart was burning with hatred towards them. I realized that I would be unable to achieve anything for our own people in that frame of mind. I equally realized that it is simply wrong to hate one's fellow men, whoever they may be. But reasoning with oneself does not remove hate. There was only one answer. I knelt down in my room and prayed, 'Lord, remove this hatred against these men from my heart; even if they are in the grip of a diabolic system, they are fellow human beings.'

During the talk, I presented my arguments objectively, and I realized that my personal aversion towards these people had disappeared. Naturally we did not agree, but they showed respect for my point of view. It had been possible to remain firm without provoking them.

It is my experience that God can help a man best if he feels helpless. And there is ample scope for that state of mind, especially in time of war!

In one respect all the *Verwalters* were remarkably similar. They did not have much time for the followers of Mussert, the Dutch Quisling. They assessed correctly the real value of that kind of person. Among our 20,000 employees there were no more than 200 Quislings, very few of them real fanatics, and none were nominated to any significant post.

This was important, as there is no better way to destroy a company or organization than by putting unsuitable people in places of influence. If, for instance, a worker is made a foreman without having the qualifications, it results in the ruin not only of the man himself but also of the people working under him. Because of the *Verwalters'* reservations about Quislings we were able to keep the promotion policy in our own hands. So the back-bone of our Dutch organization remained intact.

The *Verwalters* invariably remained outsiders. Philips never really included them, and most things were decided without their knowing it. This was true of various cases of co-operation with other companies, which were agreed upon during the occupation or altered as a result of circumstances. For instance, we took control of a cap factory in Zeeland, which after the war we made into the most modern of its kind in the world; of a cable factory in Amsterdam and of a small gramophone record plant which eventually became the foundation of our worldwide record industry.

All this happened without the *Verwalters* noticing anything. In these deals I was always motivated by the idea that we did better to put part of our money into assets, from which we could harvest fruits after the liberation, than to keep the cash in hand, risking that the Germans might take it with them when they had to leave.

I tried to put to good use the extra time I had available because production was slack and travel abroad impossible. Part of it I invested in trade association work. I was frequently amazed at how our typical Dutch perfectionism induced some in this work, no doubt with the best of intentions, to further the Germans' plans. But as industrialists we could not avoid going along up to a point with their organizational plans. I was vice-chairman of the Electrical Industries Group, and had to give some time to this organization, which came under their jurisdiction. But we used our meetings to agree how to distribute materials, and how to present a united front to the Dutch and German authorities rather than executing all the German decrees.

One such decree laid down that half of all Dutch light bulb factories had to be closed down. The Germans wanted us to settle among ourselves which factories should close, something which we resolutely refused to do. In the end a German official had to decide, and so the small factories were shut first. As this was a measure imposed by the occupying power, we decided that we would jointly supply these companies with lamps so that they could continue to satisfy their customers.

Another task I took on in this period was to improve Philips' relationship with the public and to strengthen public confidence in our company. It was my impression that our reputation was not as good as we liked to think. For example, we had a name for defending our patent rights with mailed fists. It could be said in our defence that we were faced with very tough competition, and that we had put more effort into research than any other Dutch company, so we could not take it lying down if unauthorized people used our patents without paying the licence fees. But in this context, whether we were right or wrong was beside the point. The main thing was that our reputation was not very good.

Then there was the price of our light bulbs. The former manager of our sales organization for the Netherlands and her colonies had firmly believed in high prices for our lamps and would never budge. The result was that, at the beginning of the occupation, there were in Holland no less than 23 lamp factories, large and small, which survived under this high-price umbrella. Possibly the manufacturers loved us for this, but our lamps were more expensive in Holland than abroad—a fact which the public knew. I decided that we would lower our prices after the war by fifty per cent. However, the Germans were ahead of us; they suddenly ordered a substantial cut in retail prices.

There also was the aftermath of the Depression. In 1932 we had been forced to dismiss some young engineers. This had started the rumour that we were in the habit of lightly dismissing our engineers, which was not at all true. All in all, I felt we must fight for a better public image, and I believe we eventually succeeded. My own attitude was, I think, of some significance, particularly through my work in FOEGIN, where I met our competitors in the radio branch, and succeeded in creating better understanding.

I also tried to improve our relationships with the dealers. They were our longest-standing business connections, and in this time of scarcity it was impossible to provide them with all the products on which they depended for their livelihood. Fortunately, we were able to keep supplying our oldest product, the light bulb, throughout the occupation—in itself something of a miracle. Besides this, we made every effort to keep our dealers in business.

My basic conviction was that we, as a company, should offer help wherever it was needed. Of course, it was a bonus if this also enhanced our reputation, but that was never to be the over-riding motive. Naturally we worked with the resistance movement. But there were good civilian causes to be thought of as well. Jan van Walré de Bordes, Mayor of Middelburg, a good friend of mine, provided one of these. He enjoyed great popularity, especially for the way he had conducted himself after the German attack. When hostilities ceased in May 1940, Middelburg was in bad shape, with the ancient town centre almost totally destroyed. The Germans, in their initial attempt to get the Dutch on their side, provided large-scale assistance for the reconstruction of the famous Town Hall. In order to refurnish it, de Bordes wanted to acquire two famous Flemish tapestries made in Bruges in 1640. They were for sale, but the city did not have the necessary money. Philips gave it, and one thing led to another. We also donated a particularly beautiful antique Flemish-Brabant cabinet to furnish the building and later added a monumental mantelpiece. When Rotterdam was being rebuilt, we enabled the maritime museum there to acquire some items. We also paid for repairing damage in some historic buildings. And all this without the *Verwalters'* knowledge.

I tried all the time to look ahead to the post-liberation period. One of my most far-reaching decisions was to double the number of students at the Trades School. My expectation was that we would need a great many skilled workers after the war, and I was proved right. But even in the short run, doubling this number had its advantages. Boys thus brought into training would not be called up for forced labour in Germany. Also, later on, we could select the bright ones for our own school from a much larger number.

The question we constantly asked ourselves was how to preserve our organization in fighting fettle until the liberation. I like to compare it with keeping a park in order. A well-managed industry grows like a big park. There are trees everywhere, but they have to be in the right number, place and pattern. New trees have to be planted in time to replace less good ones. But if a storm ravages the park, you realize how powerless you are. Afterwards you can plant new trees, hoping they will grow, but knowing you have lost many years. It was, therefore, a great satisfaction after the liberation that, despite the storms, the layout of the park was left untouched. In spite of German interference the Dutch Philips organization was immediately able to start flourishing again right along the line.

Chapter 10

Tension Mounts

As German fortunes declined, the difficulties of Philips in Eindhoven increased. In the beginning the Nazis had hoped that the Dutch nation would take their side in the battle against Russia, or rather against Communism, but this did not happen. The Eastern campaign was demanding a tremendous effort from the German war industry. Hitler had to draw continuously on his reserves of manpower to replenish his armies, and so the occupied territories were constantly squeezed, under Fritz Sauckel's leadership, to provide labour for German industry. In Holland this was officially termed 'employment abroad', but the people themselves called it 'forced labour'. In 1942 we at Philips were for the first time confronted with this 'Sauckel action'. Of course we resisted it with all our might. We told Sauckel's assistants that they were acting against international conventions, and we refused to comply. But they had ways of exercising pressure. So, despite resistance at all levels in Philips, about 3,000 employees were forced to work in Germany, most of them young men between 18 and 20.

We responded to these measures in several ways. First, we used them as a pretext to reduce the production of equipment which the Germans considered important. Whenever they complained about slow or small deliveries, we would point out that they had removed necessary manpower. Next, a section of our social affairs department called 'Office Workers Abroad' kept in touch with the abducted men, and was able to send them correspondence, literature and gift parcels.

We knew that the occupying power would step up its efforts to send Dutch people not engaged in the productive process to Germany. Another part of our job was, therefore, to employ as many people as we could and to produce as little as possible. For this various methods were employed, involving several training courses and a physical training programme. I thought that training courses would in any case encourage our employees to educate themselves more fully during the occupation years.

For example, our sales department had hardly anything to do. So it was turned into a planning office. This led to a lot of difficulty, because salesmen like to sell, and planning is below their dignity. But planning groups could be justified to the Germans, while sales departments could not, for there was nothing to sell. We also had language courses for our office personnel, who had little work to do and would find them useful later. Large-scale courses were organized to teach French, German, English, Italian and Spanish. Anyone could enroll, and the lessons were given during working time. Special attention was given to acquiring conversational proficiency. In the canteens there were special tables at which French and Italian were spoken, while people 'enjoyed' the canteen's wartime concoction, 'Phili-hash'.

Food supplies were diminishing all the time, so we thought we should give our personnel a meal during working time. Potatoes were the principal ingredient of these meals, but we tried to mix some meat or meat extract in with them, for which we were given a special factory meat ration. Nobody would claim that those meals were very tasty or nutritious, but they did help to fill people's stomachs half-way through the day and they were an extra. There were lots of jokes about our Phili-hash, but whenever it was dished out, people turned up in throngs.

Then there was our physical training programme. This had no precedent. But by telling the Germans that it was 'good for people's health' and 'a morale booster', I succeeded in convincing them that it was necessary. Every employee had to take part in one quarter of an hour's gymnastics, but it took three-quarters of an hour because people had to go to the special halls arranged for this purpose.

This programme served as a pretext to employ more people, including an army captain previously in charge of the off-duty programme of the armed forces, who organized it for us excellently. We also had other military gymnastics instructors, and employed a relatively large number of former officers to organize the company's air-raid protection. These former military men were more or less safe in our employment.

First Air Raid

The two air raids by Allied air forces on our Eindhoven factories were among our most shattering war-time experiences. We felt that our deliveries to the Germans were so small that they did not justify such bomb attacks. Also, they came without any warning. The first raid occurred on 6 December 1942. Nobody had previously informed us, nor had our staff in the States been told. Later my father told me how upset he had been that there had been no such consultation, for they knew the situation intimately and could have indicated what to bomb to produce maximum effect. For instance, our transmitter factory was at Hilversum. If a pilot had dropped a single bomb on that plant, our people there would have declared all important projects inoperational. After the war, however, we learned that the Allies had decided not to bomb that particular factory because it was located in a residential area.

The 6 December raid was caused, as far as we could judge, by our impressive charts. They had been produced for the German committee from Berlin and showed plans that were never carried out. These charts were seen by all sorts of staff members, some of them active in the resistance movement, who passed them on to groups in regular touch with the Allies. So naturally people across the sea would say to each other, 'Look how much they are producing at Philips in Eindhoven.' The fact that we were sparing no effort to avoid making these things was not as readily passed on.

That fateful Sunday, Sylvia and I and the Van Riemsdijks were calling on a cousin whose baby had been baptized that morning. We were just drinking the usual cup of *ersatz* coffee after the church service when we saw low-flying squadrons approach. As we were on the outskirts of the city, we could see everything very clearly. The large number of the aircraft made us suppose they were British, and our first thought was, 'Are they going to bomb the railway station?' Then we saw bombs falling and heard the noise of the explosions. Terrified, we realized that our city was being bombed! As fast as we possibly could my brother-in-law and I went by tandem back to De Laak, where we fortunately found everyone unharmed. From a distance we could see the Demer, Eindhoven's main shopping street, on fire. My wife and sister followed later on the second tandem.

From our home I went straight to the city centre. Only then did I realize that our factories had been the target. As all was now silent, I thought that the attack was over, but when I was on my way to the head office the final wave of bombers came over. I took shelter in a bicycle shop. From there I saw that our office building had been hit, and that fire had broken out. I was especially keen to save two portraits which Jan Veth had painted of my father and Uncle Gerard in 1916. The portraits hung in our Board room on the ground floor. I put on a helmet and climbed through the window, accompanied by Philips firemen. As I opened the door of the Board room a big piece of the ceiling fell in. The firemen would not allow me to proceed, so I had to leave the portraits to the flames. The building completely burnt out.

The damage to the city and to our factories was enormous. The time for the raid, the Sunday morning after Holland's popular St. Nicholas family evening, had been picked because people would not be at work. Yet more than a hundred people died in the city, and the hospitals were full of scores of wounded. Part of Eindhoven was destroyed by fire. Sylvia and my sister Jetty visited all the wounded, so we heard first-hand what people had been through. One thing was remarkable: nobody in Eindhoven uttered a word of reproach about the Allies. One man lost his wife and three of his seven children, but he made not one complaint about the bombers.

I was filled with deep emotions when I saw those factories, built with so much care and representing employment for so many thousands, in flames. It brought home to me the ruthlessness of war. But I also realized that the battle against the Germans had to be ruthless if it was to be won. That reconciled me to the infernal spectacle of destruction. I decided not to be thrown by this experience, but to see it as a proof of the Allied strength which enabled them to strike wherever needed. I had heard of Philips people who had secretly wept in a corner at the sight of the destruction, and this I could well understand. Part of our life's work had been destroyed. Now we had to learn to take this in the right way and I felt I had somehow to give encouragement to our employees. I decided that we should use this reverse to rebuild our factories better, and that we should start planning this on the day after the raid.

I was especially interested in having our factory buildings restored first, and I wanted our own employees to be used for this work so as to give the Germans no pretext to deport them. We first had to clear the rubble. Our shifts worked day after day knocking the glass remnants out of the window frames. After that we had to close up the windows with cardboard. But for the time being it was unthinkable that we could also close the gap in our production.

We gave two interpretations of the raid. To the Germans we said that the damage was limited. Our production, we asserted, had undoubtedly suffered, but we felt we could get back to normal soon. We said this to protect our people from deportation to Germany, and it succeeded. The other interpretation was put about in the hope that it would reach the Allied side through the underground—that the raid had been so terribly effective that there was no need for the squadrons to return. The truth was in between the two. With the occupying power we used the fact of the raid to the utmost to explain arrears in all sorts of deliveries. And in fact the damage was not to be underestimated. We have learned that, in calamities like air raids, there are always three phases. The first is when everyone says, 'Oh, what terrible damage!' The second follows when you realize that it is not all that bad. For instance, some heavy machinery turned out to be repairable. (Incidentally, the same thing happened in Germany, and this was one reason why the incessant Allied raids on German factories had caused less damage than aerial photography had suggested.) Finally, there is the third phase when you come to the conclusion that the damage is great after all.

Because of the threat of raids we now had to disperse the various departments, as it was no longer allowed to work on the top floors of buildings. We rented vacant buildings wherever we could find them, and housed our smaller development divisions there. One of them, incidentally, was working on stereophony. One advantage of this decentralization was that we could work without being disturbed by German curiosity.

Freedom in Decline

Being a large company, we needed all sorts of materials. As we had many of our purchasing department shopping around to obtain the necessary vouchers and then to get the vouchers traded in for materials, we had been able to collect considerable amounts of scarce metals. Indeed we had amassed quantities of copper and aluminium which factories in Germany could envy, and we used these materials for a variety of products, like X-ray equipment, which had nothing to do with war production.

In the beginning of 1942 I was informed that a mission from the *Rüstungsinspektion* was going to visit us. In preparation I had a look round. When I walked through the machine factory, I noticed large supplies of scarce materials stacked up in the so-called 'daily-use containers'. I knew how much the German factories needed copper, aluminium and nickel. The gentlemen from the *Rüstungsinspektion* would be even more keenly aware of this. So I agreed with the factory manager, Wim de Vries, that we would, as far as possible, remove these materials from sight by putting them into the lower containers. Some days later this manager was unexpectedly arrested by the Germans. His order to make materials disappear had been carried out too thoroughly. Things had even been stored in the toilets, and a Quisling had reported it. Even though we could prove with the vouchers in hand that there was no question of black market dealings, De Vries was sent to the notorious gaol for political prisoners in Scheveningen. His wife was a German who was completely on the Dutch side, and the Germans assured her at various intervals that he would be freed immediately if she would declare that it had been I who had ordered the concealment of the materials. But she steadfastly refused. In the same period another senior Philips man, Gerard Jenneskens, was arrested because he had always objected to German requests, and so provoked their wrath.

It worried me greatly that these men were detained for so long. I had been told about a certain Mr. Bodde in The Hague who was able, he asserted, to influence the Germans. So I went to The Hague to see Mr. Bodde. He was very talkative and poured statements over my head to the effect that he was a good patriot and that he knew many important Germans. His office was richly decorated with pictures of noteworthies, often signed and with personal messages. Powerful names reeled from his lips. At long last, I put forward my request to get our two men freed. In order to make my point even more clearly I told him that I would be back the following week with thirty thousand guilders in my pocket. And, in fact, one of our men was released soon afterwards, while the other was moved to the concentration camp at Vught, where he was allowed to work in the Philips workshop, which I will describe later in this chapter. He used his time well there by making, at my request, a draft for a new machine works. After the war a big machine shop was built according to his design, and in 1951 the building was opened by our Minister of Economic Affairs.

It is hard to tell if Mr. Bodde's intervention was responsible for getting our factory manager moved. He himself told me that the Germans eventually accepted his version that he had ordered the materials out of sight with the noble intention of not causing unnecessary embarrassment to the visitors. He regretted, he told the Germans, that his order had been carried out in such an unwise manner.

Some time later, Mr. Bodde asked to see me. This led to a somewhat secret rendezvous in a pub across from the Eindhoven railway station. There he produced his case with the thirty thousand guilders in bank-notes! On 15 March 1943, the occupation authorities had suddenly declared all thousand and five-hundred guilder notes invalid, in order to stem the flow of black market and other illicit money. Such notes had to be exchanged, and only those who could prove a legitimate source for them would get their money back. Mr. Bodde wanted to return the money to me for obvious reasons. But as I did not trust him, I told him that I was ready to certify the legal source of the money after the war. He left Eindhoven, disappointed.

Our Workshop in Vught

If I were asked what was the strangest Philips activity during the German occupation, I would probably say, 'Our work in the German concentration camp near Vught.' In this village near the town of 's Hertogenbosch, the Germans had a camp in which they imprisoned the most diverse people: political prisoners, black market dealers, people who had committed offences against the occupying power like hiding Jews, professional criminals and people who had done nothing at all. The camp was already in existence when, in the beginning of 1943, one of the *Verwalters* asked me whether he could discuss something with me. He had received a request from Berlin: Would Philips be able to provide work for the prisoners in that camp? The camp was not far from Eindhoven, so it would be a good solution if we would provide some useful work for the prisoners. My first reaction was entirely negative. My principal objection was that, by accepting it, I would provide a pretext for the Germans to present their concentration camp as a place in which people 'worked' in a normal way.

The *Verwalter* kept insisting. At last I promised that I would give it some thought. I discussed the matter with my colleagues and arrived at the conclusion that it might be possible to do something for the prisoners. I put forward a number of conditions which would have to be fulfilled. First, the workshop must be under our supervision and not the Germans'. Our responsible people must be allowed freely in and out of the camp and it must be our decision who was to work, and what work and how much should be done. Furthermore, we must be given permission to serve a hot meal at noon in the workshop—and something better than Phili-hash. Finally we insisted that we should be permitted to pay these Philips workers for their work by giving money to their dependants.

To my great astonishment these conditions were accepted, with the exception of the last one. Work started in the Philips workshop in February 1943, and ended in September 1944 when the south of Holland was freed. In that period we were able to make the lives of countless prisoners more bearable and even to save the lives of some. This last was undoubtedly true of the Jewish Philips people who had been sent to the

Sobu. That word, Sobu, assumed for Jews in the Vught camp a meaning which filled them with both terror and gratitude, as letters which I still receive testify. Sobu was an abbreviation—one of many in those days. It had two connotations. In Dutch it was the contraction of 'Speciale Opdrachten Bureau' (Special Tasks Office). In our *Verwalters'* minds it meant 'Sonderbüro' (Special Office).

Soon after occupying our country, the Germans imposed all sorts of discriminatory measures against our Jewish employees, measures which were gradually intensified. We had a choice between resisting them and seeking ways of adjustment. Had we adopted the first line, we would not have achieved anything. By following the second, we at least managed to save many of their lives. In Eindhoven, and later in Hilversum, our Jewish personnel were segregated and, towards the end of 1941, put in the Sobu. Finally, in August 1943, all Jewish employees were moved to Vught. There they were put to work in a special barracks, but they retained a close link with Philips. We systematically tried to get these Jewish men and women working on radio valves, repairing measuring equipment and other essential war work which gave them relative protection.

The Philips workshop soon became the most important section of the camp. The manager of our apparatus factory, Laman Trip, was in charge of this workshop, which the Germans called *Philips Kommando*. He went regularly to Vught where he was assisted by various of our staff. A friend of mine who was a prisoner in the camp, Van Ketwich Verschuur, looked after the card file in the administration there. He knew precisely who was entering the camp and, in consultation with Laman Trip, decided which of the new arrivals would work with Philips. So they selected only those in most danger, political prisoners and not black marketeers and criminals.

At various times I would be phoned by an acquaintance who would tell me in despair that his son had been arrested and put in Vught. He would then ask me whether I could get his son placed in our workshops. Because I was certain that my phone was bugged day and night, I would reply, 'My dear friend, I have nothing to do with those things. You are addressing yourself to the wrong person. That workshop is completely in German hands. I wish you the very best for your son.' And I would immediately put down the receiver with a bang. Then I quickly jotted down the son's name, and he was usually in our workshop within days. In this work for the prisoners the two men with whom I collaborated closely were Eb Laman Trip and Hans van Ketwich Verschuur, old Delft friends. Who would have thought of this during our carefree student days?

In the end, this Vught workshop developed into a complete factory. People were glad to work there, as they were not policed by the Germans, and our staff gave them a chance to communicate with the outside world. Many things were made there: squeeze dynamo hand torches, Philishaves, radio valves. Measuring equipment was repaired there. Calculations were made for the laboratory. Documents which had been lost or damaged by the air raids were copied on typewriters. Raw materials damaged by fire were made usable again. I still retain a vivid picture of a former Belgian cabinet minister industriously trying to clean a rusty transformer sheet with a steel brush. During a visit I started talking with him. Quite pleased, he said, 'Ah! M'sieur Philips, tout va bien!'

Prominent Dutchmen worked in our workshop, people like Professor Ben Telders. We were able to give him work in patent law, in which he was an authority. In the drawing office I also met De Vries, the machine factory manager I have referred to earlier.

Ten years after the liberation we were presented with a stained glass window by the Association of Political Prisoners to commemorate this work, and we installed it in our head office.

Unwelcome Visitors

A great sensation was caused in January 1944 by the announcement that Himmler was coming to inspect the camp. Without doubt he was among the most repulsive personalities of the Nazi regime. It was this man who had on his conscience the persecution of the Jews, the extermination camps and much else. Yet what kind of man did Laman Trip meet when he had to show him around the workshop? A small, friendly, rather schoolmaster-like fellow who peered at everything through his tiny glasses, very attentive and precise. He wanted to know whether the toilets were in order. He followed the work being done with striking intelligence, and showed great satisfaction with it and with what was being done in the Sobu. On leaving, he told Laman Trip that, if there were special needs, he only needed to ring him in Berlin direct. What an enigmatic double personality!

In 1940 I had been confronted with much the same situation when the German Governor, Seyss-Inquart, visited our factories in Eindhoven. He had wanted to see the Philips factories in 'his' domain. I might have feigned illness, but then the *Verwalters* would have acted as if they had created Philips, which I wanted to avoid. Moreover there was the possibility that I would need to appeal to him on some issue later, so I decided to receive him. I led him around and showed him our assembly lines, while I remained as serious as I could. I wanted to avoid laughter for fear of appearing in a photo joking with Seyss-Inquart. Indeed, a picture published by some newspaper did end up in London. I could imagine people there saying, 'Look how Frits Philips is trying to get into Seyss-Inquart's good books!' And it was difficult to go unsmilingly through the factories with a German-Austrian who acted in a friendly way and appeared interested, even if he was doing this only to try and win the Dutch over to his side.

But this was nothing to my meeting with Robert Ley, head of the *Kraft durch Freude* organization, a corner-stone of National Socialism's social structure in the Third Reich. This luminary also came to Eindhoven. I think this was because it had been the men of the heavy Ruhr industry who had put Hitler into power. This must have taught the Nazi leaders to take an interest in large industries, because whenever a big Nazi boss came to Holland, he wanted to visit the 'Philipswerke'. Thus Ley and his retinue turned up in Eindhoven. He was interested in our social conditions, and especially our company housing. The group arrived in a convoy of odd-looking cars. When the Philips residential areas were to be visited, he pointed invitingly to the first of these cars. 'Mr. Philips, may I invite you to come?' It was a Volkswagen, a product which was, in principle, a *Kraft durch Freude* achievement, and he was very proud of it. So I sat next to him as we drove in an open car through the Philips neighbourhood, he looking with interest at everything and expressing his admiration, I feeling as if I were sitting on burning coal. I could not jump out of the car, so my only defence consisted in keeping my face in a rigidly cool grimace. For all the money in the world I would not have been seen by the Philips people sitting next to a Nazi boss and explaining to him with a friendly face the details of our housing schemes.

A Glimpse of Freedom

In March 1943 I was faced with a curious problem. We were still exporting from Eindhoven to Philips establishments in some neutral countries, and the Germans suddenly began to insist that we strengthen our hold over these establishments. They were especially interested in Switzerland, and insisted that our people there should report to Eindhoven as they used to do. The Swiss management refused. In response, the Germans threatened to stop our exports to that country. But in order to keep our company there going, the delivery of our products was essential.

I knew that the Germans did not really want to stop exporting to a country which paid in hard currency, so I went to see the *Verwalters*. I said I would be able to negotiate a compromise, if I was allowed to go and talk to our Swiss management in person. This appealed to them, even after I had laid down my conditions. I wanted, I said, to further Philips' interest, even though this might not automatically turn out to the advantage of the Germans. Further, I demanded that I should be allowed to move as freely in Switzerland as were the Swiss. They hesitated a bit but in the end they agreed, provided I would make the trip with two *Verwalters* as my companions. So I got my *Marschbefehl*.

Again the way to Switzerland was via Berlin. Since my previous trip through Germany, hardly two years before, things had changed visibly. The air raids had had a noticeable effect, and our train moved through cities whose stations were attacked regularly from the air. At every air raid warning, the trains were moved at once outside the stations. The sirens could be heard continuously. From far away we could hear the anti-aircraft batteries firing at the passing squadrons. I was surprised to note that this did not worry me in the least. These bombs, I told myself, were not meant for me. Only now did I realize why we heard the continuous droning of so many air fleets passing over Holland. They were on their way to destroy the German cities. We had little pity for the German population; but what we refused to face at the time was that many Germans who no longer supported Hitler's war were suffering terribly.

We spent a day in Berlin. There I met our Dr. Kemna, a German who worked in both Berlin and Eindhoven, and had begun to look after our Philips workers who had been forced to work in Berlin. He had rented a big houseboat where they could live. Further, he had been able to arrange that they were put in the workshops and design departments of our factories. I visited the houseboat one evening and saw that, considering the circumstances, they were doing well.

I could see, too, that our 'Office Workers Abroad' had helped. The fact that letters could be exchanged was especially important. Our people in the purchasing department, always on the move, played a vital part. They always had with them lists of Philips employees in the region they visited, and if for instance they were working in Hamburg, they stayed on for some extra days to see where our people were allocated and how they were doing. They took letters for them and brought others back. Many of our deported workers did not wait for the end of the war but managed to walk back on foot, and started work with Philips again. Our personnel department then enrolled them under assumed names, and provided them with identity cards.

From Berlin we continued our trip to Basel. During that leg of our trip I talked with my German companions. One of them remarked, 'Mr. Philips, how can you still want our enemies to win? That could never be right! If the Russians win, they won't stop at Berlin. They will move past Hanover, even into Holland. In that case your whole country will be occupied by the Communists. And then you'll see that their regime is much worse than your people say ours is.'

Of course I did not agree with them. And I noticed that once we had passed the Swiss border, they were the first to buy Swiss newspapers. They, too, knew that no German newspaper told the truth.

After I had talked to our Swiss management, I had a secret meeting on a quay under the trees with Dr. Brümmer, an Eindhoven lawyer stationed in Switzerland to keep contact with our management in the United States. I was able to tell him everything about our situation, so that he could pass the information on to my parents. My companions knew nothing about this, but I kept a promise I had given them not to contact the Netherlands Embassy. I could understand this condition, because they would never have been able to explain such a move to the Berlin authorities.

I arranged things in such a way that we could resume our deliveries to Switzerland, agreeing that we would leave the question of authority over the Swiss establishment undecided until after the war. To the *Verwalters* I insisted that I had no authority in Switzerland, but that the main point was that we could start exporting to Switzerland again.

Up till then everything seemed to have taken its normal course, but suddenly I was confronted with a crisis. Towards the end of March there was still plenty of snow, and after coming to terms with our Swiss manager, I had agreed with him to go skiing in Arosa. But the Germans forbade me to go. Although I pointed out that they had guaranteed me complete freedom of movement in Switzerland, they kept on saying no. They even threatened to have my wife and children arrested if I disobeyed their orders. But I had tasted the difference between the situation in Switzerland and my country. I had had a glimpse of freedom! So my nerves broke down to the point that I had to stay in bed for half a day in my hotel room in Zürich. Fortunately, some good friends whom I had known for many years through Moral Re-Armament visited me, and helped me to overcome the crisis.

But we had to move on. I told my companions that I would give up my stay in Arosa, but that as I was in Switzerland I must do all that I would normally do on a working visit. In Chaux-de-Fonds we had a small apparatus factory, and I wanted to see how things were going there. The Germans agreed and we went there by train. The warm reception there did me a lot of good. On my return journey I gave my nosy friends the shivers by boarding a different section of the train, so that they did not know whether I was on board or not. Years later the Swiss told me that they regretted very much that I had not lodged a complaint about these two men. It would have been very easy to find some pretext to put them under lock and key. But if I had done this, it would have led to complications. Certainly, freedom was tempting, but it never crossed my mind to leave my family and our people in Holland in the lurch.

After my return to Eindhoven I went to see our family doctor and told him what had happened to me in the hotel in Zürich, a thing so unlike my normal self. His advice was that I should take a rest away from all business worries. So Sylvia and I spent some time in a hotel near the village of Maarn.

The Second Air Raid

Immediately this rest was rudely disturbed. On the night of 30 March I received a sudden call: our radio valve plant had been bombed! Next day I went to Eindhoven, and there I saw that, as a raid, this second one had been quite an achievement. Of the 23 bombs dropped, no less than 21 had fallen in the target area. The damage was tremendous and, sadly, people had again been killed, though as the raid took place after working hours only three people were still there.

We have never been able to find an answer to one puzzling question concerning this raid. We did not then realize that the manufacturing of radio valves, both for radio receivers and for military equipment, was a serious bottleneck for the Germans. But this was plain to the Allies, and could have been the explanation for this raid. We knew, however, that by far the most important Philips radio valve factory was in Hamburg, and that factory was built on a hillside outside the city, so that it could easily be identified from the air at a long distance. Yet that plant was never once bombed, although a large part of Hamburg was flattened.

Even though we supplied quite a lot of radio valves from Eindhoven, it is worth mentioning that they had to be returned by the thousands on account of poor quality. Our people had discovered a way of arranging that the valves would appear all right when first tested, but would soon stop working. As this was kept strictly secret, our Allies were unaware of it.

My Mother-in-Law and the Gestapo

After my return to our country hotel we were disturbed again. The Gestapo in The Hague wanted a word with me. I had some idea of the reason for this summons. Some days before something had happened in De Laak, about which I had been told by telephone.

My mother-in-law, Mrs. Digna Vlielander Hein, was staying with us in our home, and she was fervently anti-German. She knew that the Swiss consul went regularly between Holland and Switzerland, so she had dropped into his mail box a postcard for friends in Switzerland—a tacit request to have this card mailed there. On the card she had written that all the rumours about the Germans' bad conduct in Holland were not only true, but were surpassed by reality. This she had signed with her full name and address. Naturally the mail of this poor consul was checked and the postcard was found.

The Gestapo could not take this lying down. First they had tried to arrest her in her Hague flat. As she was not there, the policemen, who appeared well-informed, came to De Laak. There she was, sitting in the garden. But as soon as she saw suspicious characters approaching our home, she rushed into the kitchen where one of the maids was already signalling her to disappear. Then she ran with one of her dogs through the bushes to the gardener's house. She said to the gardener's wife, 'Here is my scarf. Put it on. Go and sit in the garden and say you have been sitting there all afternoon.' She herself put on the woman's scarf and taking the gardener's arm walked with him peacefully out into the street. After that she disappeared without trace.

Nobody in De Laak knew where she was. The Gestapo did not know either, and they were furious. First they interrogated one of the maids, without any result. When one of the police said, 'You are lying', she replied, 'All right, then I'm lying!' There was a Dutch Quisling with them who asked little Frits, a boy of three, 'Where is Gran?' In our family that word is not used for Grandmother, so he might as well have asked him where the Shah of Iran was.

But my mother-in-law had disappeared, and the Gestapo wanted to ask me some questions. I phoned and asked them whether I could stop by next week, because I had to be in The Hague then anyway. They agreed, so apparently there was nothing urgent.

Next week I was received very correctly at the Gestapo office in The Hague. Soon I was sitting opposite a gentleman who laid my mother-in-law's postcard in front of me, asking me to read it out aloud. With an impassive face, I read the text. I had decided that the best way to handle the matter would be to say that, though she appeared normal and a hard nut to crack, she was somewhat strange, to say the least. So I burst into exuberant laughter, and cried, 'What nonsense!'

'Why do you laugh?' the man asked in surprise.

'Well . . .' I shrugged my shoulders and pointed to my forehead. 'Don't you understand that my mother-in-law is a bit . . .? And it is you people who are responsible.'

'How is that?'

'Her youngest son was killed in action. Since then she has been out of her mind. As soon as she sees a German uniform she gets very excited.'

'That may be true, but still we would like to ask her some questions.'

'Questions? How do you propose to do that? She's gone.'

'But you must know where she is. Where is she?'

'That is just what I would like to find out from you. Your people ought to be able to find her. Anyhow, we don't know and you are responsible for her disappearance.'

After that I really gave that man hell, ending by asserting loudly, 'Searching my home without telling me in advance is absolutely irregular!'

'But, Mr. Philips, we could not have left this undealt with!' He pointed to the postcard.

'Pursuing an elderly woman like her? Haven't you got anything more important to do?'

He was dumbfounded. In the end I had to promise to tell my mother-in-law what he had said when I met her again. I repeated that due to their action she must have run away over-wrought—and heaven knew where to. I really had not a clue where to look for her. And until the end of the war my mother-in-law had to hide from the Germans.

A short while later, I returned from our rest in the Utrecht forests to Eindhoven, full of new courage and energy. I was soon to face even greater difficulties.

Chapter 11

In Captivity

Towards the end of April 1943 the Germans, who were being repulsed on several fronts, began to display signs of unrest and insecurity. After their victory in 1940, they had released all Dutch prisoners of war. But now that an invasion threatened they realized that former soldiers might be dangerous for them in a country with such a long coast line. On 29 April they suddenly announced that members of the former Dutch armed forces had to report. This caused consternation everywhere. There were strikes at the blast furnaces and the state mines. On Friday, 30 April, many walked out of our factories too.

At once I realized that the situation might become very dangerous, and I decided to get all my moves recorded from then on. I went to see the *Verwalters*. I contacted the *Rüstungsinspektion* and they assured me that Philips would get all the necessary papers so that nobody would have to report. Mistrust of the Germans had, however, grown tremendously, and rumours abounded in our factories. It was impossible to make the undertaking by the *Rüstungsinspektion* known immediately, and more people walked out. Towards the end of the afternoon I suggested to the *Verwalters* that we should give people the following Saturday morning off. They agreed. So notification was at once posted at the factory gates that Saturday would be free. It happened to be 1 May. The *Rüstungsinspektion*, who were meanwhile consulted by phone, also agreed. So the fact that no work was done on the Saturday could not be considered a strike.

That morning I did not go to my office, but I did attend the examinations at the Trades School. It was fortunate for me that they were being held that very day. As it was my custom to do this the Germans could not accuse me of having taken part in a strike that morning.

On the Sunday we discussed the dangerous situation which had developed, having by then appraised ourselves of the position at the blast furnaces and in the mines. As the Allied landings were not likely to liberate us soon, a protracted strike did not make any sense. It would just cost many lives, for the Germans had proclaimed a state of emergency, enabling them to shoot people without trial.

We decided therefore to do everything in our power to get people back to work the next morning. We asked the Works Committee to appeal to all neighbourhoods in and around Eindhoven to that effect, and arranged a meeting with them for Monday morning. I wanted the Monday to pass as peacefully as possible.

Unfortunately, the Germans had decided on the most stupid line of action imaginable. People who turned up for work on that Monday morning found strong German guards at the gates, so that many did not even go in. What made things worse was that the municipal authorities had, for perfectly comprehensible reasons, cut off the gas supply to our factories. The flow of gas had been briefly interrupted as a result of the strikes in the mines and had since been resumed, but the gas works had decided to have the gasometer filled for private consumption first and only afterwards to supply the Philips factories. People in the factory, however, concluded: 'No gas? So the strike at the mines is still on. So let's go home too.' Anyway, our factories were poorly manned that morning, and those who had come began to feel uneasy. Finally they, too, left.

In the centre of the city, meanwhile, there was unrest. A riot of a kind resulted in the upsetting of a milkcart. The situation was ominous. Towards twelve o'clock I was planning to go to the meeting with the Works Committee, to repeat my request that everyone should be urged to return to their jobs, when German soldiers entered my office. I was not allowed to leave.

In a short time, the Germans had assembled the whole directorate in my office, with the exception of Spaens who was on tour. I phoned Sylvia to tell her that my colleagues and I were under restraint. She soon turned up—with some packs of playing cards. So we talked among ourselves and played card games, with a German keeping guard over us. I took the opportunity when I went to the toilet of getting rid of all unnecessary papers from my wallet and notebook. Later in the afternoon we were told that we were to be transferred to Haaren, where a seminary had been converted into a special prison for preliminary judicial inquiry.

Sylvia said to me, 'That's just as well—imagine the war going by without you having been gaoled!' One of the Germans almost exploded. He shouted at her, 'So you think you'll win the war?' 'Do you think anything else?' she retorted calmly. Then she went home to pack some essentials for me in a small suitcase.

The news of our arrest was soon known all over Eindhoven. The

Germans did their best to frighten people. They put it around that Mr. Philips had been gaoled and that if the workers valued his life, they should go back to their jobs at once. And they went beyond threats. Later we learned that at about the time when we were taken off, seven men had been executed in the factory yard, among them four of our workers. One of them had been arrested while working in his small garden. When the Germans asked him if he was on strike, he told them he was on a week's leave. Then they asked him if he would have gone on strike if he had not had a week off. He replied honestly that he would have. So he was shot.

The same day some of the Works Committee, hearing that I had been arrested, went to see the Germans and offered to take my place at Haaren. Their motivating thought was, 'Mr. Philips has six children, and anyway he is not responsible for this strike.'

The four of us in the directorate were taken by taxi to Haaren, with only one guard. On the way the taxi had a puncture, so we got out and strolled around a bit. None of us thought of running away. We were sure that the Germans could not pin anything on us. As I entered the prison, I looked around and said to myself, 'Now it is 3 May. The trees are green already. What will the world be like when I get out?' Yet at that moment it felt as if the colossal weight of my responsibility dropped off. It was only much later that I realized that my life had been that day hanging by a silken thread. The SS General in charge of maintaining order in Holland, Hans Rauter, was furious about the strike and had threatened that henceforth he would execute only heads of management. The Germans were in the mood to resort to the most extreme measures to terrorize the population.

That same evening the Germans drove loudspeaker cars through the villages around Eindhoven where many of our workers lived, saying that if people wanted to prevent Mr. Philips from being shot, they should all go back to work.

My wife also realized that my life depended on this, but she felt strongly too that God had the last word over life and death. Curiously, she slept well that night. But next morning it was music to her ears to hear hundreds of clattering wooden shoes as people passed our home on their way to the factories.

The Haaren prison was under the Gestapo, but we had been imprisoned on the order of the *Rüstungsinspektion*, in other words by the German Army. Between Gestapo and Army there was considerable rivalry, so the Gestapo was not all that much against us. As a result we four had a relatively bearable time at Haaren. As well as getting normal prison food, we were allowed to receive parcels. And every morning we were allowed to walk in the garden for an hour. It almost seemed as though the prison management felt honoured to have the Philips directorate to stay with them.

That first week Holst and I shared a cell. We enjoyed this, for we shared many common interests, and neither of us was moody. During our walks in the seminary park we had long discussions too with Dijksterhuis and De Vries. So it was a blow when, after a week, the others were released and I had to stay.

One of our guards was a German who had been living in Poland, where he had been imprisoned himself. After my colleagues were released, he said that he felt sorry for me having to stay. But I was beginning to view this differently. I told him that, on second thoughts, it was better this way. After what had happened on that notorious Monday, it might have created a wrong impression if I had been released early. People might have muttered, 'There, you see—workers are shot, but Frits Philips is let off easily!' This the German understood.

I started preparing my room for a more protracted stay. On one of her visits my wife brought a tablecloth, a floor mat, and two Van Gogh reproductions to hang on the wall. I even got a power-point installed so that I could use my Philishave.

Altogether I was lucky. I was not worried about my family, for I knew that my wife was equal to any difficulties, and I had no reason to fear losing my job. These were the concerns which many of my fellow-prisoners had to live with. Small businessmen worried about their shops, about their sons who had been deported to Germany or about their wives who were completely overwrought. The greatest help was, however, an unshakeable faith. I trusted God fully to look after me. Apart from a time when an infection caused me great physical pain, I did not have a single sleepless night during my time in gaol.

I was allowed contact with the hostages who had been left behind when hundreds of others had been transferred to the nearby village of St. Michielsgestel. For in order to keep the Dutch in line, the Germans had now resorted to the large-scale imprisoning of well-known Dutchmen as hostages. The hostages left in Haaren had to look after the prisoners. Most of them were put four in a cell, and were subjected to tough interrogation. And later, often after confessions had been extorted, they were transported to War Tribunals in Utrecht where they would be condemned to imprisonment in the concentration camp at Vught, or even to death. In our corridors there always reigned an oppressive tension.

Only after three weeks in Haaren was I interrogated. I asked my interrogator his name. 'It is not the custom for you to know our names,' he said. I could only reply, 'All right.' But later I found out that he was Josef Schreieder, one of the principal personalities in German counter-espionage and the big man behind the so-called *England-Spiel*. As such he was crown witness after the war in the famous case against the Dutch-man Anton van der Waals, who was executed in January 1950 for col-laboration. Through clever collusion between Schreieder and Van der Waals, many resistance men fell into Gestapo hands.

These people came across the sea either by air or ship, believing that all had been carefully prepared for them, but instead they walked into a trap. German counter-espionage would meet them upon arrival and arrest them at once. We had heard of this tragedy and we could not understand why the responsible people across the sea did not realize something was going wrong. We did all we could to warn them, but nothing seemed to help, and a large number of them died before the firing squad. Some of them, after being arrested, were held in solitary confinement on the top floor of our building.

My interrogator began:

'Mr. Philips, how is it that each time we encounter resistance, Philips people are involved?'

'That's not very remarkable,' I replied. 'Philips is the largest company in Holland. If you take the percentage of the industrial workers who work at Philips, it is a still larger share. If you add the fact that we make radios and that resistance always means establishing communications, it becomes even more understandable that we have people like that among us. And one more thing: it is often the most enterprising people who end up with Philips. So it shouldn't surprise anybody that there is a lot of resistance among Philips people. It would be stranger if it were not so.'

'Mr. Philips, are you involved in resistance?'

'Yes, every day, in my talks with the *Verwalters*.'

'But don't you believe in actual resistance and sabotage?'

'No, I don't. That won't decide the outcome of the war. War is won in a different place.'

'Yet you are very anti-German.'

'I'm not anti-German! I'm against National Socialism.'

'Why?'

'Because I believe in what Jesus taught. He never made any difference between one race and another. It's not part of His teachings. And He always put special emphasis on man's individual conscience. In your system a man's conscience doesn't count. Only one authority is recognized—the State—and the State determines what is good and bad. That runs completely contrary to my religious convictions. I firmly believe such a system is bound to collapse.'

'Aren't you a member of the Oxford Group?'

'No, I couldn't be. The Group doesn't have any members. It is just people who have decided to live by standards they are deeply convinced about. You won't be able to find a list of members anywhere. It doesn't exist.'

He then began to interrogate me about one of our local deputy managers, who, though a good man doing a good job, had turned out to be a Quisling. I was sorry, because I had liked him. I had called him to my office and told him frankly that I could not understand why he was doing this. He had tried to explain why he was a member of the Party, and I had attempted to change his mind by telling him how the Germans had behaved in Poland. That talk must have taken place in August 1940. Later, my regard for this man diminished when he began to act strangely, and he promised the Germans that he would help them with all sorts of things without having the slightest chance of fulfilling these commitments. At last he was arrested. For days they pressured him, and so our conversation had come out. It was recorded and put in my file. Now it was read out to me. I burst out laughing and cried, 'But my dear sir, do you really believe that I would have said this to a Quisling? Do you think I am as unintelligent as that? To say that kind of thing to such a man?'

'Yes . . . yes . . .'

'After all, you ought to know by now that this man is not quite all there.'

After this my interrogation went into the events of my Swiss journey. I told him everything in detail, not sparing him criticism of my companions who had nearly given me a nervous breakdown by the way they had behaved.

Finally, the most important subject was broached: my conduct during the critical days around 1 May, which had been the direct cause of my being in gaol. My interrogator wanted to get to the bottom of this. And now the fact that I had recorded all my actions and words proved its worth. First of all I could prove that I had continued working normally myself, even supervising the final exams of the Trades School on the Saturday morning when everyone had been free. I could also prove, through my notes, that I had contacted the *Rüstungsinspektion* at a certain time and what we had agreed upon; that I had seen a particular

Verwalter at a given moment, what he had said and what our conclusion had been. It was clear exactly what I had done from hour to hour. It tallied so completely that it was impossible to pin any charge of sabotage on me. Soon I realized that I was beginning to impress my interrogator by my record of events, and that he could see little reason to detain me much longer. A secretary wrote everything down, and I had to sign the statement.

A week later I was informed that I had been promoted from prisoner to hostage, which in German eyes was a considerable promotion. In retrospect I have been able to understand better what actually happened. Schreieder was a power in the Gestapo, but the Army people, who were responsible for armaments and ammunition, did not like me too much. So they arrived at the compromise solution of making me a hostage. This had the additional advantage that it would make the right kind of impression on the Eindhoven population.

The Germans now wanted me to move to the St. Michielsgestel camp. But I did not like that a bit. In that camp the weekly visits from my wife would become monthly ones. Besides, I had begun to understand how privileged my position had been so far. I was allowed free movement in a section of the prison and was the only detainee permitted to wear ordinary clothes.

Four hostages, of whom two were doctors, one a dentist, and one a priest disguised as an orderly, told me that they had stayed behind, after the big move of hostages from Haaren to St. Michielsgestel, to look after the prisoners. So I asked to stay in Haaren, too. The Germans agreed, and I was detailed to help look after the prisoners. I went about in a white coat, helping to irradiate patients with an Infraphil, which helped against all sorts of infections, and doing other jobs of that kind. I did some housework, too, and was convinced that I was of more use there than I could ever be in the hostages' camp. I also managed to provide the small hospital ward with a gramophone and some records, which was a boost to morale.

Our prison warder was still the big stout East Prussian whose nature told him to respect people in positions of authority. One day he asked me whether I could arrange for a radio to be provided for the prison staff. My first reaction was, 'Very simple: you get me released and you'll have your radio!' But that, of course, could not be done. Still, I promised a set, provided it was put in a corridor so the prisoners could listen as well. The prison warders agreed, and so it happened. Even though only the Germans could operate the radio, we soon discovered with astonishment that many of the 'German' newscasts actually turned out to be from the BBC in

London. The casual passer-by could hardly tell the difference. He would just hear German-language news. But we noticed that in 1943, with their armies being pressed from all sides, our German warders wanted to know the more truthful Allied version of their position. For us, this positive news was a source of hope.

I was struck by the support which the surrounding population gave us. A local veterinary surgeon had organized a regular supply of butter, bread, vegetables and other food which he collected from the local farmers. In the village of Haaren itself lived Engeltje, a very simple, small, but courageous man. By horse and cart he would make the rounds of all the farmers to collect food, and then deliver it at the prison. In a large pot on a hot plate in our room we melted the butter. This was then mixed into the prisoners' food. As a result they got much more than the usual 10 grams of fat in their daily ration, which made a great difference, and boosted morale as well. We were also able to give additional nutrition to the exhausted, underfed prisoners arriving from the main political prison at Scheveningen. In our small hospital ward German doctors only rarely appeared, and were interested only when the thermometer showed a high temperature. They paid hardly any attention to the patients, who had to rely completely on our two Dutch doctors.

The prison director was a German who had been in the civilian police. Politics meant little to him. He always behaved correctly towards us, and he trusted us to the point of allowing one of the doctors to go once a week by bicycle to 's Hertogenbosch to collect medicine. Of course, the doctor could have stayed away after one of these trips, but neither he nor we wanted this, because the prisoners depended on our help.

As the only hostages left in that prison, we enjoyed the special privilege of being allowed to walk in the seminary garden, and not only in the inner courtyard. We gladly availed ourselves of the chance during that beautiful summer of 1943. We walked through the tennis court, outside the barbed-wire fence, and as far as a wall, beyond which was a small canal. This was the outer boundary of the property. If you climbed up on the wall, you could look far and wide over the Brabant landscape. You could even have the illusion of being completely free. In the distance, along winding roads, we could see the farm houses, and all around us the birds were singing. We really relished those walks, and they also gave us the exercise we needed.

One summer night when Dr. Steijns and I were returning from our walk, there were sudden shots. That was unusual, and we looked at each other. Again we heard shots, and this time the bullets whistled overhead.

Suddenly I saw a man with a rifle at quite a distance from us. I shouted, 'What on earth are you doing, shooting at us? We're allowed to walk here!' The shots had alerted other guards, who told the youthful sniper that he had better stop. Later, it turned out that he was a young Dutch SS man. Ostensibly he had fired thinking we were trying to escape, but rumour had it that he had boasted more than once to his cronies, 'Wait and see. I'll get that man Philips!'

Shortly afterwards I got an infection on my left thigh, a furuncle which caused me much pain and forced me to stay in bed for weeks. It was an unpleasant experience. But I thought it would not hurt me to endure these throbs and stings. During the attacks of pain I used to say to myself, 'Damn it, it does hurt, doesn't it? But all right, so be it. . .' This increased my powers of resistance at once. In prison they did what they could, but it was very little, as of course there was no penicillin yet in Holland. The furuncle produced a hole big enough for a tangerine.

Just at the time when I was beginning to walk again, our small medical team's stay was abruptly ended. The reason was the discovery of a secret warning system. The German interrogators were trying, by every means available, to extort confessions from the prisoners. In addition, they wanted to know names, names and even more names. Under such circumstances it was natural that some people gave names away. And it was then urgent to warn the people concerned as fast as possible so they could save themselves. There was an agreement that the one who did give names away passed this on to the underground. In Haaren this information travelled a strange road. The names were written on bits of paper which were taken away by the floor attendants, who were themselves prisoners. These bits of paper were smuggled into our hospital ward, often by slipping them into the pockets of a doctor's coat. I used to hide them under my mattress and Steijns, when he went on his regular shopping trip, would take them with him. So the information reached the resistance movement, and they did the rest. Once in a while Sylvia also smuggled out information.

There was also another warning system, which functioned differently. As I have told already, quite a few victims of the *England-Spiel* ended up in our prison. We realized that many of these men would be shot. If any of them were ill—as many inevitably were—a blood test was sent to the University Hospital in Utrecht. The tubes of blood were stuck down with a plaster. The way this plaster was put on would tell the initiated if the blood was from a man whose life was in danger. In this case the report would invariably read, 'Patient is so seriously ill that he cannot be transported.' This would temporarily prevent the prisoner's transfer to the Utrecht prison.

It was therefore important that our medical team stayed together. One evil day a floor attendant was caught carrying a bit of paper to Dr. Steijns. Steijns happened to have his birthday on that day and his wife brought some fried chicken, which we all shared. Each of us knew what might be in the offing, but we did not show it. That same evening Steijns was summoned to the phone. He did not return. Next door to us was the store-room where the blankets were kept. If prisoners arrived at night, blankets were fetched from there. We heard someone in the store-room. So blankets were required. They must be for Chel Steijns! None of us slept a wink that night. There was a great likelihood that we, too, would be interrogated the next day. We destroyed every piece of paper still in our possession.

Next morning the furious commandant came to see us. He had had the fullest confidence in Steijns and now it had been betrayed. He felt deceived and his mind was made up. 'You'll all be transferred as soon as possible to the St. Michielsgestel camp.'

That was quite a relief. Things seemed to be working out relatively well for us. But what would be Chel Steijns' fate? In addition, we were worried that the prisoners would now have to do without most of the medical and other care which we had been able to give them.

I had an additional concern. I strongly suspected that one of my close Delft friends, Dick van Driel van Wageningen, was also in our prison. Before the war he had been KLM manager in Rotterdam. My friendship with him dated back to our Christian Student camp days, and in Delft he had been one of my best friends. One day when we were skiing together he had said to me, 'Frits, I feel awful, I've completely lost my faith.' 'You can get it back,' I answered. 'It depends on whether you really want to. It's very simple. Just take a quarter of an hour sitting quietly every morning, and write down your thoughts, whatever they are. This will give you ideas you haven't had before. When you begin to experience this, you may come to believe that it is really God speaking in your heart.' So he did. After a fortnight he told me that he had in fact experienced miracles in his life.

This was quite a while ago. Now I suspected that Dick was in that terrifying upper section of our prison. It was very hard for us to find out who was up there. The only way was to get access to the central card file, which was in the keeping of a man who always kept his mouth tightly shut, as it would cost him his life if he were found to have let out any information. Only after my release did I learn that Dick actually was in Haaren. I then began corresponding with him there and he wrote me remarkable letters, showing how real his faith had become. He wrote once, 'I can say that, whatever happens to me, I have the fullest confidence that it will be what ought to happen. I am whistling here in my cell and I have a peace in my heart which is not of this world.' I managed to arrange for his mother to visit him. Sadly, he later died in a concentration camp in Germany. It has remained one of the strangest experiences of my life to have been gaoled for months in the same building as one of my best friends without knowing for certain that he was there.

Although as a hostage I had no part in the Philips management, my wife's weekly visits kept me in touch. A few people like Theo Tromp and Woltersom also visited me. Woltersom told me once that I had a chance of being released if I would live in Arnhem and keep outside Philips' managerial decisions. I consulted Sylvia and we both agreed at once that it was out of the question.

Hostage

The change to St. Michielsgestel was a big one. In Haaren I had been in a prison. In St. Michielsgestel I was in a camp where, apart from the barbed-wire fence, personal freedom was considerable. About a year earlier, the Germans had shot ten hostages, but now they had changed their tactics. They had started seizing people at random from places where there was sabotage or resistance, and having them shot without trial on the spot. This method was terrible, but it had removed the atmosphere of impending danger from the hostages' camp.

My left leg had been weakened so much that I had difficulty in walking. I shared a small room with Father Herman Gall, the priest who had been disguised as an orderly in Haaren. After my recovery I was delighted to be able to take up drawing, under instruction from the well-known portrait painter Karel van Veen. Dr. Brugmans, later Vice-Chancellor of the European University in Bruges, gave us a refresher course in French, and later I was able to play hockey. Some of my best experiences were on the tennis court. Some time earlier, when I could not imagine becoming a hostage, I had provided the hostages with the materials and labour to build this court. Now I could enjoy the result myself.

In many ways my stay in St. Michielsgestel was interesting, and I derived a lot of benefit from it. The occupying power had carefully gathered the elite of various social groups in one place in order to forestall sabotage. It was natural, with so many well-informed Dutchmen together, that we discussed and planned a great deal about what should happen after the liberation. One important consequence was the post-war co-operation between management and labour organizations. Thus, after the war the Foundation of Labour was started in which the presidents of the various organizations met weekly to plan how to solve the social problems of our plundered and impoverished country. We had got to know each other so well in the camp that this Foundation was built on mutual trust.

Hostages were being released all the time. The Germans would give the names of the fortunate ones to the administrative office, who had their seat in office No. 1 together with the hostages' spokesman, Professor Schermerhorn, who later became Prime Minister. If the sound system announced that someone had to report to office No. 1, there were two possibilities: either he was being given some days' leave of absence, or he was being released altogether.

On 20 September, I was called to office No. 1. The Germans had decided that I had had enough. Suddenly I was released, almost five months after my arrest. People congratulated me all round, but I had mixed feelings. Of course I was more than delighted to be free again and to see my family. But I also thought of the many friends I was leaving behind. And, curiously, I was also thinking of the forthcoming tennis matches . . .

After my release I needed relaxation, so Sylvia and I spent a week in Limburg and afterwards went sailing. As we were not allowed to sail on the Zuiderzee (now the IJsselmeer) or on the estuaries, we were limited to the rivers. Sailing on the rivers was in itself an art, because an auxiliary engine was out of the question, and you had to take wind, current and rising and sinking tides into account. We found new courage and strength there, wonderfully free on the water and far away from the Germans and their henchmen.

Chapter 12

Back at Philips

By the beginning of October 1943 I was back in my office. Colleagues and employees came to welcome me with happy faces. But when I met the *Verwalters* I sensed that something was afoot. They wanted to discuss their plans with me, they said. As I expected nothing good from them, I went on the attack.

'What have you done to me? Do you know that nobody has even told me why I was arrested? I can imagine that in the confusion of the strike some things got out of hand. But I don't understand why I was not released with the others. And what have you been doing to help me all this time?'

For a moment they were caught unawares, but soon the truth came out. They hoped I would realize how much the situation had changed. It was unthinkable that I should exercise the same authority as before.

I answered that the Germans possessed the power to relieve me of my office, but that in that case they must announce at the factory gates, 'Mr. Philips is no longer in charge.' Then everyone would know the true situation.

No announcements were posted at the factory gates. But this did not mean that the transition from prison life without responsibility back to being head of Philips under German occupation was easy. When I was released I had asked myself how long I would need before I would fully find my way back into the Philips situation. In fact it took six weeks. In the first weeks my thoughts were often with my camp friends. Is Piet's wife still ill? Has Jan got his leave? Has my friend Einthoven got his better radio to pick up the BBC news? How did the tennis matches go? Are Karel van Veen's drawing classes continuing?

After a prison term of almost half a year you especially enjoy normal things. First of all, of course, the family. To be with my wife again, not just for one hour a week, but with enough time to discuss everything, was a wonderful thing. And I enjoyed the company of my children, fascinated to see how they had each developed.

I was, of course, immediately involved in all that was happening in Philips. One of my daily concerns was: Can we keep our people working? Every day I had the railway trucks counted as they brought in raw materials. On them depended the amount of work available. Nothing had been transported by road for a long time because of fuel shortage, and we hired horses and carts for our internal transport.

Our workshop at Vught also required attention. The Germans had changed the camp commandant several times. Each time a new man was put in charge, Laman Trip alerted me. He always wanted me to make the new man's acquaintance so that we retained the relationship which would keep our workshop's special position. I had made it a conscious habit to shout as loudly as possible over the phone at these commandants. When the change of command occurred I would ring the new man and yell at him,

'Mr. Camp Commandant, this is Mr. Philips speaking!'

'Who?'

'Director General Philips!'

In my imagination I could see the man at the other end bowing to the telephone. I shouted to him that I wanted to visit the camp.

'But of course, Herr Director General! You are most welcome!'

Again the telephone in Vught boomed,

'If convenient I shall come tomorrow at 3 p.m.'

Each new commandant received me politely. None of them seemed aware that until recently I had been the involuntary guest of his masters. Visiting the workshop, of course, meant more to me than an ordinary factory inspection, as I would meet friends and colleagues. On one occasion, to my great surprise, I met Chel Steijns, the Haaren doctor. He had just been through a terrible time in Vught, but was now the prisoners' doctor again. Fortunately he could not foresee what was still in store for him. As a result of help he gave later to some prisoners who managed to escape, he ended up in one of the worst concentration camps in Germany, an experience he barely survived.

As Hitler did worse and worse on all fronts and the air raids obstructed German war production more and more, the situation in Eindhoven became even harder. Germany increasingly lacked manpower, so the Sauckel men came to strip Holland of yet more people. Our *Verwalters* were put in charge of squeezing hundreds of young workers out of our factories. We refused all co-operation. That created bad blood, all the more so because the *Rüstungsinspektion* was very dissatisfied with our performance. As always, our excuse was that we could not keep our delivery deadlines when our personnel was being taken away.

The Germans refused to accept that argument any longer. But our *Verwalters* were also unhappy about losing more young workers. They realized it would meet with resistance and that it would affect production adversely. They suggested we should tell them which young people could best be spared. We refused. Then they turned the thing around—we must tell them who could *not* be spared in the production process. Again we refused, despite threats that we might be accused of sabotage. Our people had gradually become aware of what was going on in Germany and knew that workers taken there might be killed in air raids. Apart from objections of principle, we wanted no responsibility for a choice which would expose some people to risks others would escape by staying at home.

Though we did not budge, the threats were not carried out. Sauckel's men pushed their plans through without us. But this conflict aggravated the situation.

The *Verwalters* began to meddle more and more in our affairs. One day a *Verwalter* came to inform me that all the aerials on our physics laboratory had to be taken down. I feigned surprise, though I had expected this kind of command long before. I asked why this had to happen all of a sudden. He replied:

'Each time bombers take off from the airfield here, there is an immediate reaction in Britain. There must be people here who send an immediate signal.'

I shook my head, saying that this must be nonsense. Our people were fully occupied. They had other things to do besides observing German bombers. Knowing the kind of radio artists working in the laboratory, the complaint did not, of course, surprise me. The aerials were removed, but I was sure that they would be replaced by something equally effective.

The *Verwalters* came another day to discuss a big order for thousands of magnets which they wanted to place with us. We were experts in manufacturing magnets for loudspeakers, but we sensed that these magnets were wanted for land-mines of which the Germans needed many thousands to defend their positions in Russia. Needless to say, we did not want to make them. We told the gentlemen so. They threatened that a refusal might be regarded as sabotage. But according to the Land War Regulations they were not allowed to demand ammunition or weapon components apart from what the occupation army needed.

'Gentlemen,' I said, 'you must know that we are not legally bound to accept such orders. You have the power, so you can accuse us of anything you like, you can even shoot us. That is your responsibility, not ours.'

'Mr. Philips, we assure you those magnets are not intended for land-mines or ammunition. It is of great importance for Philips to accept this offer.'

'All right, if you submit a letter to us, signed by the head of the *Rüstungsinspektion* in The Hague, certifying that these magnets are not to be used for land-mines or other weapons, then we are prepared to study whether we are able to make them.'

The letter never came and the magnets were never made. It interested me to see that the years of Nazi lies had not yet completely destroyed old-fashioned German honesty. Many Germans, especially the non-politicised army officers, would still refrain from putting their signatures to a lie.

I also found that many German business people, even among our competitors, kept a straightforward attitude to us. I had a talk in The Hague with Dr. Lüschen, one of the top management of Siemens, who wanted to buy our valve factory in Hamburg. I said to him,

'At the start of the occupation I decided not to enter into any transactions on behalf of Philips which I would not want to hold to after the war. In dealing with Germans I have to be especially cautious, because I am not free, so please come back after the war to discuss this with us again.

'Of course,' I added, 'you can turn to our *Verwalters* and enlist their help in a take-over. But I doubt whether you'll succeed, because one of their tasks is to see that the capital and assets of Philips Ltd. remain intact. You can go over their heads and try your luck with the government in Berlin, but that is completely your business.'

'I understand your viewpoint completely,' replied Lüschen, 'and I shall respect it.'

I should like at this point to pay homage to the men and women of Philips who lost their lives in the resistance movement. Their names have been inscribed on Carasso's monument in our works. And besides them there are dozens of others who, while sacrificing and risking as much, came through alive. Those names are often so easily forgotten. If people in occupied Holland began to call Philips in Eindhoven the 'British fortress', it was not without justification.

Our Family

In this very difficult period, my family was a kind of counter-weight. I was still able to devote more time to them than before the war. We were able to help each other and we had much to be grateful for. We faithfully had our Sunday morning times at De Laak, in which our children's friends also took part. Equally faithfully we went out for country rides on cycles and tandems.

Food was not always easy. Even though our secret cow yielded her daily gallon, this did not compensate for the ever-shrinking rations for our large family. It was our principle not to buy on the black market. Nor did we take part in the favourite trading sport—we never traded radios for steaks. In the spring of 1944 we made the painful discovery that two of our youngest three, little Sylvia and Frits, had caught a light degree of tuberculosis from our driver. Lack of the right kind of food must have played a part in this. Fortunately, by keeping them in bed and giving them extra food, we were able to deal with it.

Sylvia was meticulous in dividing up the rations to the point of providing each member of the family with their own dish of butter, with their name on it. In the beginning of 1944 the weekly ration—actually of margarine—was 146 grams for adults and 175 grams for children. How it was to be consumed was everybody's own affair. Some finished the lot in the beginning, others spread it thinly at first so as to make it last longer.

One luxurious commodity was freely available to us: wooden shoes! We got them by supplying wood from our own trees at De Wielewaal to the clog maker, and were able to provide many people with wooden shoes. Our children, too, mostly went about in clogs. After the liberation some of them protested vehemently against wearing proper shoes again. 'Oh no, do I really have to wear *shoes* to school?' they would say.

In spite of all the worries we did not neglect our vacations, and took our elder children sailing on the rivers. But we kept those holidays brief, for I never dared to stay away from the factories for long.

The children turned out to have an enormous capacity for adapting to new circumstances. They moved from one place to another without a whimper of complaint. When I was in prison in the summer of 1943, I asked Sylvia to move away from Eindhoven for a time, for fear of air raids. That summer the family stayed in a village hotel and then on a farm near St. Michielsgestel. My eldest daughter, Digna, would wave at me as she cycled by at a prearranged time, when I was on the seminary's flat roof. The Germans, who did not approve of this, invariably chased her away.

My wife believed so strongly that all our lives, including mine, were in God's hands that her attitude of good-natured trust permeated our whole family. Later, in June 1944, my eldest son, Ton, had to sit for his secondary school admission exam on the very morning when there had been, at seven, a raid near Eindhoven. Ton and all the boys went to school as usual for the exam.

At times, too, we had our narrow escapes. One winter night in 1943 a British incendiary bomb dropped on the Eindhoven gasometer, only a few hundred yards from De Laak. Many people living nearby evacuated their homes, but we took shelter with some neighbours in our cellar. The situation was quite tricky. The risk was enhanced by the fact that wrong handling could have resulted in a highly explosive mixture inside the gasometer. The head of the public utilities had the courage and presence of mind to readjust the inflow of gas when the oil in the gasometer was already burning overhead, so as to avoid an explosion.

Meanwhile we were in the air-raid shelter, but after an hour I had had enough of this and went outside to see what was happening. At that very moment the gasometer lid blew off. With a roaring sound all the gas burned up in a few minutes, in flames as tall as towers. But because of this, the explosion which might otherwise have erased a large part of the city, including our home, did not happen.

The Invasion Comes in Sight

My last visit to Vught was in May 1944, shortly before the Allied landings. The Germans were getting nervous, because they were uncertain where the Allies would launch their big assault. I went to Vught because there was talk of a precipitate evacuation of the whole camp. That was exactly what we feared most, for if the Germans moved the camp, a great many workers for whom we had been able to do something would be deprived of our protection. And sure enough, the commandant confirmed that the Germans might be forced to evacuate the camp. I tried to reassure him.

'But, Herr Kommandant, those people won't come here! Suppose they really reach the French coasts, that is still a long way off. An invasion on the Dutch coast, say near the Hook of Holland, is out of the question. The supply lines across the sea are too long. Nobody here should worry about that.'

Meanwhile in Eindhoven we were expecting the invasion any moment. At home we had discussed it thoroughly. De Laak was near the railway station, and it was likely that such an important junction would be bombed by the Allies. So we had decided that as soon as the invasion started, we would move into the club house at the golf course, using the dressing rooms as bedrooms.

The sixth of June started like any normal day. I tuned in at seven to the BBC news as usual, and heard nothing special. Our radio, incidentally, was hidden behind the bath-tub, and we discovered later that all our children had known where it was, but none of them had told the others. When I arrived at my office at eight-thirty there was great excitement, for at eight o'clock the BBC had announced that the invasion had started. And I had missed it! At once I returned home and discussed with Sylvia what we should do.

On reflection, we were inclined to tell ourselves that things might not move as fast as we had anticipated. But we had decided to move, and we felt we had to go through with it. So we started for the Golf Club, Sylvia and all six children on their bikes, and I took my small gas-fuelled car, stuffed full to the last corner with blankets and baggage. At the Golf Club we installed ourselves as best we could. And from there I would go every morning the nine kilometres to my office, either by bike or—if possible— by car.

So the invasion had come, with its uncertainties for the occupying forces. I, too, felt far from safe. Rumours abounded of a list of Dutch people whom the Germans wanted to take with them to Germany, and my name was said to be on it. So I began to think of going into hiding.

On the morning of 20 July I had the strong feeling: 'You should go into hiding!' Tension was mounting from hour to hour. That same morning I discussed with my personal assistant and with the doorman how a warning bell could be installed in my room, to be operated by the doorman's foot as soon as he noticed suspicious people approaching.

The bell was never installed. That afternoon I was told that some Germans wanted to see me. They said they wanted to discuss *Wehrmacht* orders. That sounded suspicious, because this kind of thing was always cleared first through the *Verwalters*. So I decided to disappear. At that same moment we were told on the phone that other Germans were posted at the other entrance as well. I arranged with my personal assistant that he would receive the visitors in my room and tell them, phone in hand, that I was probably somewhere in the plant. Then he would phone to one factory after another, asking whether I was there.

This 'search' took more than a quarter of an hour. That was enough for me. A long time ago I had had some steps built which enabled me to leave my office by the window. In the fence surrounding the building was a gate, to which I had the keys. Now this arrangement came in handy. I asked my personal assistant to send my car to the municipal trades school, where I knew I could wait unseen in a deep doorway. I jumped out of the window, went through the gate, moved along the back of some gardens and then walked, outwardly calm, into the road, over the footbridge to the street where the trades school was located. Suddenly I heard a cyclist catching up with me from behind. It was the doorman, who told me that I had gone off with the car keys in my pocket. I gave him the keys and said I would go on to the school. All went according to plan. The driver came to collect me, and from then on I disappeared from sight.

Chapter 13

In Hiding

I was now in the same position as thousands of other Dutchmen hiding from the Germans and their henchmen—a process for which we had invented a specially expressive word, *onderduiken*—to dive below the surface. But this process was especially difficult for me because so many people knew me by sight. I went first to the Eindhoven home of a maternal cousin who was married to one of our Philips people, Ton Huizinga. I spent only one night there, but it gave me a chance to plan my next moves in peace. That night I wrote a letter to my wife which was mailed in The Hague, stating that I had felt nervy lately and was going to do some sailing in Friesland to regain my peace of mind.

Meanwhile Weber, the head of the Gestapo in Eindhoven, and his cronies were looking for me. I had agreed with my personal assistant how he should explain my sudden absence. He was to say that I had a meeting in The Hague next day and that, as often happened, must have left a day ahead. My wife was told the same story. All the same, the Germans went to the Golf Club to look for me that same evening, but Sylvia could tell them only that I was in The Hague.

That happened to be the day on which Stauffenberg tried to kill Hitler at his headquarters. Whether there was any link between the move to arrest me and that attempt on Hitler's life, I don't know, but one of the *Verwalters*, Dr. E. Löser, who formerly worked with Krupp's and was not too keen on the Nazi regime, was arrested some time after. That could happen to any suspect person at that time. Anyway, I had beaten the Germans to it, though the danger was still there, for it had been announced that hiding from the Germans would be regarded as sabotage and might be punished by death.

Huizinga found me a hiding place in his neighbourhood with a family called Van der Weerd. A Jewish girl was hiding there, too, but in two weeks there I only saw her once. My letter from The Hague duly arrived saying I could be reached Poste Restante at Grouw in Friesland. Sylvia handed this letter to Dijksterhuis, who showed it immediately to the

Verwalters. The thing appeared simple: I was somewhere in Friesland.

I was lucky in the weather. But because it was so temptingly beautiful outside, I found it hard to stay in my attic room. I wanted to get out! And by bike. My brother-in-law, Frans Vlielander Hein, was also in hiding, in the region between the two big rivers, on a country estate near a village called Zoelen. There I hoped to find a place too, somewhere really in the country. Before moving to Zoelen, I spent another twenty-four hours at Huizinga's home, where Sylvia joined me. The Huizingas had three children, and they never knew that their Uncle Frits and Aunt Sylvia were stowed away in the attic. There we were able to talk things over and say goodbye to one another for nobody knew how long.

At 6.30 a.m., amid the hundreds of cyclists going to work, I went on my way, accompanied by Huizinga. I cycled behind him, my briefcase, containing a toothbrush and a shaver, on my rear carrier. I had on a raincoat with the collar turned up and thought nobody would recognize me. But that same evening a cousin of our housemaid told Sylvia, 'Mr. Philips is in Eindhoven!' My wife shook her head: 'That's impossible. He's somewhere in Friesland.' But the girl insisted, 'My husband is sure he saw him this morning on his bicycle.'

Towards noon, I reached Oss, thirty miles away. At the local Philips factory I asked for the plant manager, but he was away. I also went to have my hair cut, because I knew it could be dangerous for people in hiding to show up at the local barber. It was a very fine day and, in the best of spirits, I pedalled on to Zoelen. I enjoyed the ride greatly. In my pocket I had a fine identity card in the name of my deceased brother-in-law, Warner van Lennep. The central identity card records in The Hague had been destroyed in a specially planned British air raid, so details could not be checked back there. And, if I were arrested, I would be able to tell them all about Van Lennep.

While I was moving to a new address, my *alter ego*, who had been sailing somewhere in Friesland, was also moving. The night before in my attic I had written another 'letter to my wife', to be mailed in Belgium. In it I said I had moved to the Ardennes, to wonderful surroundings, amidst quiet, dreamy woods, an ideal place to continue my rest cure. I said I was beginning to feel better. This letter, too, landed on the *Verwalters'* desks.

In Zoelen I enjoyed myself with my fellow fugitives. We played ping-pong in the garden, and felt so safe that we were apt to get careless about security. My wife and younger sister were more danger-conscious: they decided that safety demanded the removal of my protruding front teeth.

These teeth, they thought, made me too conspicuous. I would have none of it. Such a change in my appearance would be like giving up part of my identity.

But my situation was not as secure as I had wanted to believe. Suddenly, on 16 August, I heard that the Germans had arrested Sylvia. That knocked me out. I was powerless. All I could do was to pray for her.

One of the German stratagems was to lock up wives and children to force men in hiding to give themselves up. We had considered this possibility beforehand and decided that I should in no circumstances emerge from my hiding place. But now we were faced with the reality. Some Quislings had come to collect her from one of the Golf Club dressing rooms which she shared with our three daughters. Orange dresses made from part of a flag were hanging up there in anticipation of the liberation, which annoyed these unwanted visitors. After waiting for half a day in the Gestapo offices in Eindhoven, she was taken with three senior Philips men to Vught. But let my wife tell her own story.

My Wife's Account

We asked ourselves where we were being taken. In Vught the road forks —one road leading to Haaren, so well-known to me; the other to the concentration camp. In the village we made a brief stop at the local Gestapo office. There the four of us, left by ourselves for a few minutes, listened with a certain recklessness to the BBC news.

It was the camp in Vught after all. An NCO took me from the camp entrance to the heavily guarded gate, about half a kilometre further on. As soon as we were on our way he asked me,

'Mrs. Philips, how is it that you're not afraid?'

I looked at him in surprise.

He explained, 'Last year I was with you when your husband was arrested.' In the few minutes left I was able to tell him why I did not fear. It was forbidden to talk with prisoners, and when we arrived at the gate, he was given a sharp reprimand by his superiors.

I was kept waiting some time, and then suddenly I heard a well-known voice from a window: Frits's close friend from Delft, Hans van Ketwich Verschuur, a prisoner in charge of administration, was trying to encourage me.

I spent the first night in a cell. Next morning I was taken to barracks containing nearly a hundred women, who sat all day at long tables, twisting rope. I was welcomed particularly warmly by those from Eindhoven. It was an odd feeling to go to bed there. The iron beds were arranged in long rows, two abreast and two on top, all tied to one another so the whole row would shake if anyone turned over. I did not get much sleep that first night.

I saw a nurse, a fellow-prisoner, going from one bed to another looking after the women. How wonderful, I thought, that she can do something for the others. Immediately a thought flashed through my mind, 'You, too, can do something for them. You can teach them to listen to Me.' That was a hopeful thought. During the day we whispered to each other while we worked (it was forbidden to talk, but who can stop a hundred women from talking to each other!) and at night, when the guards were withdrawn, we gathered in a corner near our beds. We had one New Testament, a forbidden commodity, but a great help. Having no priest or minister, it was even more important for people to experience the fact that God can speak to us in our hearts.

I told them how much change this listening had brought in my own life, change in my attitude towards my husband, towards my children, in fact towards everybody. I also told them how I had only now, while in this concentration camp, realized that the new purpose which I had found for my life could not be taken away from me. My purpose had at first been to have a happy family. Gradually, almost imperceptibly, it had expanded to become taking part in the building of a world as God intended it to be, certainly one without wars and concentration camps. Again and again, our talks reverted to that new world and to everybody's part in creating it.

After about four days I had got accustomed to the daily routine: roll-call at 5.00 a.m., when our captors liked to keep us standing outside in rows for an hour, one dry slice of crude brown bread for breakfast, twisting rope, rather inedible soup for lunch, twisting rope again, one evening slice of bread with something like margarine or jam, and finally to the dormitories.

One afternoon I was fetched to be interrogated. I realized, of course, that I was going to be asked where my husband was. I had been wrestling with that problem for some nights. Was it right to tell a lie and say that I did not know?

I was put to stand in the centre of the big square, in the hot sun, and kept there for two hours. The aim was to destroy my morale. But how inspiring those hours were! A camp like that is porous. Rumours circulate at great speed. So my presence on that square was soon universally known. First I saw my dear cousin Ben Telders moving along the edge of the square, making cautious gestures of greeting. I was the last of our family to see him: he died in Bergen-Belsen shortly before the liberation. Then after some time two other prisoners came by, two of the men with whom I had been arrested. After half an hour, the main gate was opened to admit a group of men in striped prison gear who had been made to work outside the camp. There I suddenly recognized our friend, Chel Steijns. He saw me and I saw him. 'Chel!!!' I yelled. At once I was told to leave the centre of the square, and spent the rest of my waiting with my face turned to the wall. But what a radiant peace had entered my heart! I was thinking of a hymn:

> If God, my God, is for me,
> Who is then against me?
> Then the tears and trials turn
> To blessing for my soul,
> Then the angels keep me safe.
> At night I'm cheered by stars,
> By day by flowers along my way.

All those friends I had seen: stars at night and flowers along my way! Suddenly I knew for certain that I was free to say whatever would save my husband's life.

In the room upstairs I was interrogated by a German officer. A secretary with a very low-necked dress typed out the conversation.

'Where is your husband?'

'I don't know.'

'I don't believe that.'

'I understand. If I were you, I wouldn't believe it either, but that doesn't alter the fact.'

'Don't you know that we are going to put your children in this camp if you aren't prepared to talk?'

'You can do whatever you like, but I don't know where my husband is.'

After this fruitless conversation, repeated with variations for perhaps a quarter of an hour, I was taken back to our barracks.

I remember vividly how one of the other women offered to give my back a good hard scrub. Once a week we were marched to the bath building. There we had to wait, stark naked in single file, before the gentlemen prison warders permitted us to refresh ourselves in threes or fours under one shower.

One of our jobs in the barracks was to mend the clothes worn by people who had been executed. There were bullet holes in waistcoats and jackets, sometimes a lot of bloodstains and bullet holes at abdomen level. Once there was a coat marked v.L.—van Lennep? I would never know.

On 22 August while we were being exercised, quickly marched to and fro along the same stretch, I was suddenly called out of the line. I was marched outside the camp, put into a car and taken to a Gestapo office somewhere in the neighbourhood. There to my delight I met not only the men with whom I had been arrested, but also our good friend Mr. Steensma, a notary public—and another gentleman, Mr. Bodde. I remembered the latter as an enigmatic figure who had possibly played a part in getting one of our Philips people released and our machine plant manager transferred from the prison to Vught. Now my fellow-prisoners and I heard the notary public reading a document which stated that Mr. Bodde had been appointed Director-General of Philips, and that it was he who had arranged for us to be released!

That same afternoon I was allowed to collect my belongings from the camp, though of course I left as many of them as I could for my fellow prisoners. So, soon, with incredible gratitude in my heart, I was able to embrace my children again.

After my arrest a group of Germans had come to the Golf Club three days running, each time with a different excuse. Fearing that they might arrest the children, my brother- and sister-in-law, the Van Riemsdijks, had sent the three youngest to the village of Heeze, while the three eldest were taken into the home of friends.

A week after my release, the camp at Vught was evacuated and all the prisoners were transported to Germany. Of the hundred women in my barracks only seventeen survived Ravensbrück, and none of them without a chronic infection of lungs, kidneys or other vital organs. How immeasurably grateful I was that I had been freed just before that mass transportation!

A Few Changes of Address

From my wife's account it is clear that hers was by no means 'gentleman's imprisonment'. Of course I was unaware of this. But because a fugitive, forced to stay put in one place, has ample time to imagine unpleasant things, I had a terrible time.

I had the clear thought to disappear from Zoelen, so I had to move house again. I decided to go to Tiel, where I was given a hiding place with the Van der Feltz family. As a result of the evacuation of the Isle of Walcheren, Willem van der Feltz, Counsel for the Prosecution in Middelburg, had moved to the house of an elderly cousin in Tiel. It was a big rambling house which was also used as a nurses' residence for the local hospital. Though I had been billeted under the name on my identity card, a brother-in-law of Van der Feltz's, also in the judiciary, happened to be a good friend of mine, so my true identity soon became generally known. Before long I learned, to my great relief, that the Germans had released Sylvia from Vught. In addition, the news from the battle areas was encouraging. When, on 25 August, we heard that Paris had been liberated, I was in the mood for a proper celebration, and I had discovered that the cellar below the house contained excellent wine. I suggested that the occasion justified our using some of it, but Van der Feltz, being a straightlaced Dutchman, felt we should not touch his cousin's fine wine. I told him that if, after the war, he wanted to repay his cousin he had only to tell me and I would guarantee him something good; besides, Paris would be liberated only once. So we drank an exquisite bottle. Later, in the confusion of the evacuation of Tiel, all the remaining wine was stolen.

Meanwhile, strange things were happening in and around Philips. Tromp, Laman Trip and J. C. de Vries had gone into hiding, and for over a month there had been no President. Then suddenly Mr. Bodde was installed.

He had always indulged in a great deal of self-advertisement in his contacts with the Germans. He told them that they would not be able to talk Mr. Philips around to anything, and that this was because, among other things, they had nominated the wrong *Verwalters*. If they needed a man who could do this job, they should consider him. And thus, as the position of the gentlemen of the *Rüstungskommission Niederlande* (Armaments Committee Netherlands) was getting increasingly precarious, they suddenly thought of Mr. Bodde. On 17 August they empowered him by letter to take charge of Philips.

Mr. Bodde was clever. He saw the pitfalls and opportunities of this job quite clearly. He would only accept it on condition that Mrs. Philips would not be moved to a German concentration camp, but released forthwith along with the three Philips men arrested with her. The Germans agreed. Mr. Bodde did not leave the job half-finished. He ordered the notary public to record what had happened. As my wife has already related, this document was written out formally and signed by all concerned, including our *Verwalter* Dr. Nolte.

Mr. Bodde was now sure he stood in high esteem with the Germans, and also expected appreciation from the Philips community in Eindhoven. So he tried to get me and other members of the management to surface again. He even discussed with some of our people how one might, as I had 'sent a letter from the Ardennes', advertise in a Belgian newspaper saying roughly, 'Frits, come back! All is forgiven!' After her release, he summoned my wife and warned her that Mr. Philips had got to come back. 'This is his last chance,' he insisted. 'Otherwise the big hunt for him will start. And then it will be too late. I won't be able to do anything for him then!'

My wife acted her part well. She asked him to help her to find my address in Belgium. He promised her to do his best, and then exclaimed with a blissful expression on his face, 'Who would ever have thought it? Me, head of Philips!'

On 4 September, he made his first official appearance in Eindhoven. About thirty senior staff members whom he had called together were waiting for him. Mr. Bodde entered. Nobody stirred. He said that Philips had manoeuvred itself into a difficult position. His own nomination was entirely due to the fact that Mr. Philips had cleared out, a thing he should never have done. The authorities in The Hague had put him into the vacant position and he expected the strictest obedience from all present.

His speech was greeted with ice-cold reticence. A terrifying silence followed. After that Mr. Bodde withdrew to the President's office. A short while later he departed back to The Hague, ostensibly for health reasons. In Eindhoven people whispered, 'On account of a political gastric haemorrhage.'

All this happened while I was hiding in Tiel. There I lived through the 5th of September, which later became known as Mad Tuesday because it seemed that the Allies, who had conquered most of Belgium in only five days, would keep up that same pace while advancing into Holland. I saw German columns pass through the city and heard that the Allied armies had reached Brussels. I still deeply regret that our Allies did not pay more attention to messages sent by the Dutch Underground, for at that point the Germans were in such disarray that a few hundred parachutists, dropped at the crucial Moerdijk Bridge, might have turned the liberation of Holland into a walk-over. How differently it had to happen in the end! Anyway, that Tuesday I foresaw an early liberation of Eindhoven and so wanted to get south of the big delta rivers as quickly as possible.

Then I had another proof of how God was guiding me. While getting up a thought struck me with great clarity: 'You must get out of Tiel today!' One of my acquaintances was a Mr. Daalderop, an elderly gentleman, who had at one time been a major supplier for Philips. At my request he came at once to my place of hiding. I told him I wanted to get across the Waal that very same day and asked him whether he happened to have a truck moving that way, so that I might get a lift next to the driver. His remaining truck had just been shot up and was not in working order, but luckily he thought of another solution.

Shortly afterwards he came to collect me. With my bike I boarded the ferry boat to Wamel. There was only one very young soldier on board, who did not check anything or ask anybody to show his identity card. It was the last ferry to cross the river for some time, as the Allied air force had just started firing on ships plying the river Waal.

My next job was to cross the river Maas. Confusion reigned on the Maas ferry, for a tugboat captain had not heeded Allied warnings, and his ship had been shot at. He and his wife were killed; their baby had survived. So it was doubtful whether the ferry would sail, but in the end the ferry captain decided to cross once more. So I reached the other side, with my inseparable bike! I cycled to Oss, where I stayed for some days with our local plant manager. But suddenly I had to move on, because our *Verwalters* sought refuge in Oss too.

So I sheltered with a farmer outside the town. It was potato-lifting time. As was fitting, I gave a hand. And was it tough! As I had only one pair of trousers with me, which I did not want to ruin by working in the usual way on my knees, I bent down to do it. At the end of the day my back ached like blazes. For the rest, I was treated kindly by those hospitable Brabanders. But I wanted to move still closer to Eindhoven and I was still north of the 's Hertogenbosch-Grave motorway, which carried an uninterrupted stream of military vehicles. In order to get across that road, you had to know the region very well.

Fortunately the local parson was able to find me a new hiding place, nearer Eindhoven, in the vicarage of Dinther, a hamlet just north of Veghel. The wife of a friend of mine piloted me through an area infested with German checkpoints, cycling a hundred yards ahead of me until we reached a place where I could safely cross the motorway. Following my cycle path, I arrived in Dinther without any trouble. On the way I passed soldiers belonging to the Volkel air base. I was afraid they might confiscate my bike, so I turned it upside down and pretended to be repairing a puncture. While I was doing this, I could not keep myself from waving kindly to the soldiers, wishing them a good trip. They seemed to feel the war was over as far as they were concerned, and responded quite civilly.

In Dinther, where I stayed for a week, a resistance group kept me more or less informed of the situation at the battle front. That Sunday, after church, we were having lunch when suddenly we saw a skyfull of opening parachutes. Paratroopers were jumping from dozens of low-flying Dakotas. It was almost too good to be true! Was this going to be the liberation, the end of those years of occupation? Would the Germans in this region resist, or would they run as they had on Mad Tuesday?

We were told that parachutists were heading our way. Now I could not remain indoors any longer. I ran into the village. And yes, there they were. What struck me first was that these soldiers seemed so fat. For we Dutch had gradually become quite thin. These young fellows seemed, by comparison, to have enormous heads! Furthermore, they were dressed in thick pullovers and were literally covered with sten-guns, hand-grenades and rations. They had already managed to get some horse-drawn carts from local farmers on which they transported knapsacks and arms. It was evident they were in top form.

As I was the only one who could speak with them fluently, I was soon talking to their captain. Shaking hands with this liberator, I was so moved that for some seconds I could not say a word. At last I asked him where he was heading. 'To the Veghel bridge,' he said. It was not hard to show them the way there. However, he wanted some bicycles to send a party on ahead. Nearby some farmers were looking on, holding the handle-bars of their cycles.

'Men,' I said, 'these soldiers would like some of your bikes. So please . . .'

This did not meet with a favourable response. 'Sir, my bike . . .'

Angrily I said, 'Are you crazy? These parachutists are risking their lives to liberate us. And you people dawdle because of a bike? All right, I'll sign a voucher for every bike you give and, after the liberation, you can claim a new one from the mayor.' So I signed receipts for about six cycles. The captain signed them too. Suddenly one farmer rushed off to go and get, as he said, a better bike. He returned with his wife's.

With intense respect I watched those paratroopers cycle along the road from Dinther to Veghel, knowing that hidden German machine guns might be waiting for them at every corner. I wanted to go with them, but the vicar dissuaded me, and the people held me by the tails of my rain-coat. As a civilian accompanying soldiers, I might be dealt with as a partisan if the battle went against them. So I returned to the vicarage. The airborne company reached the Veghel bridge that day without encountering any resistance.

Next morning we were woken very early by the rumble of British tanks on their way to Veghel. I was determined to go there too, but time and again my road was blocked by German patrols.

That night a fierce artillery battle broke out. Above our heads we heard the shells howl between Veghel and the forests of Schijndel, where German troops had taken up positions. That night I discovered that man does not always know what to fear and what not to fear. While the other people moved to the vicarage cellar I stayed in my bed. I had the strong feeling that those shells were not meant for me, and had a pleasant sleep.

The next afternoon, an American patrol marched into our village. When I asked where they came from, they pointed to the road to Veghel. This told me enough. Quickly I collected all my belongings, thanked my host and hostess, jumped on my bike and cycled to Veghel, where I found the headquarters of the 101st American Airborne Division, the 'Screaming Angels'. I wanted to continue immediately to Eindhoven. Some people managed to dig a motorcar out of a garage where it had been hidden, and this car left brimful with two nurses, two hide-away fugitives, one underground fighter and the garage-owner—and lots of luggage. I had one nurse on my knees. We left in the early evening for Eindhoven, but had only been under way half an hour when we heard the noise of a heavy air attack approaching. To be on the safe side we moved off the road and dispersed as much as possible in the fields. At last the raid was over. Darkness fell, but we continued our journey as far as St. Oedenrode, where we were stopped by a British military policeman.

In St. Oedenrode we found a pub but there were no beds. Someone tried to sleep on the billiard table, others on the floor under it; but everywhere was equally hard. In the end we began talking, and each person told his story. So we got through the night, and left early next morning, reaching Eindhoven before noon. It was just in time, because soon afterwards the Germans captured parts of that road.

At last! I was anxious to know hundreds of things. How were my family? What was the state of De Wielewaal and De Laak? I asked the driver to go past De Wielewaal. The house stood empty, the epitome of solitude. Most of the tiles had been blown off the roof and part of a wall had been knocked down. The garage was totally destroyed. No one was in sight. Later I learned that the woods had been bombed by the Allies, because they believed the Germans had stored ammunition there, and that my cousin Anton de Jongh, who lived in the flat above the garage, had only escaped a direct bomb by a minute.

Moving on into Eindhoven as fast as possible, I met a member of our company fire brigade who told us the Allies had liberated Eindhoven the preceding Sunday. The following Tuesday the Germans had tried in vain to retake the city, which they bombed later that night. The raid we had heard from the distance the night before had been aimed at Eindhoven! The Allies had not yet installed anti-aircraft batteries, so the German planes had been able to drop bombs at random for three-quarters of an hour. The city, still celebrating its liberation, was badly hit.

I asked our man whether he happened to know where my wife and children were. He believed they were in the city, whether at De Laak he could not tell. He had heard De Laak had been on fire.

I pressed on to De Laak, but the streets through the city centre were completely blocked by rubble. By all sorts of detours I finally reached the house, which was indeed badly damaged. But the car had not stopped before the children's nanny rushed out exclaiming, 'Nobody's hurt!' I stumbled into the house and was reunited with my family. Seldom have we felt so grateful to God. I cannot describe what it meant to see one another again after all those difficult weeks.

I was distressed to find that my wife and children had in those last days experienced their worst fears of the entire war. The day before the liberation of Eindhoven they had moved on bikes from the Golf Club to the town because there was heavy fighting in Valkenswaard. On their way they had repeatedly been forced by gunfire to dive into the ditches lining the road. In Eindhoven, however, the situation appeared quiet. So they went to De Laak. On Monday, 18 September, Sylvia and Ton saw the Allied tank columns move through Eindhoven's narrow shopping streets. They were struck by the contrast between the happiness of the cheering population and the tense faces of the soldiers on those tanks.

Next evening my wife went to visit a cousin, taking the three eldest children. She wanted to listen there to the radio report of Eindhoven's liberation. But suddenly the hell of the bombing raid broke out. At least twenty people sought shelter in the Leopold home, under the stairs of the small cellar. They could hear bombs falling nearby, making the house shake. At that moment even my wife was very frightened. Meanwhile at De Laak our three youngest were sheltering in the cellar with their nanny. Six bombs fell in the garden, one so near the house that all the windows were blown out, walls were damaged, and heavy pieces of furniture were thrown about. Pieces of plaster fell from the cellar ceiling, but luckily not in the part where they were sheltering.

It was impossible to go on living in De Laak, so we all mounted our bikes and rode to the Van Riemsdijks' home at the Golf Club. This house had been occupied by Germans, and now some families whose homes had been destroyed had moved in. The food for those eighty-one homeless people was cooked in an abandoned German kitchen car. We moved into the garage which we made into separate rooms by make-shift partitions. Some days later, we moved 'temporarily' into the annex to Otten's house, which had also been occupied by the Germans. There we lived until the end of 1946.

The days for which we had longed for more than four years had come. There were no more German uniforms. No threat to personal liberty. No lies in the newspapers or on the radio. No restrictions anywhere. There was freedom of expression again. We could hardly believe it. We watched the interminable columns of our Allies' armies pass through Eindhoven. What meant most to us was the fact that we ourselves were liberated.

Sadly, our joy was mixed with grief. Our city was in deep mourning. The Tuesday night raid had killed many, and death notices of friends and acquaintances soon reached us. A large number of children had been killed. So there was not just joy and cheering. We realized only too well that the war was not yet over.

Chapter 14

Liberation

The first thing I did after my return was to get clean, an aspect of life I had neglected during the last weeks. After that I went on Sylvia's bicycle to a school classroom where our management and staff were conferring. My arrival was greeted with cheers, but the discussion about what was to be done in the new situation was immediately resumed.

For the time being we were in the middle of a battle area, with Allied soldiers having taken the place of the Germans. My first task was to establish contact with the new authorities. So we decided that I should pay my respects to the British Town Major and the representative of the Dutch Military Authority, created by the Dutch Government in London to handle the country's administration in the transitional period.

Our other decision was to protect our factory buildings, to prevent things being spirited away amid the confusion. For the time being there was not much more we could do, except to start clearing rubble again resulting from the last bombing raid. Electric power was not available; raw materials had been taken away, as well as many machines; other equipment had been made inoperational. But our people were still there, and that was the most important thing.

To my great astonishment Otten turned up from nowhere shortly after the liberation. He had got himself attached to the Allied Committee under Sir Robert Watson-Watt which I have already mentioned. It was a moving reunion. Both of us had looked forward for years to the day when we would be able to shake hands again in a newly-liberated Eindhoven. Otten's return was of great value for Philips' reconstruction, even though he was a stranger to the sort of life which had developed in Eindhoven during the war. I was also delighted to greet Prince Bernhard, who, as Commander-in-Chief of the Dutch armed forces, came to inspect Holland's first liberated city. In the years of exile the Prince and Otten had become friends.

By chance I ended up sitting in a jeep of the Princess Irene Brigade when it moved into Eindhoven, so I was able to see from close quarters the enthusiasm with which the Dutch population welcomed their own troops back on national soil.

The following days were filled with rush and tension and an atmosphere of almost constant elation. People enjoyed their freedom intensely, though it was freedom with inevitable restrictions. In Philips we had the difficulty of getting people to accept order and regular schedules again. But in the beginning this was not too urgent, for there was hardly anything we could make. Everyone was filled with a sense of all-encompassing gratitude that Eindhoven was freed from the terrors of German occupation.

But it was not long before the first disillusionment and unexpected troubles made themselves felt. At Philips we wanted to get our factories moving again as soon as possible. But our Allies were completely absorbed in winning a war against a tough, desperately courageous enemy. I had at the time no clue of the extent of the difficulties which the Allies were having to overcome to keep their armies supplied with arms and food.

Soon after our liberation the airborne landings at Arnhem took place, which meant a colossal strain on the narrow Allied supply lines. The Germans had managed to hold on to the Isle of Walcheren, from where they prevented ships from entering the Port of Antwerp, so all supplies had to be moved through France. All transport to the battle theatre in Brabant had to move by the roads that led through Eindhoven. Endless supply columns moved through our streets. But, alas, they could not supply the onlookers as well. The food situation in Eindhoven steadily worsened and the calory value of the daily rations came down to 600 grams, less than during the occupation.

In October I drove to Paris to discuss this with officers in charge of logistics at SHAEF (Supreme Headquarters Allied Expeditionary Force). With some difficulty I penetrated to the British general in charge. I had already discovered that one does not get far with the British with long lists of complaints. When he asked me, after some introductory small talk, how the food supply was in Eindhoven, I merely answered, 'Not too good, really.' There was silence for a moment. Then he said: 'Is it as bad as that?'

I had got his wave-length. At once he promised his assistance. A column of trucks was just moving from Normandy to Eindhoven, driven by Dutch women volunteers. He would put this column at the disposal of the Dutch authorities to get food to the people. With this promise I returned to Eindhoven, where the news was received with delight.

The achievements of the women's volunteer corps during those days cannot be appreciated too much. Day and night these girls distributed supplies to the places of need. So our food situation improved. And none too soon, as people were beginning to rebel. It was hard for them to realize that the war was far from over: Breda was to be liberated by the Poles; Tilburg by the Canadians; a tank battle at Overloon was to free Brabant from further German threats. Even then the war was still on.

In spite of this, people walked out of our factories on 21 November to demonstrate their dissatisfaction. Our own Free Holland radio station broadcast news of this demonstration. It was dignified and peaceful, but we heard that it had created a bad impression in other parts of Holland still under German occupation.

Information also percolated through that the Germans had taken away everything in our Hilversum plant. Machines had been removed, lighting fittings stolen, even the electric wires and cables had been taken away. As a matter of fact, the occupation authorities had done much the same in Eindhoven on Mad Tuesday. Under *Verwalter* Nolte's supervision, wagonloads of our stores had been loaded on to trains for Germany. Philips people made a desperate effort to stop these trains. It cost one man his life: he was shot for sabotage. And from the machines they could not transport, the Germans removed essential components. So much of our effort to build up stores for post-liberation production had been nullified.

The activities of Radio Free Holland led to unforeseen results for us. The broadcasts required a large staff—technicians, announcers, programme-makers—and such people could be found in Philips. And it was not only the radio station which siphoned people away. The Allies also needed many civilian employees, especially people who spoke more than one language. Soon Eindhoven had been made the capital of the liberated parts of Holland, which meant a multitude of new offices. Employment by the Allies was especially attractive because it included access to all sorts of perks like cigarettes, coffee, needles, nylon stockings and other commodities which had become totally unavailable. Otten calculated that no less than forty-six different organizations were competing to attract Philips personnel. So we were faced with a veritable exodus. As many Philips people had not had a man-sized job for years, it was a relief for them to get going again. The majority of them, however, came back to us later.

Many public utilities were not functioning yet. At first there was no telephone. The mail did not function either, so letters had to go by messenger. Trains were out of the question; gas and fuel non-existent. The house fuel supply was sparse, so wood was much in demand. During the winter of 1944-45, a third of the trees in the De Wielewaal woods were cut down. This was inevitable, but soon this large-scale wood-cutting assumed an objectionable aspect, when black marketeers began to cut down our trees and sell them in the city at steep prices. So we took measures to stop this practice. Henceforth each person could cut down one tree after showing his ration card, which was then marked. The trees were cut at knee-height, so that we were left with woods full of stumps. Later a team of workers who had no other employment used a tripod and chain to pull them out. In the woods around our home no less than 1,200 bombs had been dropped, so the team filled in the craters too.

When the Germans had requisitioned our house, they had been convinced that they would live there until the end of time. So they had looked after De Wielewaal relatively well. But at the end of the occupation, as I have already told, the house was seriously damaged. Nevertheless the Allies installed the air base construction department there. These soldiers had been camping in tents since the Normandy landings, and for them even a manufacturer's damaged residence was a luxury. But whereas the Germans had been thinking in terms of a stay without end, the Allies were still camping. They cooked on petrol stoves, which produced a layer of soot more than half an inch thick on the kitchen walls and ceilings. We did not complain, because everything would have to be renovated after the soldiers left anyway, although we did not want to start on this as long as the people of Eindhoven had a serious housing shortage. We had a good home meanwhile in Otten's annex.

Otten's house itself was a solid building, painted conspicuously white and easy to identify from the air. The Royal Air Force Command had moved in there under Air Vice-Marshal Harry Broadhurst. We felt a bit uneasy living under the same roof as the Air Force headquarters, but Broadhurst insisted that fear was unnecessary. According to him there was a tacit agreement between the *Luftwaffe* and the Royal Air Force never to bomb each other's headquarters. But scarcely had General Montgomery, with his staff, moved into the village of Geldrop when Broadhurst prophesied, 'You'll see. They are bound to strike!' And sure enough, though there was never a raid on Otten's house, Monty in Geldrop did get a bomb or two intended for his headquarters.

At Christmas, the British occupants of our home wanted to show us some kindness in return. So we were invited to De Wielewaal with our children. It was an odd feeling to be guests in our own home. In our beautiful hall the British had built a colossal bar of rough planks, of which they were vastly proud. It was not all that pleasing to our eyes, but our children were not bothered by it. In our sitting room we were served such an enormous tea that the children literally ate themselves sick.

The British were sorry that the woods had been damaged, and noticed that I was keen to start planting new trees as soon as possible. The Germans had carried away all the trees they could lay their hands on to border their local airfields, and to serve as camouflage. These trees were largely conifers. In the spring of 1945 we were provided with a truck for one week to transplant as many of the conifers as we wanted. This was a charming gesture. A great many young trees were hauled to De Wiele-waal, and this was some compensation for the damage. I was very glad to be able to start restoring the forest after years of destruction and neglect.

Very slowly the factories started moving again. We had got a small generator of some thousands of kilowatts going, and with this power we started to adapt our production to new needs. Very limited power was available for domestic purposes; so we began making bulbs which consumed little electricity. The fact that they also yielded little light was of minor importance. Simply to keep work going, our people also started making small stoves, and even toy jeeps.

We needed gas for the manufacturing process. The Eindhoven gas supply came from the state mines, but the pipes from there went through territory still controlled by the Germans, so Philips engineers and city technicians succeeded in getting the old municipal gas plant going again.

A private initiative was launched by some Philips people, who formed teams to repair houses damaged by the recent bombing attack. In fact, our people acted as pioneers wherever action was taken to get the city functioning again. For they knew what teamwork meant, and above all they knew each other.

Manufacturers' Circle

One of the curious features of the pre-war years had been that manufacturers hardly knew each other. Philips, as the biggest enterprise in the city, was regarded by other manufacturers as in a special category, and they did not always like us. As far as I was concerned, I regarded all the other manufacturers as colleagues. They, too, had to run risks, to look ahead and to have the right relationship with their workers.

In the chaotic situation after the liberation, the Eindhoven manufacturers were confronted with all sorts of problems which could best be solved together. Immediately after my return I was able to do something about this. Cycling through Eindhoven, I met a textile manufacturer, Willy Bakers, in conversation with Jan van Sandick, Secretary of our local chapter of the National Society for Industry and Commerce. We greeted each other warmly, and soon concluded that we ought to get the manufacturers of Eindhoven together. Next day twenty manufacturers jointly founded the Eindhoven Manufacturers' Circle. They wanted me as chairman, though I resisted, in view of the dominance of Philips. I am chairman still, and this association has always remained close to my heart.

The Manufacturers' Circle filled a great vacuum. We met every Saturday morning in the Chamber of Commerce and discussed many important matters such as contact with the military authorities, the fuel position, the lack of window glass and above all the very poor food conditions. It soon became clear that this local co-operation was yielding excellent results.

Our example was copied, as the liberation proceeded, in most of the principal towns of Brabant, and the co-ordinating body of Manufacturers' Circles in Liberated Holland came into being, of which I was elected chairman. After the liberation of the whole of Holland, in May 1945, Circles were also started in the north. I had the illusion that we had initiated a new form of organization from which a great deal might be expected, but it was not to be so.

At one point Church opposition threatened, but this was overcome. In Eindhoven, Roman Catholic employers were co-operating with Liberal colleagues, and this at first seemed objectionable to the Bishop of 's Hertogenbosch. I had a talk with the Bishop and realized that he was in a dilemma:

'Mr. Philips, you make it difficult for me to forbid Catholic employers to become members of your Circle. I can't use the usual arguments, because I know you are a believing Christian.'

'But, Monsignor, that ought to be a reason for you to give up your objections to our Circle!'

A short while later the Bishop gave the green light for Catholic membership, which reassured even the most scrupulous Catholic manufacturers. Of course, the situation today is totally different, as Catholics and Protestants co-operate fully in all such organizations.

Real opposition to our body came, however, from the old established organizations. I had a talk with L. G. Kortenhorst, Secretary of the Roman Catholic Employers' Association, who was dead against our

Circles. He saw them as a kind of competition. The Netherlands Employers' Federation also told us that our southern initiatives were mere amateurism. Even so we, the amateurs, had achieved more than the old-established organizations had ever been able to do. From talks with the pre-war leaders I concluded that all they wanted was to go back to the good old days. As I had more important things to do than trying to push through an organization for which, under the circumstances, I could see no future on the national level, we dissolved the national co-ordinating body of the Circle at a meeting in Utrecht in October 1945.

The Eindhoven Circle is, however, still active and useful. At the monthly lunches problems of the day are discussed and, if needed, working sessions are arranged. One useful result of this organization is that people tend to consult and help each other much more quickly than they used to.

But I have digressed from the autumn of 1944. We had to keep on paying our employees. It was impossible to do this from sales of our products, but our London Government, through the intermediary of the Military Authority, helped out. Through its office in Eindhoven we were provided with the money to continue paying wages and salaries. We were, of course, running up debts of millions.

As there were also other matters to discuss, I went several times to Brussels, where I used to stay in Prince Bernhard's headquarters. There a typical headquarters atmosphere prevailed. I had a great respect for the way the Prince had provided leadership for the resistance movement. He was enormously popular.

You met a mixed bag of people at headquarters. I remember a big fellow who told the most exciting stories of his adventures north of the big rivers. He was always on his way to or from German-occupied territory. He boasted of his heroic acts and encouraged others to follow in his footsteps, but after a time it was noted that those who did follow always fell into German hands. In the end it turned out that he had been a double agent, and he was arrested. Later this man, who had always been referred to as 'King Kong', met with an inglorious end suitable to his deeds.

Winter Journey to Switzerland

In the second half of December 1944 I made a trip to Switzerland accompanied by two of our engineers. The Germans had carried off or rendered useless a great proportion of our machine tools. When I had been in Switzerland in the spring of 1943, I had ordered lathes and machine tools, with the secret proviso that they would be delivered only after the war. Now we needed to obtain them and many more quickly. And demand for these would be greater as soon as the whole of Europe was liberated. If I wanted to get fast delivery times, I had to get to Switzerland ahead of other customers.

To begin with we needed a car. Fortunately our purchase department manager had kept his excellent Hudson hidden under a haystack for the duration of the occupation. So that car was available. We ourselves and the car were documented with all the rubber stamps we could get hold of. The Military Authority supplied a declaration in three languages that our trip to Switzerland was in the interests of the war effort. On the windscreen and the back window of our car were stickers reading 'Special Netherlands Mission'.

So we went to Louvain, with my loyal driver Ad den Hartog. Luckily, our manager there had good relations with the British, who provided us with jerry-cans full of precious petrol. Our representative in Brussels had excellent contacts with the French underground, which led to a series of vital stamps in our papers. From Brussels we went to Paris, where an exit visa for Switzerland had to be obtained. We were told this might take weeks, but we did not have that much time. So we set out to try our luck in Lyon, where our manager knew his way around the local French authorities.

Half-way to Dijon I had the greatest difficulty in getting petrol, which had to come from the Americans. I finally found the American I needed, but according to him we did not have the correct papers, so he could do nothing. I drew his attention to the universally known French practice of drilling holes in the pipe-line from Marseilles to Lyon to siphon off petrol for private use. If that was tolerated, he could easily supply a few tins of petrol to an honest, loyal Dutchman on his way to Switzerland to buy essential equipment. My reasoning helped, and so we reached Lyon.

Still we had no visas, and the French refused to grant them. We were told we had to go back to Paris. I managed to penetrate to the captain in charge of the border guard. But he, too, said, 'Mr. Philips, I really can't do anything for you!'

I looked at him and observed,

'If I were to go to Paris, I bet my last guilder you would be consulted by the people there about our case.'

He admitted that the chances were high. So I suggested,

'Give your verdict to me here and now, then I'll take it to Paris, and that will save us a lot of time.'

Now it was his turn to look at me. He saw through my scheme, but he still gave me the document. With that I went straight to the border at Annemasse. As the border post there was directly under the command of the self-same captain, we were allowed to pass.

Arriving in Geneva in the evening was a strange sensation. For the first time for ages we saw a fully-lighted city. Not only the streets, but the shops, too, were full of lights. We got out and walked through the city centre. There we saw a shop window full of shoes, and next door another shop with two more windows full of shoes. And a bit further on, another one. After the years of scarcity this abundance was almost unreal.

In the Philips office in Geneva, Dr. Brümmer was still in charge. I could now greet him openly and in freedom. We set out at once to look for machines. I also bought some cars, including a Buick which had done only 10,000 km. In this we could transport the measuring stand which we had bought from our old supplier, the Société Génévoise des Instruments Physiques. But all this required export licences.

The Swiss had agreed with the Allies that they would export this kind of instrument only with their permission. But luck seemed to be with us. The British Consul in Geneva was married to a Dutch woman and he wanted to help. But he could not, because Holland was still listed as a German-occupied country. I insisted he take the matter up with London, and went myself to the British Ambassador in Berne, who promised to take steps on our behalf.

We were forced to wait for the outcome of these diplomatic activities. So now I had the chance to go to Arosa for a few days of winter sports to make up for those I lost in March 1943. It turned out, however, that my knee was still not fully cured from an injury incurred two months earlier in a hockey match against a Royal Air Force team in Eindhoven. So instead of skiing I enjoyed some days of rest in the winter sunshine.

Back in Geneva I waited with my companion for a reply from Britain. Nobody gave us any hope of an answer before Christmas. Unexpectedly the Consul phoned: 'The miracle has happened. The answer has come through, and the deal is approved.' It was just before Christmas.

We started home in high spirits, having ordered machines worth more than a million francs. My most valued acquisition was a 3000kw generating set which would double our power capacity. It had been standing for years, already packed and waiting to be sent to Thailand, but its export had been stopped because of the war. The management of the provincial power

Signing a collective agreement between the Dutch unions and the
management of our Dutch factories (1948).

Reception of King Bhumibol and Queen Sirikit of Thailand in Eindhoven by Frans Otten and myself (1960).

Loupart and I with Henry Ford II at Eindhoven when he saw the
Stirling engine for the first time (1948).

President Habib Bourguiba visiting Eindhoven, with our Foreign Minister, Joseph Luns (1966).

Queen Juliana looks through a microscope at a diamond die, made by us for use in the manufacture of very fine tungsten wire for light bulbs.

Talking with a girl in one of our Singapore factories.

During the 25th anniversary of the Indian Philips organization we all made a festive boat trip.

Visiting the Middle East accompanied by Guépin, Ackerstaff and Van Lanschot.

So many countries, so many customs. Nigeria.

Talking to Ethiopian students during a Moral Re-Armament conference in Caux.

plant had also asked me to visit Brown Boveri to get an estimate for a turbine and dynamo combination and the papers were in my suitcase. We had had the luck to be the first foreign buyers, so we were given a delivery time of only six months. In addition we had acquired six new Lancias, speedy and economical cars which have been very useful to Philips.

Our return trip went smoothly. The driver drove the Buick, while I took on the Hudson. It was winter, and snowing continuously. Far away the guns of the Allied armies advancing into Germany could be heard. Getting petrol continued to be difficult, but this time our friends in Lyon supplied the necessary jerry-cans, and in Paris we got enough to reach Louvain. It was still snowing in Belgium. Along the road we saw heavy artillery in readiness to repulse the enemy if the Battle of the Bulge, now at its height, should lead to a German break-through.

The year was approaching its end when we entered Louvain, and on New Year's Eve we reached Valkenswaard. During our return trip we had rarely been stopped for checks, but on our way to the Eindhoven Golf Club a British patrol did halt us. 'Advance to be recognized!' One by one our faces were lit by torchlight. Special precautions were being taken because an attack by German parachutists on Air Vice-Marshal Broadhurst's staff was considered likely.

A minute later we were home. My arrival was totally unexpected, and the joy of seeing each other again was the greater. That New Year's Eve was special, as it concluded a very eventful year. In that year we had lived through the invasion. My wife had been imprisoned. I had been forced to hide from the enemy. The liberation had come. And in Switzerland I had had a foretaste of a time of less want and scarcity. We had cause for great gratitude.

Yet the new year soon seemed to warn us against too great expectations. Next morning a low-flying German plane came straight towards our home, giving us a considerable fright. It was, it transpired later, a reconnaisance flight, but elsewhere swarms of low-flying German fighter planes had attacked British air bases in liberated territory. Evidently the German Supreme Command believed that the British would not respond immediately because of New Year's Eve hang-overs. And my impression was that the attack on our local airfield had caused a lot of damage. Though some British fighters went up, they were outnumbered. It seemed to me that the year had started badly.

That afternoon Harry Broadhurst gave a New Year's cocktail party. I felt depressed because of the morning's events, but noticed that the British were in the best of spirits. After talking with Broadhurst I understood why. That same morning the British had sent a great many fighter planes to escort bomber squadrons to Germany. These fighters had been called back by radio, and intercepted the German squadrons. The German attack had been carried out by young, inexperienced pilots who had used up all their ammunition, so on their return flight the veteran British pilots brought them down like flights of ducks. The German attack had taken the British completely by surprise, but the British response had been so effective that thereafter there were no more large-scale raids on Allied airfields in Holland or Belgium.

In Eindhoven we expected that the new year would bring the liberation of the whole of Holland. But our situation actually remained more difficult than anybody had anticipated. In many buildings the heating no longer worked. Everything was scarce. I felt it was my job to do something for our people's morale, so I talked to them in various factories, standing on a chest or table, trying to give them courage. I compared our condition to the time of the year. The nights were long and dark, the days brief, but almost imperceptibly lengthening. Our situation would now improve steadily. In a few months we would be able to tell the difference. 'At this point we are all going through hard times,' I continued. 'One of our daughters has kidney poisoning. In the middle of the night we had to take her to hospital. Shortly afterwards a British plane lost a bomb, which fell near the hospital, and her room was full of glass splinters. Luckily she wasn't hurt.'

Trip to Britain

Soon afterwards, about the middle of January, I went to London at the request of Queen Wilhelmina, who wanted to meet people from the liberated regions in Brabant, Limburg and Zeeland. I went with a fairly large group including other Eindhoven citizens such as the future Premier, Louis Beel, and a couple of other ministers to be.

We crossed by ferry boat from Ostend escorted by naval units, for German submarines were still about. It was a dark winter night. It was hard to get to sleep in those uncomfortable army berths; so we kept talking in small groups on the deck. It was cold, and my thoughts went to the many people who had lost their lives at sea during the war, to the pilots of damaged planes who had not made the other side, to the people from occupied territory who had attempted to get to Britain but did not reach freedom . . . And now we ourselves, who had dreamed of being able to cross the sea to liberty, were on our way to Britain at the request of our courageous Queen.

On the first night in London we met her over a very simple meal. A speech seemed to be expected, but no one got up. So at last I took the floor, saying it would probably be against all protocol to propose a toast with a glass of beer, but that I wanted to express how deeply moving it was for us all, after years of oppression, to sit down to dinner with Queen Wilhelmina. Many had tears in their eyes, and Her Majesty, too, was moved.

Up till then she had got her facts about conditions in the liberated regions only from the Military Authority or from people who had managed to escape. Now she wanted to hear directly from people who lived in the liberated territory. We met with her for several days and it became clear from our various statements that everyone wanted civilian authorities to take charge as soon as possible. But for the rest, ideas often conflicted. Different people had different thoughts about new structures, about alterations to the Parliament, about constitutional reforms. All these ideas, whether properly worked out or not, were debated. It was a heterogeneous group. Among them there were people who had actively taken part in armed resistance, but they were not predominant. Manufacturers were few. There was a great fear among Dutch residents in London of a Communist coup in Holland after the liberation. They believed that the Communists possessed enough arms to take power immediately. Our group could not understand this.

A half-brother of Sylvia's, Ben Vlielander Hein, was an RAF pilot. He invited me for a weekend to an air base in eastern England, where I saw a squadron leaving at 5 p.m. for a bombing mission to Berlin. On that darkened airfield I lived intensely into the anxieties of those missions. When they returned after four or five hours the planes were anxiously counted. Some planes returned with defective engines or damaged tails, and some never returned. My brother-in-law survived more than a hundred and fifty missions over enemy territory.

In London I stayed on the top floor of my hotel. Those were the days of the German V-weapons, and every now and then I heard a heavy bang in the distance. It was some consolation that you could not hear such a missile coming if it was going to hit you. British fighter pilots managed to bring down many of the V-1s, but this was not possible with the much faster V-2s, which dived down from a high altitude. Our head office in Shaftesbury Avenue, Century House, was never hit, although buildings all around were wrecked. In the end our employees said they wanted to move into Century House, because it seemed clear no harm would come to Philips!

In London I was invited to meet a committee of British civil servants preparing aid to liberated Holland, and was asked to tell them what would be most urgently required. I said transport—railway stock and trucks—was, apart from food, the first necessity. I had a hard time helping them to realize how totally depleted Holland had become, and that simple things like safety pins, handkerchiefs, socks and, of course, food were just not available. We impressed on our compatriots, too, that a great part of Holland had been starving and that therefore food supplies would have to have priority.

My stay in London lasted for two more weeks after the talks with Queen Wilhelmina, after which I was able to return to Holland by plane. There conditions were gradually improving. The next thing to expect was the complete liberation of our country.

Chapter 15

Recovery

On Sunday, 5 May 1945, we had two guests staying with us. Eindhoven had no hotel accommodation at the time, and so our guest room was permanently occupied. Among the continuous stream of guests, for instance, was Albert Plesman, the founder of KLM, who after his period of exile in the east of the country, imposed on him by the Germans, was on his way to London. He was so brimful of plans to rebuild KLM that Otten, who was sharing our guest room with him, had to catch up on sleep after his departure.

That Sunday the long-awaited news of Germany's capitulation came at last. Sylvia and I, with our two guests, were in the sitting room when the great news came over the radio. A wave of gratitude engulfed our hearts. We called the whole family in, and we all knelt down and thanked God.

The army communiques the day before had been so promising that all Eindhoven manufacturers had agreed to give people the Saturday off. The following Monday no work was done either, because nobody felt like it. Celebrations were going on everywhere, while Queen Wilhelmina addressed her nation from our Radio Free Holland studio.

We in Philips realized that much hard work was now required. Many of our machines had been carried off, a number of our factories had been destroyed, our raw material reserves were depleted, and we had no money. Also, many of our most active people had gone north with the relief columns for which they had worked so hard. In the final weeks of the war the Germans had given permission for food parcels to be dropped for the starving population there, but that had been a flea-bite. So members of our sales staff, in the uniform of the Military Authority, had acted as food commissioners in the newly liberated cities.

After the total liberation of our country we all went through extra-ordinary experiences. How a person had behaved during the war became an important issue, and there was a universal desire that collaborators should be punished immediately. The issue was not much of a problem within Philips, as we had screened our own people ourselves. All those accused of collaboration had been investigated and this had sometimes meant dismissal. But very few of our people had been guilty of it.

There were, however, other difficulties connected with people's conduct under war conditions, particularly when these people were in positions of leadership. A man might, for instance, have been an excellent head of department or personnel manager, yet fearful during air raid warnings. Or in other cases, managers had continued to insist on strict discipline and punctuality at work as if there had been no war on, while people working under them had shown more understanding of the changed circumstances. It boiled down to the fact that subordinates had at times shown more character and courage than their bosses. During the occupation they had been forced to tolerate their bosses' attitudes, but after the liberation they did not want to obey the orders of superiors whom they despised. After some time these conflicts resolved themselves, often because such a manager's ability to lead under normal circumstances became evident again. But in the meantime it was a problem.

Another difficulty came from the need to regain the old quality of working after many years of going slow. This was not always popular, and, in fact, we did have some brief stoppages for trivial reasons. However, we learned something from them. In our metal factory the working hours had been changed without anybody troubling to explain the reasons to the workers. The result was that we received a phone call at 10 a.m. to say that the metal plant had gone on strike. So I went there, and soon found myself face to face with people who had all sorts of grievances.

Of course I was willing to discuss them, but first work had to be resumed. Though this was far from easy, I remained firm. I went to a man operating a very big press and said, 'Man, get this machine going, and the rest will follow.' Some minutes later the banging of that press resounded through the factory, and sure enough, the whole factory was soon working again. Then I started talking with the employees' representatives. A lot of old grievances, some more justified than others, were put on the table. It took a long time to sort it all out. At last I looked at my watch and said,

'Now I should like to go home to lunch. I've promised my wife I will go home today, because I happen to have a birthday.'

'If only we had known, Sir, we wouldn't have done this today!'

That was typical of the prevailing atmosphere. So we came to an agreement that same afternoon. The conflict had been entirely due to lack of communication.

Some time later there were difficulties in the glass factory. Our glass blowers felt they were made to work harder than workers in other Philips plants. Equally, they believed that the rates for the different types of bulbs differed too much. This gave occasion for dishonesties: a foreman could give softer jobs to friends and harder jobs to others.

Two different issues were at stake in this conflict. We had the first complaint investigated by experts who were not involved in Philips, for we wanted to have a completely outside opinion. And the conclusion was that the glass blowers were not being paid enough. This was, of course, put right. The rates were examined by a committee composed not only of time-study experts, but also of some of our veteran glass blowers, men working daily at that particular job who could guarantee their colleagues that the matter would be properly dealt with. We naturally try to keep the right balance in pay differentials, and on this occasion we were able to eliminate discrimination which had developed without our realizing it.

Encounter in Sweden

While politicians were trying to form our first Government, Otten and I were restoring our co-operation with our organizations abroad and trying to get the money for rebuilding Philips. We had arrived at the conclusion that a Government loan of 90 million guilders, including the 30 million already advanced, would get us going properly again. For this the necessary steps were taken. Then Otten and I went together to London, and he went on to America and I to Sweden. In London I had met the manager of our Swedish establishment, so I was informed about the particular problems which had arisen in Stockholm—problems typical of that period.

The sales manager of our establishment there was a Swede, Herbert Kastengren. Our technical manager was a Dutchman, Rinse Hylkema. Kastengren had good contacts with leading politicians and with the Chief of the General Staff, and met regularly with them to discuss the situation. But he had a German secretary, which was purely accidental, and was from time to time visited by our Eindhoven *Verwalters*, more particularly by Dr. Gase whom the Germans had entrusted with financial affairs and who was the one who had made my life difficult during my trip to Switzerland in 1943. In Sweden, too, Gase tried to push through certain changes, which Kastengren resisted as much as possible. Even so, the Germans were received graciously, and this created resentment among the Dutch in our Swedish organization, and notably in Hylkema. He had sworn to himself that as soon as Hitler was crushed the Swedes, and first of all Kastengren, would be made to pay for their attitude. So Kastengren and Hylkema were at daggers drawn. In London, too, Otten had given Kastengren a piece of his mind, as a result of which he wanted to leave Philips. That was the situation when I arrived in Stockholm.

I soon discovered how difficult Sweden's position had been. Above all she wanted to stay neutral, as she was, like Switzerland, entirely surrounded by German-controlled territory, and she could not count on Allied support. Our Philips people, meanwhile, were primarily concerned with keeping the new factory and the sales organization going. But at one point money was needed which could not be obtained from Holland or the United States. So Kastengren appealed to his old tennis friend, the Swedish banker Marcus Wallenberg. He said to him one day, 'I need some money at once for our company.'

'How much?'

'About fifteen million crowns.' In those days that was a sizeable amount.

'What security do you have to offer?'

'None whatever. Only myself!'

Wallenberg knew Herbert Kastengren as an able and honest businessman. He gave the Swedish Philips organization 15 million crowns without any security and the work was able to continue.

As I had lived through the German occupation, I was able to understand both sides. I could understand the wrath of the Dutch, but I also realized that the Swedes, living in an enclave, had been forced to accommodate to the Germans. It took a great deal of effort, but in the end I succeeded in getting these two able managers reconciled. So Kastengren, who had personally vouched for our Swedish organization, was kept in the company, and we resolved a tricky situation in a country where people tended to judge things from an entirely different angle from ours in Holland.

In Gothenburg I had an encounter of another kind. In a Red Cross camp there I visited a group of Jewish women who had been deported to Germany in June 1944 from the camp in Vught. The first attempt by the Germans to carry them away had failed as a result of fierce opposition from our Philips people. Every possible effort was made, the top authorities in Berlin were approached, and at the eleventh hour the women had been rescued from a train ready for departure. But a second attempt by the Germans had succeeded, as it was a surprise move made during the night.

What those women had gone through is hard to put into words. First they landed in the notorious extermination camp of Auschwitz, at the same time as a train load of elderly Hungarians and children who were stripped of all their possessions and immediately gassed. The *Philips-Gruppe aus Herzogenbusch* (Philips Group from 's Hertogenbosch), however, ended up, after some dreadful experiences, in a Telefunken plant at Reichenbach. Working hours were from 6 a.m. to 6 p.m., but the food was relatively good.

After this factory had been bombed, the group were dragged all over Germany and Czechoslovakia. Then they were put to work in an underground factory in Minden in Westphalia. There the women had to work with tools taken from the Philips workshop in Vught, and they found the names of Dutch girls scratched in the small welding benches they were operating. At the beginning of April they were made to work in another underground factory, after being beaten into and out of countless trains. Finally they were transported to Hamburg. After the armistice, the Swedish Red Cross at last rescued these women, maltreated and plagued by starvation, thirst and lice. They were given proper nourishment, beds and clothes and were taken by ship to Gothenburg. When I visited them, their repatriation was being planned.

I knew some of those Philips employees from Vught. It was moving to see them again. My thoughts went back to 1943 when we had had to decide whether to set up the Philips workshop or not. These people were a living proof of the fact that we had taken the right decision.

After this I went for a week to Oslo. It was easier to have a meeting of hearts with the Norwegians, because both our countries had been in the same boat.

Slap in the Face

The day after my return home I arrived in my office in a very happy mood. On my desk was a cable. My eyes fell first on the signature: Lieftinck, the new Finance Minister. I read the message—that because of the Government loan, Philips was to be supervised by a Government Commissioner —and I felt as if I had been slapped in the face. The idea was an insult. During the occupation we had done all we could to frustrate the Germans. We had managed to keep our company relatively intact, but, unlike many other firms, our coffers were empty and our factories plundered. It was obvious why we needed Government help to get started again. Why then this Government Commissioner? We were rid of the *Verwalters*—would this man now take their place?

I was unwilling to accept this kind of treatment. Immediately I drove to The Hague, a difficult journey, as the main bridges were destroyed. I talked to a number of cabinet ministers, and soon began to understand what was behind the cable. It had been sent at a moment when my colleagues Otten, Loupart and Van Walsem were in America, and I was in Sweden, and was motivated by a fear that Philips was considering moving its headquarters permanently outside Holland. This was, of course, the last thing we wanted to do. I also had a talk with Lieftinck, and finally with the Prime Minister, after which they promised to reconsider the question.

L. J. Trip, who had been reinstated as Governor of the National Bank, was working out the conditions which this commissioner should impose upon us. I went to Amsterdam to explain to Trip why I regarded the imposition of such conditions as ridiculous. I felt that he, who had experienced German nosiness himself as Governor of the Bank, should have known better and could tell the Minister that this was the wrong way to go about it.

From Trip I went to Tas Greidanus, who already had been appointed Government Commissioner in Philips. Greidanus was one of the pleasantest people you can imagine, the archetype of a liberal banker and certainly no protagonist of Government interventionism. I said to him, 'You must realize that if you accept this job, we'll give you precisely the same treatment as we gave the *Verwalters*. I think it is fair that you should know this in advance.' This shook him visibly.

The storm blew over. Some weeks later I received a letter from Minister Lieftinck in which he stated he had 'the pleasure to request me to consider his telegram of 31 July as never sent'. In the same letter he reminded me of my promise to convene the absent Managing Directors of our company at an early date for a joint meeting in connection with the loan.

The end of our difference with the Government was that Greidanus was elected a member of our Supervisory Board by the general assembly of the shareholders with our full approval. It was understood that he would make monthly reports to the Finance Minister on the situation at Philips. He was a valuable member of that Board and we became good friends.

The agreement finally concluded in October 1945 between the State and Philips concerning this loan explicitly stated in Article 1 that Eindhoven would continue to be the managerial centre of its activities in research, output and the administration of its Philips establishments around the world. Consequently the seat of the enterprise would be moved back to Holland at the earliest possible date.

The Government loan was well spent. A time-table had been drawn up for amortization and payments of interest on this loan with the aim of redeeming it in 1960. We actually managed to repay the entire loan in 1948. Of course, this did not mean the end of all debts. We had increased our stock capital and had floated a loan in bonds enabling us to redeem the Government loan. The financial world's confidence in Philips had been fully restored.

Expansion Begins

Later I had contact once more with the same Finance Minister in connection with our take-over of the smallish firm Hazemeyer Signaal in Hengelo. This firm, now known as Hollandse Signaal Apparaten, has had an interesting history. Under the terms of the Treaty of Versailles, Germany's ability to produce armaments was restricted. The Germans who, prior to outbreak of World War I, had been involved in their country's rapid naval build-up and wanted to use their know-how and experience in the field of armaments production, looked for opportunities in other countries. Consequently Siemens, in conjunction with Mr. Hazemeyer in Hengelo, had started this firm, specializing in artillery guidance systems. The Dutch Navy was also interested, and these Hazemeyer systems were used in our warships. They consisted of sophisticated equipment which, in aiming the guns, calculated factors like the speed of the ship and its target, the wind force and the rolling of the ship. In those days there were no computers or electronic devices. It was done with purely mechanical constructions, which required great precision in manufacture, so the firm employed able technicians. Because it worked closely with the Dutch Navy, a naval officer, Captain Schagen van Leeuwen, had been posted to Hazemeyer's since 1935. By that time the Germans were no longer interested in the firm as they were building up their Navy in their own country, but nevertheless it had remained a predominantly German enterprise. Incidentally, Schagen van Leeuwen and Professor von Weiler, an expert in the field of radar, managed to escape to Britain in May 1940 with valuable research and production data. During the occupation the firm, with its 120 men, managed to survive mainly by doing repair jobs.

After the liberation the Military Authority took on the supervision of German firms, and Hazemeyer's was placed under the care of the Trust Institute. I was convinced Holland was going to rebuild her Navy. A new company was formed, Hollandse Signaal Apparaten, in which the bankers Mees & Sons, the Navy and Philips participated with the aim of getting the factory turned over to them by the Trust Institute. Our first concern was to preserve a factory which was important to our country. The potential commercial benefits were not yet clear, but Schagen van Leeuwen, who became its general manager, was full of confidence that his new artillery guidance systems would conquer the world.

The deal was concluded with the Trust Institute and naturally a take-over price was agreed upon. And as we were planning Hollandse Signaal's future organization, officials of the Finance Ministry intervened. They did not agree with the negotiated price and the three partners were summoned to The Hague by the Minister. The business was discussed in detail. We stressed that the take-over talks had been conducted by the head of the Trust Institute who was fully authorized to do so. At this point the Minister let drop,

'We at the Ministry of Finance would like to conduct this business as honestly as possible.'

I flared up, 'But, Your Excellency, "as honestly as possible"? What do you mean? The business should not be as honest as possible, but honest full stop!'

His Excellency went a bit red in the face and corrected himself: of course it had to be done honestly.

'If the business is to be done honestly,' I continued, 'you need to honour undertakings by men who were fully authorized to enter into agreements on your behalf. You are committed by their word. And as to the amount to be paid, it will only become clear in the long run whether we have paid too little or too much. At the moment only one thing is evident: a lot of money will have to be put in to keep the firm going with all the risks that involves.'

We parted as friends. Later Hollandse Signaal Apparaten did develop into an important company. After the war, the cruisers *De Ruyter* and *De Zeven Provincies* were ordered along with some destroyers. Our Navy put so much trust in Schagen van Leeuwen's designs for artillery guidance systems that they placed big orders. Schagen van Leeuwen's designs proved to be fully up to requirements—which did not surprise me a bit.

To me this is a typical example of how much the confidence and the abilities of a single man can mean to a company.

In carrying out this order, Hollandse Signaal acquired a great deal of know-how which has led to orders from navies all over the world. The first of these came from the Swedish and German Navies, which have bought a great deal from the Hengelo firm. As the development of electronics was increasingly influencing the design of artillery guidance equipment, it was logical that in the end Philips should take the main interest in Hollandse Signaal, and now it has become part of our Concern.

Chapter 16

Consolidation

Post-liberation Holland was brimful of new ideas, resulting from the endless discussions in the hostages' camps and in Resistance circles, as well as from the talks with Queen Wilhelmina. I was, of course, particularly concerned with developments in industry. Dirk Stikker, President of the Foundation of Labour, came to address our Manufacturers' Circle shortly after the liberation. This Foundation was a body in which employers and trade union representatives planned to work together to restore Holland's prosperity.

Some of the work Frank Buchman was doing at the time linked in with this, and I invited the executive board of the Foundation for a weekend in London to see the MRA play *The Forgotten Factor*. The play dealt with a labour-management conflict culminating in a strike and showed the disastrous effect of faulty communication, as well as a possible basis of solution. On the whole my friends responded favourably, but, when we discussed whether to have it performed in Holland, we agreed that it was more relevant to the British situation than to Holland, as, for the moment, that type of conflict hardly existed in our country.

In the Philips Concern, too, people were open to the different mentality which the war had brought. During the occupation a group of people in our social affairs section had already done some preliminary thinking on what our future social policy should be. In those discussions the booklet by Professor Alfred Carrard, *Le chef, sa formation et sa tâche*, had been a source of inspiration.

Now we invited Professor Carrard to give some lectures in Eindhoven. He proved a master at drawing his audiences into a dialogue. Otten and I then sent some of our managers to follow Carrard's course on modern management at his institute in Lausanne. This helped our top management to open their minds to modern ways of running an industry, and particularly to paying more attention to the relationships between people.

Another initiative also originated in Switzerland. In 1946 a large former hotel at Caux-sur-Montreux had been bought by a hundred Swiss families, at considerable sacrifice, to become a conference centre for Moral Re-Armament. In the course of the years 'Caux' developed into a source of inspiration leading to all sorts of new ideas and actions. At Buchman's instigation the first post-war non-political contacts between the German nation and other peoples were made there. Konrad Adenauer and Robert Schuman both participated in these conferences. It was also significant that, in Caux, many German Communists found a different purpose for their lives—a fact which played a major part in frustrating Communist plans for the take-over of the Ruhr. The Communist leaders evaluated the influence of Caux so highly that all members who went there were expelled from the Party. But the Ruhr workers realized that the ideas of Caux would lead them on a more effective road than those of Moscow, and within a few years Communist representation in the works councils of the Ruhr coal mines dropped from seventy-five to eight per cent.

Frans Otten and I several times attended these conferences in the village above the Lake of Geneva, and many of our Philips people went there too. In 1948 Albert Plesman made a KLM plane available, thus enabling a delegation of industrialists to attend a week-end conference there.

My Parents' Return

Meanwhile, in November 1945 conditions in Holland had improved to such an extent that my parents could return. They arrived by boat in Rotterdam, accompanied by my elder sister Annetje, Mrs. Otten, and her youngest son Frans. For the moment they could not return to De Laak, as the house was still not repaired. So they moved in temporarily with my sister Jetty near the Golf Club.

The first weeks were very difficult for my father. There was so much to digest. First, there were the partially destroyed factories, and then the sorry sight of the battered woods around De Wielewaal. A spontaneous gesture by the Philips personnel made up for a great deal. They marched by De Laak as they had done on festive occasions before the war, the house being the traditional spot for this kind of demonstration. So once more my parents stood there, profoundly moved, but shocked by the sight of those emaciated faces. As textiles were still in short supply, people were dressed in pullovers and other informal clothes. Ordinary shirts were rare.

My father had bought great quantities of textiles and hundreds of pairs of shoes in America to share out in Eindhoven. But now he realized that all this was no more than a drop in the ocean. However, the American consignment was gratefully accepted. People would say jokingly to one another in the factory, 'Now I'm walking in Ton's shoes.'

Father had been abroad for over five years, long enough to become a legendary figure. Many of the older ones were convinced that soon everything would be fine again because 'Mr. Ton' had returned. But not even Mr. Ton could make bricks without straw. And it was not easy for him, after such a long stay abroad, to enter into the great changes which had come about in Dutch society.

He scarcely said anything about the warehouse we had built during the war—a thing of which I was very proud. It did not seem to interest him. A 'self-help' building scheme which I had initiated he regarded as a waste of time, and said that a proper bricklayer could have done the job in a third of the time. This negative verdict in itself was unimportant, as it did not alter the real value of the scheme. But my father's opinion carried a lot of weight—and hurt me—although I was now a man of forty.

Fortunately my father did not respond as luke-warmly to everything he saw. He was delighted to be back in Holland and appreciated the fact that the Concern had been kept in one piece and that we were feverishly at work in all directions, even though he thought nothing was going fast enough. He did not realize how much the fashion of going slow during the occupation had undermined people's discipline and pace. Unlike Uncle Gerard after his retirement, he still felt deeply involved in the company, of which he was now Chairman of the Supervisory Board, a position he took very seriously. Once when an important deal had been concluded with a Dutch machine factory before he had been able to read the small print of the contract, he gave everybody hell. He often performed the opening ceremonies of new factories, and did so with much enthusiasm.

In addition to his chairmanship at Philips he was active in other supervisory boards, and when I visited these establishments with him I was struck by his grasp of their situation.

Gradually he began to withdraw, and started making more trips with my mother. In summer he would always spend some time at his beloved Crans-sur-Sierre in Switzerland. When he returned home he would go and have a look at the newly planted trees around the golf course. Then he would visit one of his children for a cup of coffee, and on these occasions he would visibly enjoy himself. Looking around the house he would say, with a smile, that there was still space for some fine antique, and on his next visit he would bring along a tankard or jar, always just the right thing for the spot he had selected.

Board of Management

In the post-war period, important changes were carried out at Philips, resulting in the establishment of a new Board of Management. Initially, we had reverted to the pre-war structure, which meant that Otten, Van Walsem, Loupart and I were actually in charge. In this arrangement neither Otten's nor my position was easy. Otten, as well as Van Walsem and Loupart, had been abroad for years, while I had managed Philips in Holland as President with the Directorate. As the loan contract confirmed, Holland was our home country again and Eindhoven our base. There people had become used to dealing with me. But now Otten had returned.

Part of the trouble was that people objected to having Otten reinstated in the top position as a matter of course. For many of our employees he was a newcomer, while the older generations were reminded of the harsh, unpopular measures he had been forced to take to combat the Depression. I knew his exceptional abilities, and felt he had to be put back into a place senior to me. I suggested that, as a temporary arrangement, we should jointly sign all documents committing the firm and all official management announcements. So gradually he was moved back into the position of President, which then became accepted by everyone.

It was soon plain to us that management problems were becoming too complex and time-consuming for four people to handle. We simply needed more manpower at the top, and in order to make this possible we had several options. We could, as was often the practice abroad, have had only a few full members on a Board of Management, aided by a great many assistant members. But we felt that the members of such a Board would be apt to become reduced to an exclusively supervisory function, without being personally involved in day-to-day business. We were accustomed to doing many things ourselves and to conducting negotiations personally. So we decided to expand the Board in such a way that there would be enough people both to head up the different sections and to be able to take on business deals and see them through. In this way we could remain in real touch with business life from all angles. This enlarged Board of Management enabled us to cope with the great difficulties of that time, and is still in operation.

In choosing the new members it was natural to consider first the war-time directorate. Dijksterhuis took charge of development, Holst of research, De Vries of finance, and Tromp of technical management. Pieter van den Berg, a newcomer, took on the commercial side, and Anton Guépin became responsible for the legal section with Van Walsem. With this team we started work and it soon proved a strong combination.

Within the Board of Management was a Presidium, consisting of Otten as President, myself as Vice-President, and Van Walsem and Loupart. Opinions have differed as to the value of such an institution, but I think it has worked well. Of course a Board of Management can operate presided over only by a President and Vice-President. But for us a Presidium has been very useful. It was easier to discuss certain problems there, such as the appointment of new Board members, conflicts between members, demarcation of the different fields of competence, and so on. Membership of the Presidium does not necessarily mean a superiority of rank, but it does offer an opportunity to talk over certain matters in a smaller group without the risk of confusing or hurting the other members. Another advantage is that the Board of Management can meet in the absence of both the President and Vice-President without there being any doubt about who is to fill the chair.

The Board was later slightly reduced again, for interesting reasons. A Board of Management seat may be the highest position in Philips, but two members of our Board turned out to be unhappy with that position. Van den Berg constantly felt upstaged by Loupart and unable to use his abilities fully, while Dijksterhuis, who had been in complete charge of the technical management during the war, now had to share this field with Tromp. This might have led to conflict, but we managed to find the way out.

In America, our staff had been considerably reduced after our top management had returned from there to Holland. Yet industrially that country continued to be of the greatest importance for the future, not least as a television market. Van den Berg and Dijksterhuis were therefore put in charge of that operation.

We had developed in Eindhoven a new TV system of which we had the highest expectations. By means of a small high-power cathode-ray tube the image was projected on to a flat plate, and this produced exceptionally good visual quality. Moreover the Protelgram, as this set was named, was particularly attractive because it needed only a small amount of precious raw materials. We sank a great deal of money into developing this in America. The public, however, preferred the big electronic tube with its more brilliant image, so we finally gave up the Protelgram.

Dijksterhuis later returned to Holland and, with E. B. W. Schuitema, built up our gramophone record industry, which has become a business of world dimensions. Van den Berg remained in the States. There the American Trust was kept going and, through the take-over of a series of companies, assumed great importance. These companies were allowed to function as much as possible as separate units under their own management, contrary to normal practice in America. The American Philips Trust has developed in its own way independently from Eindhoven, and this has yielded excellent results.*

Later our new structure was developed further. Following the custom in America, where they are termed divisions, we established what we call 'industrial groups'. But we did not, as in America, put one man in charge of a group. Instead we put a technical and a financial manager in charge of each, thus following the practice of our founding years when Uncle Gerard was in charge of the technical side and my father headed up the commercial side. Except for some minor changes, this structure has been continued until this day.

Building Activity

Meanwhile, I was also given a special task. This covered all social matters, including housing, which was no small job. The bombing raids had destroyed hundreds of housing units, and, worse still, the construction of new houses and flats had been practically at a standstill. As early as 1945 Philips started employing thousands more people, and 1946 brought additional increase. From all sides I was asked the desperate question, 'When are we going to get a house?'

We did what we could. During the war we had already worked intensively with a building society on a plan for 380 housing units. The architects had designed these houses using mainly bricks and steel, as wood was desperately scarce. In those years the granting of building licences took a long time, but this was in fact the first big building job completed in Holland after the war.

*The North American Philips Corporation now includes some thirty-two major divisions and subsiduaries, with net sales in 1976 of $1,723,627,000. In addition to the full range of electrical and electronic products, which are sold under a number of brand names such as NORELCO and MAGNA VOX, its operations include companies making carpets, furniture and a range of chemical and pharmaceutical products, as well as a major long-distance coach company.

Meanwhile I began to consider how I could get people involved in the construction of their own homes. We launched a plan whereby three applicants built a house together, which, when completed, was raffled between them. The two 'losers' were then put on a priority list for another house. Participants in this scheme built in their spare time according to a simple system using cement blocks. The advantage was that people felt that they could do something about their own situation. It also meant that participants could rent the houses cheaply or buy them at a low price, and, in fact, many ended up buying them. The actual building cost, however, was not low, because construction normally requires skilled labour, so all sorts of special arrangements had to be made for these unskilled people. This activity, which was outside the normal scope of our company, was organized by the same ex-army officer who had run our physical training programme during the war.

The Housing Ministers took all kinds of measures to tackle the housing shortage. They produced new designs, which our Philips building staff were capable of carrying out; so we were allocated hundreds of houses to be built in and around Eindhoven.

We also made an interesting experiment with 200 semi-detached houses which we imported from Sweden. We assembled these simple bungalows, made from good Swedish wood, on a stretch of heath land. They were meant for young families, mainly from university backgrounds, and as the houses were pleasant, the area developed into a particularly sought-after neighbourhood. It became a real community with its own 'mayor', and it had its own kindergarten and other facilities. The atmosphere was so good that people still talk nostalgically about the 'Swedish village'. The houses, however, were not durable. They were meant to last only fifteen years, and actually survived twenty-five. Then the upkeep became so costly that the entire village had to be cleared away.

We did a great deal of building at Philips in those years. Factories and private houses went up, and our head office was rebuilt with a small new wing. This required the closest collaboration with the municipal authorities, and our relationship with them improved greatly. In the old days clashes between Philips and officialdom had been common. An angry mayor once remarked that he wanted to know once and for all whether Philips was located in Eindhoven or Eindhoven in Philips. The city and our firm regularly had to trade plots of building land. For instance, the muncipality needed land which it bought from us for one guilder per square metre, but if we wanted to buy a piece of that same land back a year later they would charge us ten guilders.

Of course we did not appreciate that kind of treatment. So a 'master plan' was drawn up by Tromp aiming at smoother land transactions between the two parties. A delegation from our Board of Management now has an annual meeting with the Mayor and his councillors. Both sides submit their points and they are jointly discussed, so that both parties are informed in good time about each other's plans. Since 1945 we have built 400 factories and company buildings in Holland, of which over 130 are in Eindhoven and the immediate vicinity, and we have been, directly or indirectly, involved in the building of 25,000 housing units in and around the city. We have also provided 11,000 mortgages to Philips employees to enable them to buy their own houses.

At one point the authorities insisted that we should build blocks of flats; I opposed this as I do not believe that this kind of housing suits our Dutch temperament. Our people love to live on their own plots of land, however small. One-family houses are ideal for us, and I am glad that most of the houses built or owned by Philips are of that kind. If we were unable to build that kind of house inside Eindhoven, we did it in nearby villages. Around a one-family home there is always space for a small garden to sit in, to put the pram in and to grow some greenery.

I have always regarded parks and gardens as very important, not least on our premises. After the war we paid more attention to using them to create a congenial atmosphere. We also looked more closely at details like the colour of the workshops and of the machines, as well as at the outward appearance of our buildings. Traditionally factory buildings are concrete colossi without much variation. I have tried to change this a bit. In the post-war reconstruction years money was short for major changes, but our buildings had suffered from the raids and looked shabby, so Otten and I decided to spend 25,000 guilders on paint jobs. This created an interesting reaction in people. Events like the Berlin airlift, the Communist coup in Czechoslovakia and the Korean war kept fear of a new war alive, but our painting activity did much to counteract this. People said to one another that war must be out of the question if Philips had started paintings its tower; for if war was really likely, Philips would know.

Teamwork with Frans Otten

Our sixtieth jubilee, which we celebrated in 1951, was the first such milestone free from major external anxieties. In 1916 World War I was on. In

1931 there was the Great Depression. In 1941 there was little cause for celebration, though it did burst out all the same. But in 1951 a celebration was really called for. The Concern was back on its feet again. By 1948 we had already attained 1939 production levels, and in 1950 we had exported more than twice as much as in 1939. Other figures were equally encouraging.

All through Philips people were working hard again, and the Board of Management was no exception. It was a remarkable team. I have already described Van Walsem's and Loupart's qualities. Guépin, an excellent lawyer, was a particularly balanced and wise man, qualities of great value at the top of any large enterprise. Theo Tromp was a go-getter and an excellent manager of the factories under him. J. C. de Vries kept a vigilant eye on our financial position and saw that we kept both feet on the ground. And of this closely-knit, strong team, Otten was the undisputed leader. I worked with him as Vice-President.

Otten and I were very different, both in approach and mentality. When economic issues were at stake, there was never any difference of opinion between us. In matters of co-operation with others and of introducing new products, our ideas almost always ran parallel. Otten was a tactful leader of men who yet had the courage to tell people exactly what he thought. Some felt he could be very rough, but I do not believe that anybody really suffered from this characteristic. I, too, sometimes had to take sharp criticism from him when I irritated him by my way of operating. But the basis of our friendship remained intact, even after a tough clash.

Otten was a hard worker, who did everything with exceptional precision and whose tendency it was to go into the minutest detail regarding facts and figures. So during his presidency we did not need anybody on the Board of Management in charge of keeping an overall eye on figures and data. At regular staff meetings Otten himself was able to quote practically all relevant figures from memory. For such meetings he would prepare himself meticulously at the expense of his sleep at night. I was different. When later I became President, I said that I could not fill Otten's place in this respect. Absorbing and analysing figures and data in detail was not a natural gift of mine, so I needed the assistance of someone who would take on that side of the work, and Pieter Breek came to reinforce the Board. In matters of finance, I considered a correct interpretation of trends more important than detailed knowledge of facts.

The details which I regarded as important were different. For instance, in the appointment of people or in the mapping out of new developments I was very precise. Otten took these things seriously too, but he approached them from a different angle. I preferred to look for right solutions with a team of people. I was good at heading up such a team and I enjoyed it. I was very interested in things when they were going well, but less so when they were going badly, whereas Otten preferred to turn his attention to difficulties, and when things were running smoothly his interest flagged. When new ventures were proposed, I wanted to be present at the discussions in the department concerned to try and look into the future. It was often said of my father that he was a man for booms, and possibly I have inherited this characteristic. There was nothing I liked better than starting new companies and factories, whether close at hand or in remote places. Equally I have been at my best when new products were launched. All in all, Otten and I were good at making up each other's deficiencies.

Both of us realized that after the war we were going to be faced with a difficult job. Of course differences of opinion did arise at times within the Board and then a real tug of war could ensue, but to the outside world we always preserved our unity. That was not difficult, because the decisions which were eventually taken were always loyally sustained by all. Outsiders may believe that if the leader of a board of management is a strong personality, this automatically means he dominates everyone, with disunity and tension as a result. That did not happen in our case.

Otten had a great interest in sports, as he felt they were important for the training and education of young people. He passionately loved mountaineering, and I used to play tennis, ski and mountaineer with him. He did a great deal for the promotion of sport, and paid particular attention to the Philips Football Club (PSV).

At one point, he had difficulties with his health which forced him to go to Switzerland for treatment. During these periods I had to preside over the Board of Management in his place. I knew his views in detail about all the issues, and if I had to cut knots on my own, I always did it after consultation with my colleagues. As far as my memory goes he only once, after returning from Switzerland, disagreed with a decision. Those periods were a good preparation for the time when I would have to succeed him as President.

Collective Labour Agreement

In the years of post-war consolidation, 14 December 1949 was an important date. On that day no less than fifteen trade unions and Philips Gloeilampenfabrieken signed a document about collective labour agreements which opened up a new era at Philips.

The history of this event goes back long before I had any say in Philips management. At an early stage the trade unions realized that Philips was going to be a very large enterprise, and they made great efforts to expand their influence in our company. Collective labour agreements were the best way of achieving this. Contacts with the unions were mainly in the hands of Evelein, head of the Social Economic department, which was under the supervision of Assistant Managing Director P. N. L. Staal.

Piet Staal was among my father's oldest collaborators. He had joined the firm as early as 1898, as a former sergeant-major. He had not had any university training, but he was hard-working, exceptionally practical and possessed a keen intelligence. My father had always liked to give him tough jobs. Nothing was ever too difficult for Staal. In the end he had become Assistant Managing Director, the highest rank in the Philips army, a really amazing promotion. Staal was, among other things, in charge of personnel, and the management was in those years dead against collective labour agreements. Whatever the trade unions said year in, year out, Philips remained squarely opposed to them. We said that we had our own contacts with our employees, that these had worked well for years, and that we were sure our personnel did not want such agreements. Actually, we feared we would have to negotiate afresh every year and that this would offer too many opportunities for trivialities and hair-splitting, which would not be conducive to a right climate in the company. We also took into account that only a very small percentage of our personnel were union members.

All this had produced a difficult situation. The trade unions continued to demand collective labour agreements with increasing urgency, and Philips responded with a growing determination not to give in. When Staal retired in 1938, I took over personnel affairs from him. This led to thorough-going discussions with Evelein and I decided to take a new, objective look at this issue, which was so important to the unions. My training in Moral Re-Armament played an important part in this attitude. After reflection I arrived at the conclusion that the issue of collective labour agreements should not be a matter of prestige. It ought to be settled exclusively on the basis of what was fair for all.

In this spirit I talked with the trade union leaders, starting in 1939 and continuing into 1940. The subject was not simple and the negotiations made slow progress. Evelein took the initiative to spell out in detail what a good personnel policy in Philips should entail, and this study was accepted as a starting point for further talks.

During the German occupation the talks were continued, until events took a more dramatic turn. The trade unions were faced with a choice between either joining the Quisling Labour Front or dissolving themselves. Neither the unions nor we wanted to settle our long-term relationships under foreign pressure. Thus, in great secrecy, through talks on the phone between ourselves and the unions concerned, we arrived at an agreement. This was the 'Undertaking in principle to conclude collective agreements', which I consider an important fact in our national social history. This document, dated 11 March 1941, could only be signed by some of the contracting parties and was considered a 'gentlemen's agreement'.

In this undertaking a number of Philips factories and seven trade unions declared the belief 'that consultation, developed over the years into a fruitful co-operation based on mutual appreciation and trust, has moved to a point when the time has come to lay down labour conditions for the personnel of the companies enumerated below, in a collective agreement'.

Of the principles of the 'gentlemen's agreement' I would like to quote the following:

'The undersigned, in concluding and carrying out collective labour agreements, are aware that the interests of employers and employees run parallel to the point of being practically identical. All who work in a company should, in the interest of the community, invest their full energies in a spirit of co-operation to help the company to prosper. In return, there should be a system of labour conditions in accordance, among other things, with the financial potential of the said company. In agreeing on these labour conditions, the undersigned should aim not only at preserving the social services as they have developed in the different companies in the past, but also at expanding and perfecting them within the limitations of the financial potential of those companies and according to social needs. For their part the personnel needs to show its preparedness to make sacrifices as agreed upon by the undersigned in consultation, if in the estimation of the management the company's position so requires.

'The undersigned recognize that the community's interest requires first and foremost the continuation of the social peace which has been kept intact for years, and moreover that satisfaction at work and the usefulness of this work should be increased as much as possible. In this, co-operation and trust between all who are working in the companies, whether in high or low positions, are indispensable. The undersigned therefore declare that they, both individually and collectively, will use the means at their disposal to strive for the realization of this purpose.'

As far as I know this agreement has been unique in Holland. If you examine these principles, you can see clearly how much what is now called the 'harmony model' predominated in those days. It is still my belief that such harmony is in the last analysis best for the interests of all concerned.

During the occupation the collective labour agreement issue was put temporarily into cold storage by Philips and the genuine trade union movement. In the winter of 1943-44 a group under Evelein had discussed the right social policies for our firm after the liberation. This led to the report, 'General consideration of a correct Social Policy in Philips Gloeilampenfabrieken NV', much of which was put into practice after the liberation.

That does not mean that after May 1945 the Collective Labour Agreement could triumphantly march to the finish. First, Philips had to get going again and the trade unions too had to restore their organization, which had been dismantled by the Nazi Labour Front. In the middle of 1949 the so-called 'frame agreements' were at last concluded. This new agreement drew heavily on the principles of the 1941 undertaking. Of the six principles I quote here the first three:

'1. A company only fulfils its social function in the proper way if the realization of its primary economic object is pursued with due regard to the common well-being and is accompanied by the furtherance of the welfare of all those engaged in the concern.

'2. With a view to a lasting fulfilment of its social function a company should, after previous deliberation with the trade organizations coming into consideration therefor, build up and maintain a system of labour conditions and social provisions on the one hand directed towards what is socially desirable and on the other hand brought into line with what is economically justified and financially possible for the company, wherefore the aim should be to attain the most useful possible result from the joint labours in the concern, whilst further, if at any time the state of affairs of the company should render it impossible to maintain the existing juridical status of the personnel then that personnel should be prepared to accept such measures as may be deemed essential by the company in consultation with the aforesaid trade organizations.

'3. The most useful possible result of the joint labour in the concern can only be attained when all connected with it, from the highest to the lowest, give their utmost energy in a spirit of cooperation and good faith, while promptly and strictly observing the rules fixed within the concern to that end.'

There were eight guide lines for wages, of which the first was this:

'Remuneration of labour shall be based upon the nature of the work, the personal performance, the age and, unless parties should agree otherwise, the sex of the worker.'

Finally, careful arrangements were made concerning promotion, distribution of work and classification of jobs, the fixing of standards, piece-rate work and vacation bonuses. The vacation was to be at least twelve working days, which meant two weeks because there were then no free Saturdays. Further, there were agreements about absenteeism, internal personnel representation, pensions and the maintenance of factory discipline.

Otten and I also agreed with the Board of Management at about this time that we would define our company's tasks more broadly than just manufacturing and selling, and that our primary aim should be our company's continued existence. This was not only in the shareholders' interest, but at least as much in the interest of our personnel, our customers, our dealers and our long-term suppliers—for all would suffer if Philips were to disappear.

So we were strongly aware of the responsibility of our enterprise to society, and we decided to have this embodied in our Articles of Association. Consequently in 1946 a social paragraph was inserted in these Articles: 'In order to promote the interests of all those connected with it the Company shall aim at a long-term welfare policy and maximum useful employment.' This was formulated not in order to throw slogans about, but because this was the firm conviction of the management. This step was taken without any outside pressure. Our employees and the trade unions knew that we had inserted this paragraph of our own accord, and this had its effect.

These ideas have been a guide-line and a touchstone for all our subsequent decisions. We got into the habit of asking ourselves whether a certain decision would actually further long-term prosperity. And whenever we set up new factories, we aim at a healthy undertaking providing good and permanent employment for years to come.

Incomes Policy

During the years in which Holland, through hard work and thrift, was struggling back to her feet, successive Governments maintained a firm policy of wage and price control. In general this was a good method, but it was impossible to avoid prices and wages going up in some cases. In a company like ours, which needed a lot of skilled labour, the situation became difficult. There was a strong tendency towards levelling wages down, but that was no good to us as we had to rely on highly qualified workers. We were ready to pay higher wages to have our factories run better, but neither the Government negotiators, nor the Minister of Social Affairs would agree to this.

I went to see the Minister, Mr. Willem Drees, who held his portfolio with a firm hand, to try and persuade him that too strict a control of wages and prices would lead to great difficulties, and was unfair to people who were making a special effort. The draw-back of the policy of levelling wages down was that extra effort was punished rather than rewarded.

No matter what I said to Drees, I made no headway. Meanwhile dissatisfaction and tension among our workers increased. They simply wanted more money. I saw trouble coming. One morning I phoned Dr. Beel, the Prime Minister. He could not act as a sort of director general ordering his ministers about, but I told him my concern. Beel mentioned the matter to Drees and I got the green light, but Drees was very angry with me for having involved the Prime Minister. In the end we talked the whole thing out, and our good relationship was restored.

When I think back on these social developments and remember that absenteeism on account of illness was only four per cent, despite the hardships of those days, I realize how much conditions have altered in a quarter of a century.

Chapter 17

Father's Passing

As late as 1951 Sierk Schröder painted an excellent portrait of my father, which hangs in the room where our Board of Management meets. In his twinkling eyes and active expression you recognize a man of stature. That spring, he began to lose his active pace. Together we attended a meeting of a supervisory board of which he was chairman, and then I persuaded him to visit a factory where he had purchased a number of prefabricated houses. He looked around the factory, which was managed in a very up-to-date way, and showed great interest. Nobody suspected that it would be his last trip outside Eindhoven.

He was unable to attend the festivities for Philips' 60th jubilee, though of course he followed them on the TV screen. The high point of the celebrations was the unveiling of the statue of himself by Wenkebach, made on the initiative of the mayor of Eindhoven. Those who knew my father think this statue particularly good. Normally statues are made of people after their death. Emperors, kings and generals are often portrayed on horse-back, and they all tend to look the same. But a man's bearing, the way he normally stands on the ground, generally typifies his character. Father stands there as a simple man, in a characteristic pose, ready to meet anybody, a man who succeeded in inspiring confidence and was able not only to sell his products, but also to convince people of his ideas. And that was at least as important.

When his condition gradually worsened that summer, I felt I must take ample time to visit him. I often sat with him, which both of us enjoyed. Of course we discussed the company. Until the very last, Philips' future held his interest.

In those years a lot depended on how television would develop in Holland. For two years we had been giving experimental television broadcasts, an experience from which we had learned a great deal. Those who made our programmes—the directors, technicians and artists—and the several hundred viewers who had systematically seen these broadcasts, had also acquired a lot of experience which could be used the moment the traditional radio broadcasting organizations started using this new medium. This happened at last in autumn 1951.

Our government was understandably not enthusiastic about our people spending a lot on expensive TV sets, as it wanted to maintain post-war austerity. But for us it was essential to amass experience, acquired in our own country close to the place where the sets were being developed and manufactured, if we wanted to keep our pioneer place in this field. At the time we were already making technically excellent sets.

On Tuesday, 2 October, the first official TV broadcast in Holland was scheduled. I attended the event, and next day I told Father what had happened. He was still full of interest, and was firmly convinced that the development of television, both in Holland and in the surrounding countries, would be of immense significance for Philips.

Immediately after this event my father's condition worsened. The last words he said to me still ring in my ears: 'Goodbye, my dear boy . . .' Even though I was a man in my mid-forties, to him I always remained a boy. At that moment I realized how my life was linked with his. After this he became unconscious for several days and it was no longer possible to communicate with him. On 7 October, early on a Sunday morning, he left us.

The blow was hardest for my mother. She had nursed my father with exceptional care, which was typical of her, and now she would be without the man whose comrade she had been through life.

Our Youth

At that moment many episodes of our youth came back to my mind. It was a fine youth, with two marvellous parents. As children my two sisters and I had been very fond of Dad. He had a heart overflowing with warmth. When we were naughty he gave us hell, but you could always creep back on to Father's lap. Mother gave us good fun. She always took time to play games with us, and helped us with our homework, for we had to practise the piano and to write our homework neatly. When we finished an essay, she would go over it with us, paying special attention to style. She was the more philosophically inclined of our parents. When I grew older I had wonderful talks with her on holiday walks. Dad was a big lump of warm humanity, but Mother always let her mind speak as well. This was particularly clear from the different ways they reacted if we had done something wrong. When Dad was angry with us, he would really blow his top, but afterwards it was all over. But if we had done something which Mother did not like, she would make us feel we had done wrong without getting excited herself. We found this more disagreeable than Father's outbursts.

Mother was a great sportswoman. She used to swim, row and play tennis in her Rotterdam years. Mountaineering too was one of her favourites, and she played golf until she was 84. Both my parents were enthusiastic cross-country riders, and enjoyed going over the wide stretches of heath around Eindhoven where church steeples were the only points of orientation.

On Sundays we went for walks, which were always planned minutely with maps. We would drive to some village and then walk along dust roads to a neighbouring village where the driver would collect us. So we got to know our beautiful Brabant well. Then we had car rides with Father himself at the wheel. How wonderful those excursions were! Father always drove a Renault—'our' make. Once every few years a new chassis was collected from Paris, which was then turned into a car, using the same windows as a railway compartment, by our car body maker in Arnhem. We were always wrapped up well for these rides, with blankets and scarves, because we had convertibles which would sometimes be left open even in winter, and heating systems were then unknown. Usually our driver Jan went with us, and I was always keen to sit next to him. The average speed on main roads was then only 30 miles an hour.

Dad often had to travel abroad, and he never forgot to send us a post-card. Usually they were far-away trips and as a rule they ended in Brussels. He was then met in the evening by car at the Brussels railway station. Back home, he first had something to eat while we sat around him at table, eager to hear his stories. At last he would begin to talk and talk, with full flavour and colour, of what he had experienced in Spain or Italy or wherever he had been, while we hung on his lips. When he became older and we had children of our own, I realized what a gift he had for interesting children. Whether they were our own children or beggar boys on the Nile, he knew how to joke with them and was always genuinely interested in them. Children of Philips people with keen minds also awakened his interest. He cared deeply that young people should grow up well and achieve something.

Life started at De Laak early in the morning, for my parents were early risers. They talked many things over together. I often heard later of men who never discuss business matters with their wives, because they want to be free from the day's worries in the evening, or they feel the wife should not be involved, or may gossip. In our family such fear was baseless. My mother, as well as my sisters and my wife, understood that certain things ought not to be discussed outside.

Even while he was getting up Dad had all sorts of ideas and plans for the day. He would go downstairs and ask the maid to ring up some people—which meant that our maids had to be intelligent girls. So there was a talk with Mr. A. and then with Mr. B., when each was told what my father had been thinking that morning and what he wanted done. I, too, was often given my assignments at breakfast. Sometimes he would ring people outside the company, business acquaintances who were also friends, like a young textile manufacturer whom he would ask to come to his office at nine. The young manufacturer would turn up promptly, and Dad would tell him, 'I was studying the wool prices this morning. If I may make a suggestion, I think this is the time to buy wool!'

I grew up in a home where we entertained a lot. We often had guests because there were few suitable hotels in Eindhoven. David Sarnoff stayed with us, as well as artists like the pianists Elly Ney and Dame Myra Hess, and the violinist Bronislaw Hubermann. They were interesting people for a young boy to talk to. Mother was musical and played the piano a great deal. With some friends my parents had started to organize chamber concerts. The local cinema was then converted into a concert hall, the arm-chairs from the balcony being moved to the ground floor. And if a grand piano was required, our Steinway was transported to the cinema.

Father was always exceptionally generous. Whenever he visited Paris and bought gloves, ties or the like, he would always bring back some for us. But he disliked ostentation. For him it was normal to enjoy a good income on which he could live pleasantly, comfortably and free from care, but he never gave expensive parties or balls at De Laak, except for family weddings. My parents never indulged in what one might describe as 'high society' activities. My father wanted to give a good example in Eindhoven, and he expected the same from us.

As an art collector he loathed publicity, and never had impressive catalogues made of his collections. But he usually bought well, and never hesitated to seek expert advice. Once I had bought some jars which I had liked. The price had not been high, and I wanted to know what Dad thought about them. He was sick and in bed, but he was curious to see my acquisitions. He looked at them, touched them, looked again and began to smile to himself, saying:

'How very interesting! They are nice jars, but they are genuinely, genuinely . . . false jars!'

The man who, on that Sunday morning, found eternal rest had been a great man and a good father. I had felt most keenly the combination of those two qualities when a disastrous thing was found to have happened to part of his art collection. Before 1940 he had made arrangements to store it in safety. He was proved right, but the Germans' hunt for art objects turned out to be much more intensive than anybody had anticipated and I felt that some of the most valuable paintings should be even more carefully hidden. In practice this was difficult, as it had to be done in the greatest secrecy, and I had to leave the supervision of this work to others. Mistakes were made, and some of his most valuable paintings were damaged by humidity. The repair work could not undo the damage. For Father this must have been a great blow, but he accepted the fact without a murmur of complaint or reproach.

Farewell

Father's passing left a deep impression on Eindhoven. Of course people had been aware that he was ill, but it was not until the inevitable happened that they realized that the man who had contributed more than anybody else to the city's remarkable rise had gone for ever. His funeral brought out colossal crowds. Huge throngs of people lined the streets to bid goodbye to 'Mr. Ton', and all the church bells tolled.

Father had loathed theatrical or exaggerated gestures. It was entirely in his style that there were no long speeches at his grave. But there were the flowers which he had loved so much—more wreaths and bouquets than could be counted. I was the only speaker. I said:

'You have been a great leader for us all because you always put care for people first. You demanded a lot from us, but even more from yourself. You were always ready to answer our questions and stimulate us. Whenever we left your room we had been given an inspiration for new plans. You will remain a living example even if you are no longer among us. So many of us who are here together around your last resting place owe our living and that of our families to your work. We will continue in your tradition.'

I ended: 'Dear Father, dear old man, rest in peace. Our best wishes go with you. We can be happy in the belief that you have been received in

God's arms and that you are going to partake of a glory which passes all understanding. Goodbye, Father.'

The Philips band played the chorale from Bach's St. Matthew Passion, *Wenn ich einmal soll scheiden*. All of us followed Mother in bidding Father a last farewell. Then the funeral, so impressive in its simplicity, came to an end.

Chapter 18

Network Across the World

In the post-war years we found that the situation in Philips had changed more than we had expected. During the war our establishments both in Europe and in other continents had continued their activities as far as circumstances permitted, but they had not had the close contacts with Eindhoven which had existed before May 1940. One result was that these daughter companies had become more independent.

Now we had to decide whether to revert to the pre-war system, or to continue on the road which the separate parts had already taken. We decided in the end to take the new road. Loupart, in particular, the most active traveller among us, regarded the new course as essential. His idea was to have a democratic federation of Philips establishments. On this subject he could elaborate with brilliant verbal fireworks, during which I could not help smiling, for he himself was an accomplished autocrat.

In the fifties we were not just dealing with established branches, but expanding all over the world. In one year, for instance, we built factories and offices in India, Venezuela, Portugal and Sweden. This was partly due to the trade barriers which were still being erected, but also to the nature of some of our new products. For if we were to penetrate new markets with radio sets, for instance, we had to adapt to local reception conditions, and therefore had to start producing locally. By this time we were producing in more than fifty countries and selling in more than seventy.

This tremendous expansion brought new problems. We were operating in places where different languages were spoken and where different customs and traditions prevailed, as well as different trade practices. So the cardinal question was how to preserve adequate cohesion and at the same time respect the urge towards local autonomy.

One essential was an adequate flow of information. This was soon restored to pre-war levels, thanks to the uniform systems of accounting and data processing set up by Goudriaan in the thirties. But at least as important were the contacts with the people at the head of the Philips establishments all over the world. Whether the establishment is small or large, in a village in Central Africa or a city in Brazil, the men at the head have not only to be up to their jobs, but also to have an open and relaxed relationship with the central office.

I have tried to learn from the failures of the Dutch East Indies Company in the seventeenth and eighteenth centuries, which made devasting mistakes because its governing body in Amsterdam was too little aware of the problems confronting its Governors-General far away. The head-quarters of any large enterprise can so easily slip into this mentality of 'Now we have enough facts to arrive at a decision', without having absorbed the information and assessment of the man on the spot.

There are some large companies which have departments of international affairs to oversee operations abroad, but we have never had such a separate department. We do have men in Eindhoven who co-ordinate all contacts with the foreign establishments, and who look after their interests rather like envoys. But we give relative autonomy to these establishments, and they report directly to the Board of Management. So the head office has to be able to grasp local problems in addition to the general business aspects. We have to know the conditions under which our people are working all over the world, and have a feeling for the political climate in each country. This means going to see for ourselves. So I began to travel more and more, and continued to do so all the time I was in office. It meant consciously building a network of personal relationships all over the world.

The International Concern Council

As well as giving a great deal of attention to good personal relationships with our management overseas, we have also tried to create cohesion of thought and action throughout our entire organization. For this we developed a method which has since been copied by other companies.

We started in 1954 by assembling our principal managers from all over the world to meet with the Board of Management. During this meeting, which lasted for some days, we discussed the Concern's policy in general. We found this meeting so valuable that we decided to make it an annual event. We included more and more countries, and soon the hotel we were using in Holland became too small. So these meetings of what is now called the International Concern Council are held in Switzerland, in a hotel on Lake Geneva.

About forty come from different countries, and there is a lengthy agenda. First the general position is explained, and then the past year is reviewed in detail. Prognoses are submitted for the current and following years. After that, subjects of special interest are discussed and specially invited experts may analyse the position and future of one of our main divisions, for instance, television, telecommunications or light. Discussion groups are then formed to deal with special subjects. And from these, new ideas about participation and work structuring often emerge.

The Council also provides opportunities for personal contacts. In addition to the veteran managers of twenty years' experience, you meet younger managers from countries like Salvador and Ghana. Delegates meet informally for meals at small tables, where experiences can be exchanged, old friendships strengthened and new friendships made.

The Council is also of value to arrange promotions and the transfer of managers. If we consider it useful to move the Uruguay man to Argentina, this can be discussed with him. So everybody looks around to see who the Board of Management is talking with, and as soon as people have seen one of us in conference with a junior manager, all sorts of speculations start circulating.

These meetings are expensive and demand a great deal of time from everyone, but we came to the conclusion that we could not do without them. As chairman, I always tried to get as many of the delegates as possible involved in the discussion.

The Council meetings meant a lot to me, and I felt the heartbeat of the Concern there very strongly. We all went away wiser by the experience gained from our colleagues, and with renewed courage to tackle our own problems. We all felt the strength of being part of a creative organization, and a loyalty which cannot be imposed but can only grow between people who trust and like each other, and which is the cement that keeps us together in good times and bad.

Travel Throughout the World

As I have already mentioned, I began to travel more and more in order to foster this world-wide network, as well as to break new ground for our Concern. My first such trip was in the autumn of 1951, after my father's death, when Tromp and I went to Australia and returned via Jakarta. Otten and Loupart gave us some useful tips before we left. 'Never draw conclusions immediately,' said Otten. 'Let the people on the spot tell you their full story. Listen carefully, ask lots of questions, and only come to your conclusions after you have digested all your impressions and sorted out the problems.' Loupart added, 'Try to meet as many heads of state, ministers, government people and employers as you can.'

Sometimes in those far-away countries I came across people I had got to know in Caux as students, who had since become leaders in their nations. When I met such a cabinet minister or civil servant, he knew that I was not just a businessman pursuing my own self-interest, but that I had a wider concern which included the development of his country. Young nations are, quite naturally, suspicious and do not readily believe that people from the West are coming to help them. Of course, I never pretended that this was my sole aim. I told them frankly that we wanted to invest in their countries, that our experts would come and pass on their skills, but that we could only do this if the operation would yield returns, even though not immediately. I always made it clear that our investment of money and people was proof of our confidence in their countries. And, of course, the fact that such a cabinet minister trusted me partly because of my association with Caux also put an obligation on me to live up to the standards he had heard of there.

Sylvia accompanied me on many trips, particularly after our children left home. She speaks fluent English, French and German, and also some Spanish, and was as interested as I in the people and countries we visited. She was always a happy travelling companion and a welcome guest.

Whenever I could, I visited our people in their homes and met their families, and·here Sylvia was particularly helpful. Lunches would be arranged with our people's wives at which everyday problems—children, schools, health, shops, all matters of great importance for people living in faraway countries—could be discussed. Such conversations, in addition to the normal business contacts, give our people overseas the security of knowing that we understand the background if difficulties arise. A number of our people have been confronted with crises due to riots, revolutions or enforced nationalizations, and then mutual confidence between them and us in Eindhoven becomes specially important.

India

The first of my many Asian journeys was to India. We had paid little attention up till then to this immense, densely populated country. In 1930, in the days of the British Raj, we had started a light bulb factory in

Calcutta with British partners, and, after the war, we had opened a radio factory there which was 100 per cent Philips-owned. In 1955 our establishment in India had its 25th anniversary, and I decided to attend the celebrations.

One of the first visits I made was to the Calcutta factory. As I was being taken around, I noticed some men disappearing in a rather furtive fashion and quickly hiding behind a crate on the stairs. I did not understand why. Then I was told they were sweepers, casteless people who had to stay away from my shadow. I was confronted for the first time with the evils of the caste system.

The celebration was held on the sports ground of an oil company, which had been rented for the occasion. Three ships carried the personnel to this place down the Hoogly, as the mouth of the Ganges is called. It was a festive trip, with people making music on a variety of instruments. As the river mouth widened the ships began to race each other. Two of them moved closer together, and the enthusiastic passengers rushed shouting to the side nearest to the other ship, which made both of them keel over sharply. But all three, fortunately, arrived safely.

At the grounds there were sack races, egg-gathering contests and other entertainments. The best item was the fancy dress contest. I was astonished by the inventiveness of the Bengalis. Old warriors in impressive garments walked next to strangely dressed market traders. There was a scientist in professional spectacles, stately dignitaries, and a repulsive group of beggars. One of them had an eye made of dough, dangling bloodily from one socket. His left leg had been bound up with a stump underneath, on which he dragged himself forward. In reality, this beggar was a neat office clerk. Everyone was very amused by this.

When I visited our factory, I was impressed by the quality of the women working there. Many of the girls on the assembly lines had matriculated in high school. They were Hindus who had fled from East Bengal, now Bangladesh, after the partition of India and Pakistan. For this occasion they had turned out in their best clothes, their raven-black hair beautifully decorated with flowers.

I also visited Delhi, where I later made many friends, among them the then Home—now Prime—Minister, Morarji Desai, and Gulzarilal Nanda, Minister of Industrial Planning. I went to Bombay too, on this first visit.

When I got back to Eindhoven, we sent out people to expand our Indian operation. We then wanted to build a lamp factory of our own, but the Indians would not give us a licence, so we had to wait until we were able to take over an existing factory. One day a small lamp factory in Bombay, with an annual output of five million light bulbs, came up for sale. This gave us our chance. But what to offer for a run-down old factory? We badly wanted the factory and feared being outbid. So we offered a little above what we considered it to be worth. There was another bid for exactly the amount we had first estimated. So the factory— a collection of ancient buildings—became ours. Several years later we built a new, highly modern plant in Kalma, near Bombay, whose official inauguration I attended. In India today we employ about eight thousand people in seven factories, all managed by excellent Indian staff.

With each successive visit, as I got to know more and more government people, my list of calls became longer and longer. I also got to know the Moral Re-Armament centre in Panchgani, which one of Mahatma Gandhi's grandsons established in the beautiful hills near Poona.

In Panchgani I met members of parliament, businessmen, trade union leaders, students and workers from the various Indian states, and from other Asian countries. An atmosphere of hope and trust reigned there which was in striking contrast to the general situation. Political adversaries from the hills near the Chinese and Burmese borders in India's North-east found there a basis for co-operation. Their reconciliation led to the creation of a new state, Meghalaya, without the bloodshed which, sadly, had been so characteristic of the agitations for linguistic or ethnic states elsewhere in India. On one occasion at Panchgani I had the pleasure of opening a new theatre and conference complex equipped with the latest Philips products.

Visiting Philips establishments overseas meant making a lot of speeches. After a tea in the afternoon with a group of merchants, I might speak at night to some of our staff. At times I was treated to a performance by our personnel, after which people expected a speech from me. A meeting with the representatives of the personnel, the equivalent of our Works Council, was usually on the agenda. On occasions like these I always tried to say something worthwhile.

Once our Calcutta factory was celebrating the fact that the 500,000th radio set was coming off the assembly line. The personnel sat, dressed in their best clothes, and there was I, the sahib from distant Europe. I said to them:

'Somewhere in the distant mountains lives a family. They want to buy a radio. It is a great expense for them, so they have to save up for two years. At long last the money is raised. The husband goes to the city. His trip is long and difficult. Perhaps he takes a week to get there. But finally he arrives. He buys the radio, and, full of excitement, he takes the heavy set back home. When he gets there, everyone is happy. The radio plays and people are delighted. Now the family can listen to Pandit Nehru's speeches. The house is filled with the best music. The little box brings alive everything that is happening around the world. The neighbours come, too, to marvel at the new possession. There is rejoicing around that set.

'But after a while . . . the radio no longer works. What to do now? Nobody in the vicinity knows how to deal with the complex interior of that radio. Everyone is sad. So the man has to go all the way back to the shop in the city with that heavy object. And if the people there are unable to repair it, it has to be taken back to the factory. As soon as the radio has been returned to the place where it was bought, the man has to walk to the city again. Possibly by then the radio has been away for months.

'Now let's think about what might have been the cause of all this. Perhaps one of us here has made one soldering error. This shows how important it is to do a good job. If we do, these people will be happy to have such a good Philips radio. Then the neighbours will want one too. That means that people will have good radios, and that this factory can continue to provide work for years to come.'

In the same way I would try to hit people's wave-length when I was talking to dealers. 'Even though you are not employed by Philips,' I would say to them, 'we need you and you need us. Your job is to get our products out to the customers, and I know from experience how hard that can be. So I am happy to have the opportunity of meeting you men who occupy this front-line position, because without your work we would be nowhere. I realize, as you do, that our products have their shortcomings. A radio has hundreds of components, and so do household appliances. So even if our checks are near perfect, there is still the chance of something being not quite right. And it is up to you to see that there is good service. Also, it is inevitable that some products turn out better than others. From our side we are doing everything in our power to supply you with good products on time.' Then I would usually end by offering my best wishes for their trade and for their families.

Once I was in Calcutta during a strike by our office staff. The reason for the conflict was small but the excitement was colossal. The strikers kept the local management locked up in the office premises for half a day. I intended to be in India for two weeks, and the local general manager was planning to accompany me, but under the circumstances he dared not leave. I suggested he talk to the staff. He told them how distressed I was that this incident had occurred during my visit, for I could not possibly wait a couple of weeks and then come back. So it was agreed that the conflict should be suspended until my departure, after which the issue would be discussed again. The same evening, in spite of the troubles, a performance by and for the personnel took place in a local theatre. On such occasions there are always speeches, but it had been agreed that there would be no reference to the grievances under discussion.

The night atmosphere was splendid—twanging of Indian music, beautiful dances, everyone in a cheerful mood. But the Secretary of the Works Council could not refrain at the end of his speech from pulling out of his pocket a slip of paper, from which he proceeded to read the grievances. Now the fat was in the fire! Our manager, a Dutchman, turned scarlet. The head of personnel, an Indian, lost his composure completely. And I had to reply . . .

I went to the microphone and said that it had been a pleasure to attend this performance, which had shown me how talented our personnel were. I could not refer to the list of grievances read out, because that was the local manager's business. But I wanted to make some general observations:

'Philips is at work all over the world. Here we are working not just for the sake of Philips, but also for this country, for Bengal and for Calcutta. I venture to suggest that we have acquired more experience in co-operation between people than any other concern. So it is important to realize our responsibility towards India. In the first place we want to give a good example by providing first-class quality, and we want as well to show the right way of solving problems.

'There are many industries here in Calcutta. Labour conflicts do happen. There are difficulties here as there are anywhere in the world. But what is the basic question everywhere? It is this: How can people work together? That is true for India, for her federal states, and for the industries in this city. Because we in Philips have acquired so much experience in this field, I feel your factory should be able to give an example of good teamwork. That is all I want to say. I wish you all the wisdom, strength and mutual trust you need to solve the present problems in the right way.' Even though the speech had to be translated sentence by sentence into Bengali, thunderous applause followed it.

Our manager was really worried about the incident. But I said to him, 'Don't worry. These people just couldn't miss the chance of reading out their grievances while I was here.' I went on my journey. Everything remained quiet, and later the issue was fairly solved.

On a subsequent trip I experienced real trouble in Poona. Again there was a conflict just at the time when I was visiting India. A sports competition had been organized for our personnel in the grounds of a sports club, but the unions were boycotting it. I asked the plant manager, who met me at the airport, to take me to the place where I was to stay, which was the Country Club. But he misunderstood me and thought I meant the sports club where the competition was being held. So I arrived at the sports grounds, where there was a great commotion. Soon our car was surrounded by an angry crowd. Men were brandishing banners and swinging clubs about, and young agitators were shouting slogans at the top of their voices. I looked at some of them, as if to say, 'What is all the fuss about?' One after another, they bashfully looked away. In the end our driver succeeded in breaking through the crowd, and we went on to the Country Club. The Indian manager was distressed at his mistake, and asked me whether I still wanted to visit the factory in spite of the trouble. I said that I did.

The next morning I saw pickets in front of the factory gate, brandishing banners which read, 'We want justice'. As I was taken round the factory, I did not notice anything unfriendly, but people did have a slip of red paper pinned to their overalls with the same slogan on it. Once in a while I asked, 'How's justice? Is it that bad?' The response was rather shy. When I suggested we should have a cup of coffee with the Works Council I was asked whether the trade union secretary could also be included. And I thought this a good idea.

During coffee I said that I was pleased to visit this factory, but that it would be the last time I could do so. 'For I find it hard to understand the way you have behaved. As far as I am concerned, India is a democratic country. But yesterday you did not behave like democrats. This has deeply grieved me. What should I tell people when I am back in Europe?'

Someone remarked, 'We hadn't really wanted to demonstrate, but the trade union organizer insisted we should.'

'Aren't you free people? Haven't you got a will of your own? Or do you let a few people push you around?'

I repeated that this would be my last visit. The reaction was unexpected. The people who had seemed ready to set fire to my car now had tears in their eyes.

But in this case our management was not without blame. New job demarcations had been introduced, which meant for some a drop in wages. So it was agreed that the matter would be reviewed. At the end of the coffee party a man came to me and said, 'Mr. Philips, you have gone around the factory this morning, but we haven't seen you at the plating plant . . .' So I went to visit that section as well. When I left, the workers all waved me goodbye.

Some years later I was back in Poona, this time with Sylvia. We were received so warmly that it moved us both. On the lawns between the factory buildings the entire personnel was seated, men and women in separate groups, all dressed in their best. A representative of the workers addressed us cordially and offered us a gift. This time our plant manager was beaming in the warmth of the occasion.

Taiwan

In 1962 I visited Taiwan, an island where more than fifteen million people live. The administration is efficient, and the population hard-working. The country has many universities, and made a positive impression on me. American and Japanese activities in Taiwan suggested that there were opportunities for Philips as well. After my visit, we set up a small factory in Kau Chung. Soon this was doing so well that, during a subsequent visit, I thought of starting a television tube factory there, and cabled to that effect to Eindhoven.

Such a factory requires huge investment and involves great risks. The venture would only interest us if Philips were first. I soon found that an American company was thinking on the same lines and was already negotiating. Now establishing factories in new countries takes a great deal of time. After preliminary talks, a formal application has to be submitted. The Americans had not got that far yet. I had only two days in Taiwan, and I wanted to bring things to a head, which was only possible with the co-operation of the government. On the day of my departure I had breakfast with the Minister of Industries and together we drafted the application, so that it would, we hoped, be dealt with speedily.

But it did not go all that fast. I had stipulated that, if we started producing tubes first, we would be given a monopoly for two years in view of the great amount of capital involved. Some authorities later tried to by-pass this stipulation, but we remained firm. Today there is a Philips factory in Taiwan producing three million tubes a year, with a glass factory as an annex. The greater part of this output goes to other TV manufacturers and the rest we use ourselves. No more than ten per cent of our own allotment is exported to Europe. We now also have a fine factory for transistors and integrated circuits in Taiwan.

I was greatly honoured when on my last visit to Taiwan, in 1976, the degree of Doctor of Philosophy was bestowed on me by the China Academy.

Once I made an extraordinary air trip from Taiwan. We had installed a network of radio communications between the many airfields in the Philippines. A year before I had asked President Marcos to inaugurate the new installations and had promised, in that case, to be there too. Now we were in Taipei, the capital of Taiwan. From there we went to our Kau Chung factories, and then had to return to Taipei in a hurry, because that afternoon a typhoon passed to the south of the island. The following morning we had to decide whether to continue to the Philippines, a decision hingeing on whether the typhoon moved west or east. The captain, our senior Philips pilot, who had fought the Japanese in the East Indies during the war and was experienced in weather conditions in those parts, looked at the weather reports and considered the typhoon rather inactive. He observed, 'That storm is moving neither west nor east. Our one chance is to overfly it at a very high altitude. There we will have little turbulence, and if it gets too bad we'll turn back.'

So we left, and climbed to over 40,000 feet. We passed through light mist, but the turbulence was only moderate. That afternoon we arrived in Manila in brilliant sunshine. Everybody was flabbergasted, as all flights from the north had been cancelled.

Nobody knew exactly what time the President would arrive. For security reasons he used to avoid announcing exact times of arrival. In the end he came a great deal earlier than expected, but our margin had been more than enough and I was able to keep my promise to welcome him.

Sadly, Commodore van Haarlem, the experienced captain who made this daring flight, lost his life in a street accident at Eindhoven in 1975. I had flown with him for tens of thousands of miles, and a true pilot's comradeship had developed between us.

Indonesia

Even before 1940, the Netherlands East Indies were important to Philips, but it was quite a while before I set foot in Indonesia. In the fifties I had followed with close attention the steady deterioration in the relationship between Holland and her former overseas possessions. In the agreement on Indonesian independence, the Dutch part of New Guinea had been left out. The Dutch had promised independence after ten years to the

Papuans living there, so they wanted to remain under the Dutch for the time being. But Soekarno wanted to control New Guinea himself, so there was a good deal of tension between our two countries.

When this conflict arose, I was indignant about the way the Indonesian government treated our country, especially when, in 1957, Soekarno expelled all Dutch nationals. I felt we had to back the Papuans, and also that though we had a duty to Dutch New Guinea, this did not mean we had to linger on there for eternity.

At a conference in Caux I met many Indonesians. In talks with them I began to realize that the New Guinea conflict went deeper than I had suspected. For them it was simply unacceptable that the Dutch should stay there. Some felt an instinctive fear that we would try to return from New Guinea to Indonesia. Others feared that we would help that territory to advance more rapidly than they themselves would be able to do. Confidential exchanges convinced me that Indonesian self-respect prohibited any protracted Dutch presence on the island. So I began to believe it was best to try and arrive at a solution with the Indonesians and that long-term Papuan interests would be best served that way. At the time our foreign policy was in the hands of my friend Luns. But I increasingly questioned his opinion that we should stay in New Guinea for the time being.

In a subsequent conversation with Robert Menzies, Prime Minister of Australia, I asked him, 'Can we count on Australian help if the Indonesians attack us in New Guinea?' His answer was brief: 'Have no illusions. We will not lose one soldier or one bullet over such a conflict!' I also discovered that active American support could not be expected either.

In that period, President Soekarno was continually travelling around the world. When he visited Copenhagen in 1959 I felt I had to go and talk to him. So I phoned Ole Björn Kraft, the Danish Minister of Foreign Affairs, whom I had met several times in Caux and who I knew would understand my motives, and asked him to arrange a talk between Soekarno and me, which he was able to do. I had scarcely spoken a few words of English when Soekarno suggested,

'But, Mr. Philips, let's speak Dutch. It's easier for both of us.'

He offered me a cigarette, but I told him that I had not smoked for years, and that this had done me a lot of good; during my imprisonment I had noticed how tough it had been for my fellow prisoners not to be able to get cigarettes. Laughingly, he assured me that when he had had his 'troubles' it had never been a problem. So our prison experiences created a bond. I then told him that I had come as a private citizen, entirely on my own initiative, and that I was not representing anybody or anything, and continued:

'Mr. President, I find it very regrettable that relationships between our two countries are so bad. I am not in a position to improve them, but I should like to discuss them with you. I understand what we as Dutchmen have done to you and your nation as a result of our arrogance. Of course, I am proud of what Holland is achieving, but that does not give me any right to feel superior. That is wrong.'

'Please don't worry. My very best friends are Dutch.'

'But let's be honest. We must have annoyed you tremendously.'

He paused, and then said, 'Yes, you are right.' And he began discussing the New Guinea issue.

'There isn't a soul in Holland who wants to stay in New Guinea for ever,' I said, 'but you need to understand, too, that we have a duty towards the Papuans. Besides, we have started all sorts of development projects there, and would like to finish them.'

'That is unacceptable to us!'

'But let's suppose for a moment that you agree with us that we can continue certain development projects for the next five to ten years. You know we are a nation of schoolmasters who love to tell others how to do a job properly.'

'That is true, but we could never accept such a condition.'

'But would it be possible if you, from your side, requested it? For instance could you say: "We Indonesians are taking *de facto* power over the territory, but we would value it if you Dutch could finish those projects"? Such a solution would be greeted with relief in Holland, for our people have a considerable love for your country. Everybody would rather have a face-saving solution than a conflict.'

'But I don't see how this is possible.'

'We could make a start by improving the way we talk about one another in public. There is no need to call each other bad names all the time. Take the Schmidt case, for instance.' I was referring to a certain Dutchman who had been condemned to life imprisonment for alleged illegal activities, but who had recently been released, which had caused much protest in Indonesia. 'Your press has reacted against his release, and this, in turn, has been taken up by our press, and so on. Mr. President, let's agree to this: I'll try to do everything in my power to create a better atmosphere for negotiations on our side, and you can do the same on your side.'

'I'd like to give it some thought. I'll consider it.'

We separated, promising each other that we would talk to others about this discussion only when it would contribute towards detente. I myself had not talked then to anybody except Otten. After my return to Holland, I reported to the Secretary of the Ministry of Foreign Affairs and also had a talk with Foreign Minister Luns. He told me I should never have had a talk like that, for, in his view, it had weakened our position. I replied that it could not possibly get any worse. Luns then complained to Woltersom, who tried to tick me off. I said to him,

'Listen, I'm a free man. If I'm convinced that I should do something, I'll do it.'

Curiously, for a while there were no attacks on Holland in the Indonesian press. Some time later a rumour circulated in Bonn that I had promised Soekarno that our relationships would improve. Of course our ambassador there reported these rumours to The Hague, where it fanned the flames. But I felt I had done all I could, and did not react to this.

After the dust had settled in 1964, Soekarno let me know that he would like to meet me in Rome. There I met him at a typical Soekarno breakfast. He was in the company of twenty or thirty people, all in merry mood. He said to me,

'Please come to Indonesia! I should like to co-operate with Philips.'

'I'll come if I am invited.'

The invitation came. I was eager to see what business possibilities there were in that huge country. Nico Rodenburg, then in charge of our telecommunications division, went with me, and we arrived at a basic agreement with Indonesia concerning technical aid and the exchange of technicians. This was aimed at getting the Philips factores, which had been nationalized, back into working shape. The political climate was not conducive to talks about a restitution of the assets, but I was able to make contact with a number of key people.

I visited Subandrio, the Minister of Foreign Affairs, just as the Soviet *chargé d'affaires* was leaving his room. Subandrio said to me, 'You are welcome. Now we are among friends again.'

I knew why the Russians had been there. The Soviet Union had provided Indonesia with a lot of war material for which payments were not being made on schedule. It was, however, of abominable quality. The Russian jeeps especially were so bad that they were hardly usable. I said to Subandrio, 'Why don't you put those rotten jeeps on your quays, and tell the Russians they can take them back home?'

His reaction was typically Indonesian: 'But that is quite impossible. It would be so impolite.'

In the end the Indonesians submitted a letter of intent stating that they wanted Philips to perform certain tasks in the factories for payment. This was a relatively poor result, but that was not surprising.

In 1965 Soekarno was succeeded by General Suharto. Meanwhile I had arrived at the conviction that if we were to achieve anything in Indonesia, we should be given full charge of our projects. So an agreement was concluded on the basis of which Philips was the first foreign company to enter into a joint venture with Indonesia. This plan was built on solid foundations following talks between Professor Mohammed Sadli, who was a relatively poor result, but that was not surprising. and Tromp.

During that period it was noticeably difficult for me to meet General Jusuf, the Minister of Industries, which was necessary if the new arrangement was to work. Whenever I came to Indonesia, he happened to be abroad; or if he was at home he was invariably too busy. However, at last I managed to meet him at Amsterdam airport.

'In my opinion, General,' I observed, 'the success of our joint venture depends especially upon the two of us. I view us both as uncles of our nephew, the new enterprise. If the uncles are on good terms, the young man will do a good job. But it is important that the uncles trust one another. Let's agree about this: please don't believe all the negative stories which you are bound to hear about me, and I, on my part, will believe only the good things about you.'

We shook hands on this, and a good relationship developed between us. On occasion we were able to talk very frankly to each other. Towards the end of 1974 he came especially to Holland from Rome to give me the highest Indonesian distinction ever bestowed on a foreigner. I greatly appreciated this. He declared, on behalf of President Suharto, that I was given this distinction not just because of Philips' contribution to his country's development, but also because of my personal endeavours to encourage friendly relations between our nations.

In the new company, Philips-Ralin, there is good co-operation. It has four managers, two Indonesians and two Dutchmen. First, our original lamp factory in Surabaya was put back on its feet. Then it was expanded to include the workshop of a former bicycle plant, where fluorescent light tubes, light bulbs and glass are now made. President Suharto and Sultan Hamengku Buwono IX of Jokjakarta came to Surabaya to attend the inauguration of this modernized factory. I was sitting next to Suharto, who officially uses the Indonesian language and has everything translated. When I asked him whether he wanted me to speak in English or Dutch, he replied in my language, 'You will greatly please me if you speak Dutch.

I want our relationship with the Netherlands and with Philips to be as good as possible.'

My speech then was in Dutch, and fortunately there was lots of laughter. For Indonesians love to laugh, and many understand our language well. With slightly wicked glee, I noticed the puzzled look on the faces of the foreign diplomats, who could not understand why the Indonesians were laughing so heartily.

Since then I have been in Indonesia many times, and I have many friends there. Today there is in Bandung a Philips-Ralin radio and television factory, which has grown into a sizeable plant.

Africa

The huge continent of Africa has unimaginable potential. I have made many trips there, especially to East Africa.

During my first visit to Kenya I was accompanied by my son Ton, who had been working in Africa for many months with the Moral Re-Armament programme and knew some parts well. On that occasion we met President Jomo Kenyatta of Kenya in Nairobi. I had a good introduction. Kenyatta immediately said,

'Well, Mr. Philips, when I was in detention I was able to buy a Philips radio for half-price. That is how I was able to keep in touch with the outside world.' He was referring to his time in detention in 1953 because of his association with the Mau Mau. I observed that he had been better off than I because, when I was in gaol, I was not allowed a radio. Kenyatta asked me when I had been 'inside' and I explained that I owed this experience to Holland's occupation by the Germans.

Then we discussed my son's work, travelling all over Kenya for some months to show the Moral Re-Armament film *Freedom* in the national language, Swahili, and the President exclaimed, 'Your son knows Kikuyu-land better than I do!'

Ton had been struck by the many negative slogans shouted in Africa, and he told Kenyatta, 'Mr. President, your voice should be heard more loudly in Africa. It should resound across the jungles like a lion's roar!'

This must have meant something to Kenyatta. A week later we were in the Ugandan capital of Kampala, where the law faculty of the University of East Africa—the university common to Uganda, Kenya and Tanzania —was located. An honorary degree was being bestowed on Kenyatta, and it was a major celebration. Julius Nyerere, President of Tanzania, was there to confer the degree. Here we met the African sense of humour. The large figure of Kenyatta stood in front of the small, slender Nyerere. When Kenyatta had to stoop considerably to accept the token of his new dignity, the spectators roared with laughter.

Then Kenyatta began to speak. First he joked that people nowadays needed titles to be able to fill certain posts. 'The only post you need no diploma for is that of cabinet minister, and for the President's office even less so. Up till now I have been able to cope without a title. But today it is a great honour to be nominated Doctor of Law.'

'We are grateful for being freed from imperialism,' he continued. 'That is colossal progress!' Then he raised his voice. 'But we have to beware of a still greater danger, the infiltration of false ideas. We have to keep vigilant not to embark on dangerous roads, if we are to avoid a yoke heavier than the one we have just shed.'

Thunderous applause followed his speech. We happened to be sitting behind the ambassador of the People's Republic of China. Neither he nor his wife were clapping.

I remember one of the many talks I have had with President Nyerere particularly clearly. It took place in 1967 when I was passing through Tanzania. He asked me whether I was doing business with the People's Republic of China. I told him that our trade with that country was negligible. As Tanzania has close dealings with China, he asked me why. I explained to him,

'Mr. President, in World War II my country was occupied by the Germans, and so I got to know National Socialism. That was a dictatorship. It is unimportant what label a dictatorship has, for dictators invariably want to eliminate the human conscience and replace it by the dictates of the State. I have seen with my own eyes that this can mean the death of a nation's soul. I have seen corruption, but an all-out attack on a nation's soul is worse. This has made me decide that I will never lend such a regime a helping hand, whether it be Fascist, National Socialist, or Communist. If the Red Chinese want to buy ten million lamps from me, which incidentally they can buy anywhere, I will say, "All right, gentlemen, this is our price." But I refuse to co-operate industrially with those countries.'

It was inevitable that we should get talking about South Africa, a country I had visited many times. I told Nyerere that, however much one might condemn what was wrong in South Africa, one positive aspect, which did not exist everywhere in Africa, was its free press. When things went wrong, they were openly reported and discussed in the newspapers.

I explained that I felt a certain kinship with the Afrikaners as we Dutch come from the same tribe. So I would try and help them, even if I did not entirely agree with them politically. 'Like us Dutch, they are a stubborn people,' I added, 'and you can't always get them moving fastest by kicking them.'

Yes, things needed to change in South Africa, but what about the rest of Africa? She was not the only country guilty of repression. I had heard tell of terrible atrocities in Zanzibar, but I would never judge his Government by them alone.

The white minority, I concluded, was afraid that they might be chased into the sea. I saw no other answer, short of a bloodbath, than that white and black would find a new basis of life together on a basis of trust and equality.

'But, Mr. Philips,' President Nyerere replied, 'those people want to invade us.'

'I do not get that impression. I have talked with them and they are not thinking in those terms.'

It was a frank exchange of views in good spirits, but we did not convince each other. We each stuck to our own opinions on other matters too. 'I am not a Socialist,' I told him.

'Yes, I can understand that!'

'And I think you are inclined to distrust my motives. You see me as a capitalist. But what I actually consider most important is that people should have the freedom to develop as much as possible, to take initiative and responsibility themselves. If the state wants to do everything and regulate everything, it starts a process which cannot be stopped, and people end up being slaves of the state. That is why I can't accept Socialism.'

When we said goodbye warmly to each other, I added,

'I can imagine that, if and when I am back in these parts, you will think in horror, "Here comes that man Philips again! Should I receive him or should I not?"'

'No, Mr. Philips,' said Nyerere in his charming way, 'whenever you are in this part of the world, you must let me know. I shall be glad to free an hour to spend with you. I find it interesting to talk with you.'

On our travels we went further than words. In Nairobi we now have a lamp factory and a record factory and in Arusha, Tanzania, we manufacture radios and gramophones. The plant in Arusha employs 120 people, of whom one is European. It is amazing to see how eagerly these young workers are trying to educate themselves at evening classes. The storekeeper, the cashier, the maintenance men and tool repairers are all local people. This approach is part of our policy, and Nyerere evidently appreciated this. Once he told me, 'We want a lot of Philipses in this country.'

In South Africa, too, Philips has taken many initiatives. The last visit I made was in 1974, when Sylvia came with me. The purpose of this trip was to get to know the South African homelands. We visited Gazankulu, Lebowa, Bophuthatswana, and Transkei, where the black ministers welcomed us. It became clear that they were keen for Philips to start factories in their regions. We now have a plant in Roslyn, almost on the border of Bophuthatswana. The workers come daily from that homeland and are glad of the jobs we provide. The plant looks neat and trim. Philips pays high wages, and we are succeeding gradually in overcoming race divisions on different levels. Our black friends there are amazed by the attitude of their Christian brothers in the World Council of Churches who want to boycott industrial activities in those parts.

South America

In the Andes mountains in Peru I had a memorable experience—one of the many I have had on numerous visits to Latin America. Our daughter Digna was then working with Moral Re-Armament in Latin America and I invited her to join me. She is fluent in both Spanish and Portuguese, so she was not only pleasant company, but also an excellent interpreter.

In Peru the distant past still exercises considerable influence. Inhabitants of Indian background are still living in primitive circumstances and are illiterate. Yet they know their history well through stories handed down the generations. In those memories the Inca Empire plays an important part. Its culture was brutally destroyed by the Spanish conquerors, and the mountain people have preserved to this day a deep-rooted suspicion of all that comes from the valleys.

This ancient culture possessed its technologically strong points. The Inca people lived in a volcanic region and had an effective method of building earthquake-resistant buildings. The huge stone blocks were not cemented together but were chiselled in such a way that, in case of a tremor, they could absorb the shocks without becoming separated.

In 1959 Digna and I flew to the university town of Cuzco, once the Inca capital, accompanied by our head office man responsible for liasion with Latin America, and our local manager. Our destination was that curious settlement of Machu Picchu which had been discovered in 1912 after having been hidden under vegetation for centuries. It was abandoned for unknown reasons, and the Spanish invaders never knew of its existence.

The connection between Cuzco and Machu Picchu consisted of an extraordinary little procession of four old-fashioned tram cars, each powered by a Ford engine. It left in the early morning full of passengers, mostly tourists. The rails on this stretch, leading over a twelve-thousand-foot pass, do not have the usual sharp turnings because that would have made this line too expensive. The cars climb along a zig-zag track, first forward to the angle; then the points are changed, after which the train moves backwards and then forward again. In this way the cars made their way up the pass.

Then we descended into the valley of the Urabamba River. I went to sit next to the engine driver, and got a good fright. The tracks were kept only moderately in order. A number of the sleepers were not in place, and the buffers along the track were not properly maintained either. However, it takes a great deal of disrepair to stop a train from being operational.

For the freight traffic two steam engines were used. When we arrived at the station, a bus was waiting to take us to Machu Picchu. We spent the night in a small local hotel and were able next day to have an unhurried look at the remnants of that ancient civilization. It was an impressive experience. The excursion was a welcome change from the generally over-full business programme of this trip.

The way back from Machu Picchu to Cuzco went less smoothly. At every turning we had a long wait. There was something wrong. Then suddenly, somewhere at an altitude of 10,000 feet, a broken-down steam engine was blocking our way and we had to wait until the other engine came to pull the patient away. So there we were, stranded, three tram-cars overflowing with tourists from all parts of the world, who spoke different languages—Spanish, French, English and Swiss German. We had taken ponchos with us and so we were reasonably protected against the cold. By evening it had become ice-cold, and we made a big fire from branches gathered from around. But an American working on an aid programme in Peru showed us that a smaller fire yielded more heat—the Indians had taught him that you could better warm your hands and body at that kind of fire. To our astonishment our Indian guides then began to set fire to the bush all along the mountain slope, which provided a fantastic sight, and could do no harm, as there was not a living soul for miles around. We had unintentionally met the grandiose desolation of these Andes mountains, reaching majestically into the skies and covered by trees to their summits, so different from Europe. There millions of Indians live, still filled with suspicion towards modern civilization.

After some hours the track was cleared, and we arrived deep in the night in Cuzco. On our way to the hotel we passed the short figures of Indians, weighed down under heavy loads, running in their typical trot to the market place where they would sell their merchandise. They had been on the road for hours.

I once had a surprise on a trip to Argentina. In Buenos Aires I was received by the general manager of a refrigerator company. A party had been planned at his *quinta*, an estate not far from the city, for hundreds of guests. It began with an *asado*, a barbecue at which entire bulls, cut in pieces, are grilled. In a big marquee my wife was given a brooch, and someone whispered in my ear that I was to have a surprise too. Our general manager in Argentina, Pieter le Clercq, later Vice-President of our Concern, warned me that the customs of the land forbade the refusal of any present. I promised him I would accept anything provided it was not a horse.

Outside, various impressive equestrian events followed, including tilting at the ring. Suddenly a man mounted on a particularly fiery horse came trotting along, flanked by two other horsemen. One of them bore the Philips emblem, the other the emblem of the refrigerator company. The three approached the grandstand and the middle horse was presented to me. I had no alternative but to say that it was a marvellous gift. I mounted it immediately and rode for a while. It was a jewel of a horse. But I kept wondering how on earth I could ship it to Holland. Then someone in the crowd put up his hand and volunteered to look after the transport. He turned out to be from a Dutch shipping line. I had this fine animal at De Wielewaal for some years, until it died suddenly of bronchitis.

In Brazil we have several large factories in São Paulo. There was a good Brabander working there who originally came from our Trades School in Eindhoven and was then head of our metal products division. Initially the skilled workers in São Paulo had come exclusively from Czechoslovakia, Germany and Italy. It was assumed that native Brazilians would not be able to learn these skills. But he disproved this assumption, and trained many Brazilian machine tool-makers.

I talked to the representatives of the workers there, but it was hard to establish contact with them. So I asked them, 'What bothers you specially here? I don't mean complaints about wages, because those complaints exist everywhere, but what is worrying you apart from that?'

At first nobody replied. I asked again, 'What are you thinking about when you leave the factory gate?' At last something began to come out. They were wondering how to get home. The public transport system was deplorable. People often had to wait for three-quarters of an hour or more to catch a bus.

I was invited to the São Paulo industrialists' club, and there I raised the question of the inadequate public transport and asked if it could be improved. I said my impression was that the workers' mood was still such that their confidence could be won, but I doubted whether it would stay that way very long if better provision were not made for them. I even suggested a monorail. At the time São Paulo had six million inhabitants, so there was scope for such a solution. I suggested that industrialists could fill this need with comparatively little effort by involving the authorities and a foreign partner, who should then be given a proper concession. If this problem were tackled, I said, construction could be started before the end of the year.

It is years since I made this suggestion and, at the time, it bore no fruit. But now, I know, subways are being built in São Paulo. The attitude of younger managers in South America is changing, and many realize that their responsibilities include knowing their workers' needs and taking action to fulfil them.

In conclusion I would like to mention the many contacts I have had with the port workers of Rio de Janeiro. They are tremendous fighters for sound conditions in the ports where, after their victory over gangsterism and their establishment of a democratic union in 1956, a new climate came into being. I have often met them, along with Brazilian industrialists and other trades union leaders, at the Moral Re-Armament centre in the mountains near Petrópolis. There is still much to do in the fight for justice and co-operation all over South America, but it is hopeful to see a spirit of co-operation breaking through class barriers at various places in that great sub-continent.

Chapter 19

The Philips Air Service

Many of my journeys were, of course, made by commercial airline, but many too, especially within Europe, were made in our own planes, and, for a time, we even hired a Gulfstream on long contract which was able to take me and other executives all over the world. Indeed, having our own planes has proved so useful that the Philips Air Service is now accepted as an essential part of the Concern. It now consists of twenty-one pilots based on Eindhoven, three with Pye in Britain and two Italians at Comerio.

Transport within our company became available at an exceptionally early date. There were at first some doubts about its usefulness, but it soon became apparent that it was needed as a general service and not just a privilege of top management. Every senior staff member—and there are hundreds of them—can make reservations through our travel office in our own services, which link many European capitals. In 1974 alone, this service carried 21,752 passengers.

Such a private air service must have a sound financial basis. Its justification is that things can be done because of it which would otherwise be impossible or more costly. Our planes are today in such continuous use that if I need to make a trip within Holland, I have to see whether there is a plane available between other flights. Also, when cheaper means of transport appear we adjust to them. Thus, the regular flights from Eindhoven to London and Hamburg are now served by commercial airlines, and, after my retirement from the presidency, the Gulfstream was given up during an economy drive.

It is very difficult to calculate whether the admittedly high cost of a plane like a Gulfstream is compensated for by its advantages. One has to take into account such imponderables as the effort, work and time that the passengers save. Another advantage is that such a plane does make possible journeys which would otherwise be impracticable. If, for example, the president of a concern feels he should pay a visit to Argentine, Peru, Chile and Uruguay, it takes no more than a fortnight in a Gulfstream. On commercial flights it would take so much more time and effort, and he may simply forget about it. Also, the risk of hijacking, the potential financial consequences of which should not be minimized, is avoided. Finally, the element of prestige should be weighed. It does not mean much to me personally, but it does make an impression if you arrive with your own business jet. So I thought the Gulfstream episode worth the money at the time.

Perhaps, however, I am prejudiced, because I am passionately interested in flying, and the Philips Air Service really sprang from that passion. My interest started early. As a schoolboy I subscribed to the only aviation magazine in our country and would bicycle on free afternoons to a tiny moorland landing strip near Eindhoven where military pilots practised in their Farmans.

At the first air show in Amsterdam, which was organized in 1919 by Albert Plesman, later the founder of KLM, the Philips family was present in force. My father and mother, my youngest sister and I took a brief plane ride. How exciting I found it bumping noisily over the field and then soaring off the ground! My parents and sister were equally enthusiastic. But my elder sister was angry when she heard of our escapade. From boarding school in Switzerland she wrote us a furious letter: 'Suppose something had happened! I would have been left on my own!'

I made my second flight in 1924, at the end of a cruise to the Norwegian fjords. As I had to go to a camp, I had to return before the rest of the family: by plane! This had been organized by my father in his own way. I was to fly from Copenhagen to Amsterdam. My father had asked our Danish agent to show me around the island of Sjelland before, next day, putting me on the plane. In the evening he was to show me Copenhagen. 'You can show my boy Tivoli, but do not take him to these night-clubs,' my father wrote. By then I was already nineteen.

Next day I sat in a Fokker F-III on my way to Amsterdam. The plane had to struggle against headwinds, and I was as sick as a dog. In those days there were no flights direct to Amsterdam, and we stopped at Hamburg. Back on solid ground I felt all right again so I ate far too large a steak, which wanted to get out again when we were back in the air. I had to stick my head through the window . . . We did not make Amsterdam. Something had gone wrong with the oil pipes. The emergency landing itself went well, but the meadow the pilot had chosen was too short, particularly as the wheels had no brakes. The plane plunged into a small canal and tore its way into the marshy land on the other side. The impact gave me slight concussion and fractured my shoulder. I must have been rather incoherent when I came off the plane, because the farm hands thought I was drunk. Fortunately, I felt all right again next day.

This experience did not put me off flying. In 1932 I attended the opening of the Eindhoven airfield which had been built to provide work for the unemployed. All the big-wigs of Holland's aviation world were present, people like Plesman, Fokker and Koolhoven. Members of the Rotterdam Flying Club who were there suggested that we organize flying lessons in Eindhoven and a glider club was founded there. So I began flying in a glider. Soon, this club was converted into a proper flying club and a flying course was initiated, in which I naturally enrolled.

The first flying lessons were a great and marvellous adventure. I entered a new world, which later became much more important to me than I then expected. After some months I was ready for a solo flight, and had to submit to a medical check up. This was a great disappointment, for I was disqualified on account of colour blindness. It was also a disappointment for Koolhoven, from whom I had agreed to buy a plane after getting my pilot's licence. Fortunately, he found a solution. He succeeded in obtaining a ruling at the International Aviation Congress that colour-blind amateur pilots could qualify for a licence for daylight flying. Even though the decision took a year to come through, I was mightily pleased, and Koolhoven got his order for an FK-26. This delay turned out to have a positive aspect. For a year I was forced to fly with the instructor beside me, which gave me a great deal of flying experience, and made me a good pilot.

In 1935, Koolhoven delivered the FK-26. It cost 9,000 guilders and was the same machine that the National Aviation School were using for their lessons. I had agreed with the school that they would buy the plane from me as soon as I wanted to get rid of it. In that case a sum multiplied by the number of flying hours would be subtracted from the price. It seems that I already possessed a keen business sense!

In September of that year my brother-in-law, Gerhard Sandberg, crashed. He was one of Holland's best military pilots with an international reputation as a test pilot. He was a member of the Fokker factories management and had stopped demonstrating planes to prospective buyers, but he decided to do it just once more in order to introduce the Fokker to Turkey.

He flew to Turkey with Captain B. H. F. van Lent, and they demonstrated the plane for a week. Both had prepared to return when the Turkish President, who had heard good reports about the plane, asked for another demonstration. Sandberg took it on. The demonstration ended in a nose dive, and he did not manage to get out of it again because the pressure on the wings was so great that one gave way. It was later discovered that the wing construction had been altered slightly, and he had not been told.

It was a colossal blow to us all. My youngest sister had become a widow for the second time. In 1930 she had married Aad Knappert, a promising young Philips engineer, who was killed in a car accident barely two years later. My parents found these two terrible blows in my sister's life hard to take and I realized it would be very tough for them if I continued flying, so I gave it up.

After some time my parents' objections faded away, so I started flying again, this time in a Tiger Moth, which I flew until the German invasion. In that period I enjoyed the unusual advantage that my driver, Ad den Hartog, also possessed an amateur pilot's licence. So he would bring the plane to the place from where I had to start, and if need be, he could fly the plane back. So, flying and driving, we spent a lot of time together. Each of us had seven children. Each of us eventually had a son studying at Delft. We became such good friends that it was a great shock to me when some years ago he died of a heart attack.

Emergency Landing

During my first spell of flying I had to make an emergency landing of my own. I was heading from Brussels for a Zeeland seaside resort where Sylvia was with our children. The West Scheldt became visible, so I climbed to about 3,000 feet since it is better to fly over water at a higher altitude. When I approached the Zuid-Beveland canal, my engine faltered and then stopped. I tried to get it going again, using every trick I had learnt, but it refused to function. The only thing left was to glide as well as I could, keep cool, and send up a heartfelt prayer to the Almighty. I can still see that situation before me. I saw an open bridge below, with a car waiting at it. Beyond it was an oblong meadow beside a road, which seemed to me the best landing place, considering the direction of the wind.

I glided down and approached the meadow. I just got over the ditch. Then I discovered, to my horror, that the field was not of grass, but of wheat. It was June, and the wheat was several inches high. From above I had not seen this. Though I had done everything correctly, the small wheels of my Koolhoven could not negotiate the deep furrows. So my plane made a somersault and landed on its back! Then, as I had expected, people came rushing. The first was a farmer. I was suspended, back downwards. Petrol was dripping on to my face, but luckily there was no fire. As I struggled out of the plane, I heard the farmer ask, 'Are there any more people in your plane?' The second man to turn up was a policeman on a bicycle. He asked me to show him my licence. He studied it with care, though I am sure he had never seen that kind of document before in his life.

I immediately offered to pay damages. The farmer made no attempt to get more than was his due. So the matter was settled. The plane damage too was not serious, though my friends poked fun at me: 'That's what happens if you are colour-blind and want to fly!' But I knew that I had made my emergency landing properly and that boosted my self-confidence —and self-confidence is very important for a pilot.

In the course of the years, I have flown many different types of planes. You have to get used to them in the same way as you get used to different types of motor car. I have also learned that you should not pilot with your mind alone. You cycle automatically, and you should fly in the same way, but also, of course, with due attention to navigation.

I now possess a licence for small twin-engined planes which I obtained after some weeks' practice in Ascona, in Switzerland. The head of the Philips Air Service was holidaying there too. So we were able to fly many times from the small airport there to prepare for the exam. The officials of the State Aeronautic Board examined me at Eindhoven. It was a strange feeling, at the age of fifty-five, to undergo intensive testing by men so much younger than myself.

I am allowed to fly the Beechcraft Baron, on which I obtained my licence, by myself. In practice, the planes I fly are mostly expected back immediately, so I am generally accompanied by a pilot. Almost all Philips pilots have been instructors either with the Aviation School or the Air Force, so they are allowed to let me fly in the right-hand pilot seat. As a result I have completed more than 2,700 flying hours. Whenever I am on a flight in one of our Mystères I do the take-off and landing, which I still enjoy. I have been flying in all sorts of weather, through thunder storms above the Philippines, or over the deserts of Africa, and have landed in all imaginable conditions. Once I managed to land a Fokker Friendship amidst a snow drift on the frozen landing strip of Rotterdam airport.

I still find it a wonderful sensation to move through the air high above the earth. The view is never the same. You see now a beautiful sunrise over the ocean, now an unforgettable panorama of shining white Alps. At times you catch the last sunrays as you fly high above a darkening globe where the lights of the cities are shining. Or you fly over threatening thunder clouds above the Andes. Or perhaps the desert is below you and above are the billions of twinkling stars. And these sights seem to increase in value when you share them with fellow pilots in the same cockpit. Whenever I look down on the earth, it seems as though the problems which dog us get reduced to their proper perspective, even the problems of Philips!

Chapter 20
Number One on the Bridge

During the final years of Frans Otten's presidency, I had been preparing to take over from him. It happened in March 1961. Now it was my turn to continue a great tradition, as number one on the bridge. I have to admit that at first, when I drove past the factory complexes or travelled for Philips abroad, a sense of pride sometimes gripped me that I was at the head of such an extensive Concern. That feeling soon passed and a realization of great responsibilities, mixed with gratitude, took its place. I carried the heavy burden joyfully, trusting in God. Many difficult decisions had to be made, and our Board of Management—Guépin, Tromp, De Jonge, Casimir, Deenen, Van Dijk, Hartong, Hazeu, Jenneskens, Ooiman and I—did the job together.

This teamwork gave me great satisfaction. I cannot speak for my colleagues, who probably at times thought me opinionated or wondered why I did this and not that. But my first aim was that the Board should work well together without tensions. Of course this can never be fully realized. There have to be clashes of opinion. But as long as these differences do not turn into personal conflicts, they can have a positive effect. All in all, we did not do too badly. When I became President I had the support of my older colleagues, and then as the Board was gradually rejuvenated, the new members entered into the spirit and tradition which were already established.

The effect of our teamwork is demonstrated by the growth of the enterprise. In 1961 our turn-over was 4.9 billion guilders. In 1971 it was 18.1 billion. In the same period our total personnel increased from 226,000 to 367,000. One factor which contributed to this growth was that we were working in expanding sectors. For instance, in television we had succeeded in becoming a supplier for other industries as well, and our ELCOMA division (electronic components and materials) had built up an extensive range. It was also the period of the switch from radio valves to transistors, and the great advance in television tubes.

In producing television tubes after the war we had had to follow

American techniques, but we gradually made important discoveries ourselves. We put a steel band around the tube so that protective glass to safeguard against implosions became unnecessary, and this method has now been generally adopted. We also improved the fluorescent materials which make the colour television image, and were one of the first to produce flatter screens using a newly designed electron 'gun' and deflection coils. New systems were being studied and tried out all the time in our laboratory. Meanwhile we started television factories all over the world as well as factories for television tube glass in Europe, Brazil and Taiwan. We already possessed considerable experience in glass-making—our first glass factory in Eindhoven was started in 1916, and today we manage more than twenty around the world.

Integrated circuits became very important. In these, the functions of hundreds of electronic components are concentrated within an incredibly small space. We knew all about this from the purely scientific point of view, but the Americans were ahead of us in application, due to the tremendous impulse provided by space travel. This demanded miniaturization of electronic systems to an extreme degree, as they had to be very compact and light, with minimal power requirements. We got our know-how from Westinghouse, who were pioneers in this field but who after a time stopped producing integrated circuits. After that we collaborated with Fairchild. At first they were ahead of us in mass production, then later both of us expanded and we began to encroach on each other. So collaboration with them had to end, and we are now working closely with Signetics and enjoy a strong position in many markets.

The development of our plumbicon tube, designed for use in colour TV cameras, can justly be called spectacular. Experiments had taught us that a lead oxide layer in the tubes for these cameras would produce the best results. When the first plumbicon tubes were made, they had a life-span of only a few minutes, and it was eight years before it was possible to make a reliable camera on the basis of this discovery. But I was convinced of their eventual success and encouraged the researchers to continue their work. The plumbicon tube created a revolution in colour TV, improving its quality at once. This tube is now used in almost all colour TV cameras in the world, and it is hard to imagine proper colour television without it. Plumbicon tubes are made in Eindhoven, in the Philips factory in the States and in the MEC factory in Japan.

Our activities were putting a considerable strain on our resources. Philips was undoubtedly strong financially, but gradually the share capital had become small by comparison with our development. In 1962 we needed to enlarge our capital considerably by issuing new stock, so I had to face the capital market right at the beginning of my presidency. We were issuing shares with a nominal value of more than 150 million guilders which, at the time, was a large sum. Fixing the correct price of issue was therefore of great importance. Eventually it was fixed at 475 per cent. At the very last moment pressure was put on us to lower this price, but I kept to the original rate. Things did not entirely go our way, however. The New York Stock Market fell sharply just at the moment of our issue, so the operation turned out to be far from easy, but in the end it was a success. Remarkably, this has been our last big issue. Since then our stock capital has been enlarged only by rights issues. The 1962 issue made possible the financing of several new developments, and we were also able to acquire holdings in various other companies.

Take-Overs and Mergers

One of the principal events with which we were confronted in the post-war era, and more particularly during my presidency, was the creation and growth of the European Economic Community. The gradual elimination of customs barriers enabled us to divide our production more efficiently among the member countries, but this in turn produced problems. Moreover, Europe's economic integration inevitably led to numerous collaborations and mergers. Many people view this development with suspicion, but I believe that only large combinations of European companies will be able to stand their ground against world concerns, and especially American and Japanese companies. It is rare for individual companies to possess sufficient strength for a contest in world markets.

However, no company enjoys being taken over and it is even more painful if it is done by a foreign company. Often the local management are dismissed and their places filled by foreigners. The atmosphere changes and, even if things go well from a business angle, interference and tutelage are never welcome. It is not usually the strongest companies which get into this predicament. A successful company is seldom taken over, for it is so expensive that the capital involved is unlikely to earn adequate returns.

Our establishment in Britain occupied a good position in its own field, but we were trying to get a larger share of the UK market in professional equipment. An opportunity arose when the well-known company, Pye, got into trouble. Pye, established in Cambridge, was a typically British company which had been developed by G. A. Stanley, an enthusiastic pioneer. The company miscalculated when it started large-scale renting of TV sets. This set-back proved so grave that Pye shares plummeted at an alarming rate on the London Stock Exchange. We decided to try to acquire a majority shareholding, a larger transaction than we were accustomed to. My particular aim was to collaborate with Pye in such a way that its British identity would be left untouched, and so give an example for the right way to make cross-border mergers in Europe.

After the transaction, which was successful, we retained as many people from the firm's top management as possible. G. A. Stanley had already retired, and in his seat as managing director we put the Pye man who had been managing their operation in Australia. The Board was kept as much as possible in British hands too. In addition, we nominated two Philips liaison men to see to the right development of the ties with us, and to try to prevent all unnecessary interference from Philips. These two men carried out their difficult assignment excellently, and were considered by the Pye people as their allies. Of course some limited reorganization was necessary. Departments which were not paying their way were combined with Philips activities in Britain, while certain work was transferred from Holland to Cambridge to avoid overlapping. Naturally the Pye research department was given access to the Mullard and Philips research sections.

In the final result, my aim was achieved. Pye is still regarded as a British company, though it could not, of course, avoid the influence of the world concern of which it became a part. The exchange of personnel continues, which is itself a positive thing, as everyone has better promotion chances. Technical and commercial collaboration has been intensified. The same jargon—every company has its own language—has been adopted in both countries. A similar approach to problems is attempted. The most important thing, however, is that people are respected in their own ways of working, and individual aspirations and capacities are taken into account. This is important, particularly for older employees, both skilled and white-collar workers. I am glad, too, that the collaboration between Pye people and our British organization, as well as Philips world-wide, is already good and is gradually becoming closer. Fortunately Pye has within a few years become a paying concern again, and I have great confidence in the future of this fine company.

Another international collaboration is with Felten & Guilleaume, a prominent manufacturer of cables and related equipment in Cologne. Shortly after the war, Loupart and I agreed with Dr. Horatz, general manager of Felten & Guilleaume, to launch *Felten & Guilleaume Fern-*

meldetechnik (tele-communication technology) in Nuremberg. As a member of the Supervisory Board, I attended many meetings in Nuremberg, and the know-how in the field of carrier wave telephony which our Hilversum factory provided has made this new venture flourish.

In long-distance phone connections the cable is as important as the equipment. Collaboration between producers of these two elements is therefore natural. In Holland such collaboration has long existed between Philips and the Netherlands Cable Factories in Delft. In Germany Felten & Guilleaume were making excellent cables, and the opportunity arose to buy half of the Felten & Guilleaume shares held by the Luxembourg steel concern, ARBED. Having thus involved ourselves in cable manufacturing, we enlarged our interest in it in Holland as well. The Netherlands Cable Factories (NKF) were considering closer association with a big electrical engineering concern, as they wanted access to new parts of the world market and to research laboratories with a wider scope than their own. It was relatively easy to come to terms, and the take-over included the important steel plant belonging to them. This plant manufactured, among other things, protective steel strips for cables. Steel manufacturing, however, was not in our line and we would not be able to contribute much to this plant's growth. So we managed to get it linked to the German Thyssen Concern, which eventually took it over. In the case of the NKF, too, we tried to preserve the company's own identity as much as possible. This was important both for its customers, who wanted to deal with the same people, and for the employees.

Not every operation goes equally smoothly. Immediately after the war we had entered into a collaboration with the General Railway Signal Co. in Rochester, USA, for making railway safety devices, as the Dutch Railways wanted to model their safety systems on the American ones. In conjunction with this company we started a new one, only to discover that to do business with an American company trying to expand its sales abroad can be a very difficult proposition. Collaboration always depends on people, and if certain of the staff do not see eye to eye there is little a holding company can do to correct it. So the new company was dissolved. But this railway work did result in our taking over the Alkmaar Machine factory, which still produces for the Dutch Railways. And at Philips Telecommunication Industry in Hilversum we still make relays for the Dutch Railway signal system.

We worked unceasingly for the expansion of our range of electrical products for the consumer market, first small products like shavers and electric irons, and then larger ones. Market research showed that there were opportunities with washing machines and refrigerators, but you cannot conjure up such products out of the air. Here again collaboration seemed the best way.

We bought great quantities of refrigerators from the Italian factory of Ignis, and thereby got to know Giovanni Borghi, a self-made man who, through his manufacturing method and commercial sense, had rapidly built up a remarkable firm, which he ruled as an enlightened dictator. Soon we were selling so many refrigerators that, as his largest customers, we had to make sure of continuous supplies. Henk Hartong concluded a 50-50 deal with Borghi and, in 1972, Ignis was completely integrated into Philips. This company, too, with its thousands of employees, has retained its national character. I always felt the greatest respect for Borghi's qualities as an entrepreneur, and our relationship was genuinely cordial. Sadly, this romantic character died in 1975.

Washing machines and refrigerators have now become mass consumption products, and they will be followed by others.

Social Aspects

In my years as President I devoted much attention to our social policy. For instance, in our overseas establishments I tried to get employees' representation organized, and encouraged work structuring. So there was a continual exchange of experiences between our central personnel division and the local personnel departments, although ultimate responsibility has always remained in the hands of the local management in the country concerned. For in every country customs and practices relevant to labour conditions have their own history. If you discontinue a section of your company in America and have to dismiss people, this is seen in an entirely different light from our way of thinking in Holland. And labour conditions in France are very different from those in Sweden. Before we can hope to get co-ordination in this field a lot of water—and preferably pure water—will have to flow down the Rhine, and an equally abundant flow of words will have to be poured over international conference tables.

Trade unions naturally tend to hold to established rights in their own countries and consequently are in no mood to give anything up. This is one of the principal reasons why international harmonization is so difficult to achieve that one wonders whether it will ever really happen. Until this harmonization has been achieved, it makes no sense for European concerns to negotiate with a group of international trade unions about labour conditions in the different countries. For these and similar reasons it is also impossible to have the works council in the head office participating in decisions about investments and labour conditions in other countries. We have to be cautious, therefore, about extending co-determination by labour representation across national borders.

I had given the representatives of our personnel my fullest attention when, as a member of the Board of Management, I was responsible for personnel affairs. Philips has always played a pioneering role in this field. Since 1923 we have had representative bodies in the various factories. We have also always made the effort to keep our employees informed. Immediately after the war we started annual meetings between the complete Board of Management and the employees' representatives. At these meetings, lasting half a day, we explained the Concern's position with the aid of diagrams and charts, and this carefully prepared information was much appreciated.

After the war Parliament made works councils statutory and defined their rights and duties. At first the Eindhoven Works Council represented all Philips employees in Holland. Then, understandably, the need was felt for greater co-ordination between the works councils in the various factories. Thus the CCO, Central Contact Works Councils, came into being. As President, I presided over the CCO and over the Eindhoven Works Council, and if I was absent the director of our social affairs department took my place.

We used to have an annual 'fireside talk' for our Eindhoven Works Council at Christmas time, in our conference centre near Eindhoven. There I would give a survey of the past year, and anybody could ask any question. I answered these questions as well as I could, and then it was my turn to put questions. This atmosphere of mutual trust produced worthwhile discussions. Then, after a good meal, some talented members would recite poetry, others would make speeches, and we would return home with a better understanding of one another's problems and with a firm resolve to work together in the coming year.

That was the way we used to work in Eindhoven. So I had a rather unsettling experience when I began presiding over the new CCO. I was accustomed to being believed by our people when I told them something. In the CCO, many members representing the factories across the country did not know me nor did I know them. And some of them made it plain that, at times, they did not believe me. In the course of time, however, more confidence was created in that body too. The practice of joint meetings of the Board of Management with the Central Contact Works

222 45 Years With Philips

Councils, at which the company's position and future prospects are explained, has survived to this day. After my retirement I received the Works Council members with their wives one summer afternoon at De Wielewaal, and we had ample opportunity for reminiscing about the 'good old days'.

Apart from these contacts with representatives of our personnel, I also felt the need to meet people at their work. In between conferences and discussions I had to get out and just walk through a factory again. I always find it refreshing to look around places where things are made and where new products can be seen in preparation. It is good for a company president to visit the factory floor often; but I found it steadily more difficult to do this because of an increasing number of management meetings.

In the course of the years one thing became plain to me: the way we dealt with our employees had to change drastically. First, we must give them greater responsibility; secondly, we must regard them more as colleagues and treat them accordingly. I wanted to talk about this not only with our plant managers, but also with departmental chiefs and supervisors, so I arranged with our Social Affairs Department to make a one-hour speech to 1400 men from the various levels of lower and middle management. Initially this suggestion met with a certain amount of cynicism, because people doubted whether one could establish fruitful contact with so large an audience, but I felt it would work, and I think it did. I explained my ideas first to a group of Eindhoven people, and then to the staff of other factories across the country.

It is impossible to assess the effect of such a speech, but I regard it as the manager's task to explain his views on certain subjects to a wider audience than his close associates. I also believe that sometimes I discerned certain developments earlier than some of my colleagues in industry. On this occasion I talked about work structuring, now a common-place topic, and about how a divisional head can involve an employee in fields where he has a special contribution to make.

The European workers of today are quite different from their counterparts forty years ago. Education and information by radio and television make people much maturer and capable, if they will, of carrying greater responsibility. It is irresponsible towards the man himself, as well as towards the company he works for, if we in management do not allow his qualities to be used. We have started on this new approach in many places, but are still at the beginning.

In many places we are trying to adapt our manufacturing methods to people rather than, as formerly, to find the right people for the kind of work to be done. We used to have long assembly lines for radio and television sets, where every worker had only a few manipulations to make. Anyone with a will to work could do these simple jobs, but they were often monotonous and required no special skill.

Our modern way is to involve the production workers and give scope to their inventiveness and other qualities. We break up the assembly line into groups of four to twelve people, who make a whole television set, including the trimming and inspection. They divide the work among themselves, and the supervisor is only called in when something does not work. He is an experienced advisor rather than a driving boss. The people involved feel much more a part of the whole operation. There are regular round-table work discussions, and there they have a chance to make suggestions and to have an active influence on how things are done. The results have been excellent, although the process is not cheap.

I also gave my mind to internal communication. I have noticed that many people in managerial positions love to receive a maximum of information, but are apt to forget to pass it on to colleagues who need it just as much. So a lot of information gets stuck half-way down the company hierarchy. People can never do enough to keep the communication pipeline open to employees below them. I am not advocating unlimited participation in decision-making in all fields. But I do consider it important that information is supplied and that people are open to suggestions from below. Of course the man engaged in the production process knows some details better than his boss, and if the right information is handed down from above, the flow from below upwards follows automatically. On all levels of an organization there is so much talent, knowledge and experience that it would be a waste not to make use of it, and employees always derive satisfaction from being able to offer suggestions.

This cannot be imposed by any system, for it depends on people's inner attitude towards their colleagues. If there is a genuine interest in people, this attitude follows naturally and there is also the right approach to management problems.

This ideal of a continuous flow of communication in two directions does not eliminate the need for additional co-ordination with higher level management in an enterprise like Philips. Since the war, we have held regular meetings with the top management staff. Originally they numbered only a few score, but later this group grew to a hundred and then two hundred. The Board of Management would give extensive information just before making the quarterly result public. Questions were asked and answered. Often a topical subject might get special attention, certain policies might be discussed and aims formulated. These meetings still take place and they are greatly valued. For our Board of Management they are an indispensable means of keeping in touch with the people who jointly lead the Concern. In addition, the Board of Management arranges annual meetings with all administrative heads and chief engineers, today about a thousand people, at which the company's current position is surveyed and the background of current management policies explained.

On top of all this, there is an important group who are also entitled to proper information: the shareholders and the general public. We give this in the first place through our annual report, which gives a bird's eye view of the enterprise. It must be frank, clear and businesslike. It must give enough details to enable readers to judge the company's current position, and it must also look attractive and be impeccably printed. For me the Annual General Meeting of shareholders was an important event, and not one to be dreaded. Philips Annual General Meetings are among the best attended in Holland: sometimes more than two thousand come. I always worked hard on my twenty-minute presidential address, endlessly checking, improving and rewriting. In my last address as President I gave an outline of the history of Philips, and I was impressed myself when I saw how much had been achieved since the war.

Visits

Our Concern receives a continuous flow of visitors of the most diverse kind, every one of them entitled to attention, hospitality and information. When royalty, heads of state and other personalities come to Holland, a visit to Philips is often included in the programme. So we have a special department whose job it is to look after visitors.

If Philips was included in the schedule for a king or a president, I regarded it as a duty to give the visitor a royal reception. So I was frequently rather a pain in the neck to our visitors' department. I would go into minute detail about what had to be seen and who was to give the explanations. When the officials of a department had prepared their programme and felt it was all ready, I might still upset the apple-cart, for I had the habit of taking over during a conducted tour and myself explaining how things worked. But that is the manufacturer's privilege. He believes that what is interesting to him must also interest others. That may or may not be the case. But I do think I give a more interesting explanation than the specialist, because I can better imagine what it feels like to see a thing for the first time. This made me rather notorious. Whenever I was present on a conducted tour, the scenario allowed extra time for my spontaneous digressions.

In 1954 Emperor Haile Selassie, then still surrounded by glory and authority, was to visit Holland. The Foreign Office included Eindhoven in his programme, but this time it was the DAF factories which had been selected. I told them that this was impossible, but they answered, 'We have put Philips in our schedules many times. This time it is DAF's turn.'

I replied, 'Gentlemen, I am only too glad that you should visit DAF, but then you must put in just one minute for Philips. Perhaps people in The Hague do not realize this, but in Ethiopia the name of Philips is universally known, and some realize it is a Dutch firm. If the Emperor doesn't visit us, people in Addis Ababa may conclude that the Dutch Government and Philips are at daggers drawn.' In the end the party spent an hour with us.

When the Shah of Iran visited us, our youngest daughter was asked to hand him the traditional bouquet of flowers, and she was bowled over by his charm. Our visitors' department excelled themselves on this occasion by organizing a serenade by the Philips band, who were standing on the lower laboratory roof at the moment when the Shah was led to the top of one of our taller buildings.

King Baudouin was another visitor, and we arranged for him to meet some of the many Belgians working with us. Several workers come daily by bus from Belgium to Eindhoven and have been doing so for twenty-five to thirty years.

Every diplomat accredited to our country also wants to visit Philips at least once. So we had the idea of inviting groups of diplomats once every two years to come by special train to Eindhoven. We prepare a good and effective programme, and the Philips band gets its chance on these occasions too.

Our list of visitors is very extensive, and we are keen to make the most of their visits. So we try to include time for relaxation and to avoid explanations which are too long or too scientific. To show warmth of heart is for us as important as a display of technical perfection.

Our Relations with Japan

Around 1950 few Dutch foresaw that Japan, despite her defeat, would be playing an important role as an industrial nation in so short a time. However, Loupart did have some inkling of the opportunities, and posted a Philips man there. Today Japan is significant for Philips in many ways, and we attach great value to good relationships with our Japanese partners.

Among our friends there, the remarkable figure of Konosuke Matsushita occupies a prominent place. He is no ordinary manufacturer. His motive as an industrialist is to make the world a better place. He feels that people ought to help one another as much as possible, and his slogan is 'Peace, Happiness and Prosperity'. On his initiative a monthly magazine is published, in Japanese and English, to propagate these ideas. He started before 1940 as a small manufacturer of bicycle lamps, helped by his wife. This small factory became the foundation of Matsushita Electric Industries, now one of Japan's largest concerns. Later, Matsushita started manufacturing light bulbs, then radios; and he then built up the usual range of electrical products. In 1951 he visited the United States, as he wanted to expand his factories with the aid of foreign know-how. In the States he met a Philips man who asked him, 'If you are really on the lookout for a good partner, why not go to Philips in Holland?' So he travelled with some of his people to Eindhoven, where the foundation of a long co-operation was laid.

As a result, after fairly tough negotiations, Matsushita and Philips started a light bulb and radio valve factory in Japan, called MEC (Matsushita Electronic Corporation). The plant is managed by Matsushita and the results, helped by the flow of know-how from Eindhoven to Osaka, have been remarkable. As they acquire more and more experience of their own, it seems to make ours less essential. So each time that contracts have to be renegotiated there are friendly tussles, sometimes resulting in a reduction of the fees for our technology. But then we regularly bring them new products and techniques, and many a glass of sake has been raised to new successes. The collaboration between our two companies is not just one of convenience but of trust and friendship as well.

I have visited Japan myself many times. When I first went, their cars were far from impressive, but now they have conquered a sizeable share of the world market. They also deserve great admiration for their achievements in shipbuilding, optics, electronics and the like. What is the key to their success? They are, of course, a hard-working people and keen to learn. Whenever I talked to Matsushita's employees, I was astonished how eagerly everything was noted down. But this does not fully explain Japan's success.

To me the key lies in an industrial approach which the Japanese have in common with the Americans. Throughout American manufacturing, production and selling, the same systems, on the whole, are applied. The same is true in Japan. But each European country follows its own system, and within each country working methods differ greatly from one concern to the next. Besides this, when the Japanese undertake a project, they first study all stages of it very thoroughly. Then, having arrived at a decision to go ahead, they work with unbelievable speed and strict discipline, without deviating from their agreed scheme. In America, too, when a company president has said, 'This is the way it is to be done,' it is done that way. In other countries things are done very differently, with people constantly changing their minds and submitting counter-proposals. This has advantages, especially if unforeseen difficulties arise, but it does slow things down.

Another advantage of the Japanese system is the way in which their government tries to stimulate industry. But it is above all the Japanese character which spurs things on. In Japan, once a man is employed in a company, he reckons to stay there until his retirement. There is a high degree of company loyalty and hard work is regarded as a virtue, and if a Japanese takes anything on, he will see it through to the end.

Germany and Japan, the poorest of the industrial nations just after the war, are now the richest. Why? Through the capacity and will of those peoples to work hard. We in Holland had the same characteristics just after the war, but today they are less evident. If they disappear altogether, it will mean poverty in the future.

I have gained a more intimate knowledge of Japan on the purely personal plane. I quite often met the then Prime Minister, Nobusuke Kishi, and I know how hard he tried to make amends for the wounds his country had inflicted on her neighbours during the war. And through meeting many Japanese at Moral Re-Armament conferences and also through business contacts, I have found a greater understanding of the Japanese as people, and now have the same warm and frank relationship with many of them as I have with friends in Europe and America.

Computers

Computers have taught us one thing: that a new product, launched under apparently favourable conditions, can bring disappointments. In the early fifties everything looked very promising. A research group in our laboratory had been one of the first in the world to make its own computer, which employed radio valves. We made experiments with it and used it for all sorts of calculations. Our second computer employed transistors, which was a considerable advance. In all directions, the computer offered new opportunities which we made use of—for instance, in artillery guidance systems and in our machine tools. As computer factories, large and small, came into existence everywhere, we managed to win a strong position as a supplier of components. In America we even had a small plant manufacturing by the million small cores for magnetic memories.

By the early sixties we knew a great deal about computers. We had some ourselves, but we still saw our part as being limited to the supplying of components. But then this business began to slacken. IBM no longer placed orders for magnetic cores but started to manufacture them themselves. Other manufacturers did the same. So we saw that, as far as this originally promising area was concerned, we were being shunted on to a dead-end track. What to do? Should we withdraw from the computer market or enter it fully?

We set up a small committee to advise us, which concluded that we should start manufacturing ourselves. The estimates of world needs in computers were so high that it looked attractive to get into the game. Besides, as a big electronic firm we would have to forgo a great deal scientifically if we were not active in this field. And our own company was going to need computers itself to the value of 250 million guilders.

So we decided to start manufacturing. We were late starters, but we hoped our excellent sales organization would help us to catch up. Scientifically we knew a lot. We possessed know-how and experience. We were able to make our own components. And our own needs were so great that we would, for the time being, absorb half of our production ourselves.

Some of our best men began to work on this. Apeldoorn was chosen as the seat for the new operation, as it was centrally located in Holland, especially in relation to our factories which had most to do with computer production. People in Apeldoorn worked day and night, including weekends, with colossal enthusiasm and zest, to design a computer which would best fit the requirements of the market. I am still full of admiration for the way they succeeded in so short a time in making a computer which could stand the test of competition.

We tried for years to get our big computers on to the market. We were at a disadvantage because the Dutch Government was not giving its own national computer industry the priority which the German, British and French governments were giving theirs. In these countries the national computer industries not only bagged large government orders, but also received subsidies of many millions of guilders a year. Our Government limited itself to passing round a recommendation to government agencies encouraging them to include Philips in their list of possibles when looking for a computer. The Posts and Telegraph Department did buy one of our computers for their giro system. We also fought hard to get an order for a very special computer from the Ministry of Waterways, and succeeded.

Even so, we were out of luck. The special sales organization we had created demanded tens of millions of guilders. Prices fell. Each computer we sold cost us hundreds of thousands more guilders than we took. And each time we calculated when the break-even point would be reached, we arrived at a date further in the future. So it became clearer and clearer that international collaboration was inescapable if we wanted to build a viable European computer industry. In 1971 we arrived at an agreement with the French CII (Compagnie Internationale pour l' Informatique) and the German Siemens, which we expected would result in this. Unfortunately this group, Unidata, soon had to be dissolved for reasons which had nothing to do with us. After we had tried in vain to continue with one of the two partners, we were faced with the choice of either continuing on our own or leaving the big computer market altogether. We decided we had to stop . . .

For all of us this was a great disappointment. But I do not want to make too much of it, as in the same period countless industries went bankrupt all over Europe. It was worst for those of our people immediately involved in the project who had staked their future on it. When it had to be discontinued overnight, they were hit more painfully than those of us finally responsible who, of course, also had sleepless nights over it. It is a poor consolation that the computers we delivered are still giving excellent service to their users in many countries.

Fortunately we had previously taken over Siemag, a German company making small office computers. This has become a success and we have captured a sizeable part of that market. We will certainly try to develop further in this direction. In addition, we possess in France a factory which is manufacturing a particularly good small computer for process control.

We are now going full steam ahead with office computers, bank terminals (developed in Sweden), computers for process and traffic control and for defence purposes, as well as computer-controlled telex and telephone exchanges. This is a sizeable field of activities, and I am confident we will be able to make a success of it.

Cassette Recorders

As President I had to turn my attention to so many things that it would not be interesting for the reader nor much fun for me to list them here. So I will limit myself to a few projects which have had special significance for me: the cassette recorder, the hot-air engine, telecommunications and the Evoluon.

The cassette, originally launched under the name of 'pocket-cassette', was a Philips invention. In our Board of Management this project was handled by Hartong, who foresaw that the cassette, along with the recorder developed in our Austrian factory, would become an important product. We were confronted with a fundamental decision: Should we or should we not keep the cassette to ourselves? Hartong advised us not to. He thought that if we kept the cassette in our own hands, even under the most favourable circumstances we would capture only a small part of the world market, as it is very exceptional for a single firm to capture or dominate a world market. But if many manufacturers were permitted to make cassettes and recorders, it would become a world product. This would maximize the demand to such an extent that, even if we supplied only part of the market, we would sell a great many more cassettes and recorders than if we kept the invention to ourselves.

So the decision was taken to leave it open to everyone. The Japanese at once entered the field, and now this small machine is being made according to our system all over the world. But a lot had to happen to make this possible. Our Austrian factory manufactured most of our recorders. In the summer of 1963 the pocket recorder was to be launched in Vienna, with the usual hullabaloo. Hanneman, our manager in Vienna, had arranged everything. A press conference had been called. Invitations had gone out. We were all set. Then there was a sudden phone-call from Max Grundig. He urged us to wait with the demonstration, as he was working on a similar product.

Now Grundig was not only an important competitor, but also a significant buyer of our valves and components. Besides, we hoped he would eventually switch to our system. As we did not want to offend him, we asked our Vienna manager to postpone the demonstration. But he strongly resisted this. He was not bothered by the financial consequences, but he feared he would look ridiculous in the eyes of the press. He also feared that information about the new invention would be prematurely leaked, as all the prospectuses had been printed. So we really were in a predicament. I had to decide. After ample consultation with Hartong, I said on the phone to Vienna, 'Hanneman, I am very sorry. You may call me all the bad names you choose, but the demonstration has got to be postponed. I take full responsibility. Max Grundig isn't ready yet. If we come out now we lose the chance of getting him on our system.'

This postponement enabled Hartong and Le Clercq to come to an agreement with Grundig, who eventually did switch to our cassette system.

When we came out with the cassette recorder, the normal non-professional recorder had already been universally accepted. Before Philips started producing these sets, we carried out a market survey and made an estimate of the numbers of recorders Philips might sell. In fact we sold double that amount. This confirmed again my theory that, whatever market surveys and prognoses may say, you only get to know the market by entering it.

The Hot-Air Engine

I am convinced that the Stirling motor is one of our research projects which the world will talk about for a long time. As I have mentioned earlier, this motor has interested me from the beginning. It causes hardly any pollution, its fuel consumption efficiency is significantly higher than that of the petrol motor, and it is not choosy about the sort of fuel it uses. Theoretically it can even run on salad oil.

In collaboration with Werkspoor (diesel engine specialists) in 1948 we started Thermomotor Ltd., which built an engine of 400 horse-power. Our hope that the Dutch Navy would place an experimental order proved to be vain. So Werkspoor dropped the project, which had already involved a substantial outlay. In the early fifties we had managed to develop a small 200-watt generator. These small generators, incidentally, proved very useful during the 1953 floods in supplying current for the radio transmitters used for communications in the affected areas. However, if we had wanted to improve these to make them adequate for the mass consumption market it would have taken an estimated six million guilders. We did not have that sum available, because television, then newly emerging, was already claiming our financial resources.

In 1958 a new laboratory at General Motors showed interest in the Stirling engine. This led to a long period of experimentation until 1970, when the conservation of the environment began to claim people's attention. General Motors felt it had to do all it could immediately to improve its existing engines, and dropped the long-term Stirling engine product. But it has not yet been proved that the gas turbine offers an alternative, and since steam or electrical cars, with their heavy, dangerous batteries, have not provided any solution, so Ford's has taken on the Stirling project again and decided to collaborate with us. Jointly we have made considerable progress. Stirling engines have been installed in some Ford cars on which tests are being made. We have concluded licence agreements with a Swedish group, and with MAN and DMW in Germany. Quite a few engines have been made already. One has been installed in a modern bus with a DAF chassis, in which a number of trips have been made, with excellent results.

I am confident that this quiet, clean, economical, vibration-free engine will win in the end. But nobody realizes better than I that the road towards universal use of this Stirling engine will be long and costly. It took decades and huge capital investment before the 'Patent Benz Motorcar' of 1885 became a relatively reliable vehicle.

Yet these applications are not very interesting for Philips which, after all, will never be manufacturing cars. The licence fees from car engines will not keep our factories running. The sums paid are—contrary to what many would expect—insignificant in comparison to our enormous research expenses. Normally speaking, we can redeem our research outlay only by manufacturing the products ourselves. The Stirling engine will only benefit Philips if as a result of its improvement for use in cars it becomes a small, practical engine useable for . . . household appliances! It is, for instance, an ideal generator for a caravan. The present generators produce more noise than power. It may also be useable for boats which are at present propelled by roaring motors. All sorts of applications are conceivable, but normally these would emerge from practical experience, preferably in our own field. I could well imagine, for example, that it might be useful as a spare generator which switches on as a power station stops, for there are quite a few areas in the world where this is a normal occurrence. And if things develop that way it is conceivable that these small engines may be sold by the same dealers who now supply our washing machines, refrigerators and other electronic products.

Today this may still seem pure fantasy. But who would have dreamed, thirty years ago, of cassette recorders, colour TV, motorcycles and all those millions of cars in a small country like Holland? I firmly believe in the eventual wide application of this Philips Stirling engine. And this could mean the greatest revolution in the field of traction in our century.

Telecommunications

Another area in which we have done a great deal of work is telecommunications. After Loupart's dreams, Tromp and I went to work to plan our activities in this field. We started with transmission valves for short-wave radio broadcasting, then with amplifiers and Pupin coils for telephony, and carrier wave systems for long distance connections. In the Netherlands we improved the existing telephone exchanges after the war and in other countries we erected carrier wave radio systems. A lot of work was done in telecommunications in France, and the acquisition of Pye opened new opportunities in the United Kingdom.

In Africa and Indonesia, Nico Rodenburg and I constantly tested the ground for future possibilities. After many years as managing director of our telecommunication division he was nominated to our Board of Management and has in 1977 succeeded Henk van Riemsdijk as our President.

At this moment we are the first to offer the most modern computer-governed telephone equipment for switching exchanges all over the world, and I hope our company will succeed in bringing its technique in this field to many countries.

The Evoluon

At the Brussels world exhibition of 1958 Philips gave an unusual show in a striking modern pavilion. We had wanted to let the usually exhausted Expo visitors have an 'experience'. And what we offered was so popular that we registered one and a half million visitors. But after the exhibition it all had to be taken down.

It was hard to establish whether the million guilders this had cost had been well-spent. So I suggested that we should no longer take part in world fairs, but put the money aside. Then we would save enough to erect a permanent exhibition building in Eindhoven which would also be suitable for instruction, demonstrations and lectures. This proposal was accepted and we waited for the proper occasion to erect such a building.

After becoming President, it occurred to me that our 75th anniversary as a company in 1966 would provide such an occasion. Philips was having good years when I made this suggestion, so everyone agreed. But what should the building be like? What architect would design it?

During a luncheon I discussed this with Lo Kalff, who had always looked after our exhibition plans. Le Corbusier had designed our Expo pavilion in Brussels, but we did not feel we should ask him again. We first thought of an international prize contest, but soon dropped the idea. We talked around and around, until I asked Kalff how he would picture such a building. On the back of the menu card he sketched three possibilities: a kind of flying saucer on legs, a cube balancing on one edge and a ball-shaped structure. The flying saucer seemed to me particularly attractive. I asked him how he would conceive of such a building. At once he gave his imagination free rein: it should look airy and light with modern, flowing lines. Suddenly I broke in:

'But why shouldn't you design this building yourself?'

'I have already retired. Do you think I should get involved in such a large project?'

'You'll do a splendid job!'

'But then I'll need a younger architect as assistant.'

'Nothing against that. Have you got anybody in mind?'

'That young men De Bever here in Eindhoven might fit the job.'

Kalff made a sketch which I liked immediately, and the Board of Management were also in agreement, but it would cost an estimated 9 to 10 million guilders. However, as we had meanwhile skipped a few exhibitions, there was something in the savings box. We had our eye on a beautifully situated plot which largely belonged to the municipality. I submitted our sketch plan to the Mayor and asked him what he would think of that kind of building on the plot. He had felt it was the right place for a new head office, but agreed to this new suggestion.

The plan was to be carried out. My colleagues liked the idea, but I was the most enthusiastic about it—I saw it as a crown for our jubilee. And it was a grand gesture when the Eindhoven municipality presented us with the plot we had wanted as their anniversary gift to us.

The plan was for the building to be made of concrete. When calculations were complete, it seemed that the bottom part of the oyster-shaped structure could be of concrete, but that it was too risky for the upper part, which would have to be made of steel. But I would have none of it. Philips would hardly create an up-to-date image by building in the style of the Eiffel Tower. So the technicians started their calculations again and asked the cleverest brains in the building profession for advice. Even so, one day they came to see me again with long faces, for it plainly was not possible. I still insisted we had to find a way out. At long last a solution was found which was as unique as it was beautiful. It became a roof composed of hexagonal panels, which had a skeleton of concrete staves and was light and yet strong.

The question of time began to be urgent. In 1965 I had a talk with the Housing Minister. It was scarcely eighteen months before the jubilee date, and high time to start excavating the foundations. I explained to the Minister that we had to begin as soon as possible, and requested permission to use the building workers allotted to us by the Government for this project. The Minister refused, as he wanted to give priority to housing needs. I suggested that he give me an extra quota of houses to be built. We could start on them at once, as sufficient plans were ready. But in return we would like permission to start on our new building immediately, too. He said,

'Mr. Philips, if you see fit to build that number of extra houses, I'll grant you permission, but I cannot give it before the middle of June.'

'All right, I think I can manage. But then we've got to start excavating now!'

'You can go ahead, because for that you don't need permission, but you must realize that you are taking a great risk.'

'Agreed, Sir, I'll take that risk. But we are in agreement that construction on our building can go ahead if we show satisfactory progress on the houses?'

He agreed. I returned home highly pleased, for the extra housing quota was very welcome too. And, besides, we could start on the foundations. We began work with all the energy we could muster. The construction presented us with many unexpected difficulties, but they were all solved. I followed the various stages closely, as architecture is so great an interest of mine, and on Sundays Sylvia and I would go with our boys and climb the ladders to see what progress we were making.

Gradually a sizeable exhibition space came into being, which then had to be filled. Meanwhile a creative group had been involved in this project. Professor J. F. Schouten conceived the main theme of this permanent exhibition: the removal from men's minds of the fear of the irresistible march of technology, by putting the general public in touch with this technology and its development and by showing what a beneficial influence it has had and is still having on food, health, shelter, communications and education.

To portray this message we engaged James Gardner, an Englishman with a reputation for communicating ideas through images. Then what he had conceived had to be made. Nineteen working teams were formed, each taking on a section, and starting working with tremendous enthusiasm. The name for the exhibition—Evoluon—was the brain-child of Jacques Kleyboer, and derives from words like 'evolution' and 'electron'.

We had to decide what average educational level to aim at, and settled on the standard of a sixteen-year-old high school student, who would know enough about physics to understand the greater part of the exhibition. But people with less education had also to find enough of interest. We agreed that the name of Philips would be hardly in evidence at all. Only on the last of the three ring-shaped floors would we show something about the organization of the Concern.

It became a race with time. On Monday mornings, before the weekly Board of Management meeting, the people responsible for the Evoluon came into my office to discuss where we stood. Time and again I was told that this or that section could not be completed in time. Then I would say, 'Don't worry. Even if it is not quite ready, we'll ask our exhibition department boys to fill up the empty spaces with cardboard.' That was the worst fate these men could imagine. Whatever happened, they would never allow any cardboard to be put in as window dressing. So this little stratagem worked quite well.

The building ended up by being more expensive than we had budgeted for, and, even with about half a million visitors a year, the Evoluon will never become a gold-mine. But the deficit is less than one per cent of our publicity budget and, for that sum, we are getting a lot in return. Furthermore, the Evoluon has a budget of its own for keeping the exhibition up-to-date—an advantage which science exhibitions rarely have.

The inauguration of the Evoluon by Prince Bernhard on 24 September 1966 was a great event, and the fact that my mother was able to attend this occasion gave it additional significance. There she sat in the front row, eighty-eight years old, and when I spoke I could not refrain from asking her to stand up, so that all who had heard so much about Anton Philips, the 'father' of the Concern, could now see its 'mother'. The thunderous applause obviously warmed her heart, and for me it was one of the high points of the occasion.

That same day the beautiful carillon in the tower next to the Evoluon was presented to the company by the personnel. The bells were initiated with the help of the Philips band, which provided people with an unforgettable combination of music and spectacle. It was a fine summer day, and the sun reflected from the shining instruments as the band turned out for the first time in their new scarlet parade uniforms.

The next day, our family received a surprise present. We were told that all our managers outside Holland, 141 in all, had personally given it, and in the afternoon Sylvia and I with all our children stood in front of De Wielewaal to receive it. We had no inkling what it was to be, and our imaginations were running wild. A tractor appeared, towing a cart on which a carillon was mounted, which at once began to chime. It was given to us to be placed near our home. The names of all the donors were on the bells, and we were delighted with this present. Every day we enjoy it all over again, when it plays a tune every hour on the hour. And whenever we walk through the woods, the carillon in the distance has a magical effect.

Sorrow

1966 was a year of joy for Philips, for my wife and for myself. Some years later we were overtaken, in the purely private sphere, by sorrow. In the early morning of 4 January 1969 Frans Otten died, a few days after his 72nd birthday. In April 1968 he had resigned as Chairman of the Supervisory Board, with a truly masterly speech to the Annual General Meeting. Speaking at his grave, I remembered him as a great industrial leader and as my close friend. The real monument to Frans Otten's achievements is, in my view, the many factories and activities at home and abroad which arose under his inspiring leadership.

In December of that same year my mother-in-law, Mrs. Digna Vlielander Hein, passed away. She had been staying with us at De Wielewaal during the last ten years of her life. We loved her very much, as did our children and many others for whom 'Granny Digna' was almost an institution. Her wish that she would be spared a protracted illness was mercifully granted.

Shortly afterwards, my own mother died at the age of 91, on 7 March 1970. She had been a hard-working person motivated by a strong social compassion. Until an advanced age she retained her remarkable will power. As a result of her work for the Red Cross in World War I she was awarded both Dutch and Belgian decorations. On the occasion of the Philips 60th anniversary, the Minister of Labour had decorated her with the cross of a Knight of the Order of the Netherlands Lion, an unusual honour for a woman.

In her last years she still actively corresponded, as a real head of the family, with her numerous nieces and nephews. When she was well on in her eighties she still enjoyed playing a few holes of golf. At least one night a week I would go to her for a chat, because she remained interested in the company's affairs and I could never tell her enough about them. Factory inaugurations, nominations of managers, experiences during business trips—all this continued to interest her.

She never complained about the inconveniences of her advancing years, even when she was unable to walk and had to spend her days in a wheel chair. But it became increasingly hard for her to communicate with us. Fortunately the end came gently and painlessly.

Farewell as President

My fortieth anniversary with Philips was celebrated in January 1971 with a large meeting where the Minister of Economic Affairs decorated me with the Grand Cross of the Order of Orange Nassau. The occasion ended with an impressive parade during which representatives of each country where Philips is at work marched past with their national flags, handing me a present typical of their country. Of course my Carnival association, 'De Emmers', consisting of people from my beloved machine works, were present on this occasion to congratulate their honorary member! Two days afterwards a special variety show was given in the Philips Recreational Centre in which Philips people from all over Europe took part.

After the performance we got another surprise. My wife and I will never forget the moment when a neatly-dressed gentlemen's chorus lined up in the entrance hall, and we suddenly recognized the well-known faces of many of our senior staff. A musical company formed for the occasion under the eminent directorship of a famous Maastricht chorus director, Kockelkoren, were singing songs which had me as their theme. The senior staff, all men loaded with time-consuming and weighty responsibilities, had formed this chorus—rightly described as 'the world's most expensive men's chorus'.

For my wife and me another very memorable event was when we were invited to the Royal Palace, where the Queen decorated me with the Gold Medal for Enterprise and Ingenuity. At the time the only surviving Dutchman awarded this medal was Professor Thijsse, the great pioneer behind the Zuiderzee and Rhine-Maas delta works. My father had been awarded this decoration too, but I had never for a moment thought I would qualify for it, and I was speechless.

On my 70th birthday we had a 'fourth floor' party. This kind of party goes back to the days when the top management had their offices on the fourth floor of our former head office. At times, for instance on the occasion of a personal celebration for a Board of Management member, parties are organized in which everyone working in the four top floors of our new head office building takes part—members of the Board, secretaries, doormen, coffee girls, cleaning women, everyone. Now that it was my turn, I suggested a fancy-dress party. So my Board colleagues staged an entire fashion show, using all the exotic clothes that I had been given on my travels. People dressed as Arab, Indian, or African appeared as texts were read which mercilessly poked fun at me. My own office staff were not a bit kinder than my colleagues. They performed a sketch called 'A day in the life of the President', at which we could not stop laughing.

Then the moment came when I had to pass on the presidency to my successor. I have often observed how otherwise capable captains of industry have completely failed when it has come to picking their successor, thus largely nullifying the good work they themselves may have done. I was able to look forward to this change with peace of mind, because we on the Board of Management were all agreed that Henk van Riemsdijk was the best man to take over. He had acquired a great deal of experience as the managing director of our sales organization in Holland, and as a member of the Presidium had been able to observe the duties of his new office from close quarters. He is a man of sharp analyses, who prefers to take decisions on the basis of a consensus among his associates, and possesses the ability to give leadership without fear or favour. He enjoys excellent health, has a cheerful character, and being a former sportsman —as a football player he was decidedly above the average and he is good at golf and tennis—he has the advantage of a sporting spirit. We knew he was highly respected abroad, both because of his abilities and his character.

My successor did not have an easy start, for in the second half of 1970 we experienced a rather serious business recession. Le Clercq and I went on an extensive trip through the Far East, and on our return, we realized that the autumn was turning out worse than we had expected. In 1971 our company had to adjust to difficult circumstances, which was far from easy for Van Riemsdijk, but he and his team came through triumphantly.

It was rather hard to say goodbye to the International Concern Council. For the last time I was seeing all these good friends as a body together. From now on Henk van Riemsdijk would lead the meetings, and I had no more part to play there; and, having always participated in these interesting discussions since 1954, I felt all the pain of the parting of our ways. The farewell party at the end of the conference was given a special character by an impressive fly past of all the Philips planes.

As far as I am concerned, the ten years of my Presidency sped by. Looking back on them, I realize it must have been a substantial period all the same, for so much happened. During my entire tenure of office I enjoyed the inestimable boon of good health. Thanks to that I was able both to travel a good deal and still look after my responsibilities in Eindhoven. Above all I was grateful for the daily teamwork with my friends on the Board of Management. To say goodbye to them was hardest of all, and I am not ashamed to say that I was deeply moved when I shook hands with them, one by one. My successor Van Riemsdijk was all set to take over with a splendid team—men like Le Clercq, Van der Putten, Noordhof, Casimir, Breek, Pannenborg, Wijns and Van Mourik. I was able to hand over to them with the fullest confidence now that I was leaving my post as number one on the bridge.

Chapter 21

Outside Philips

When it came to responsibilities outside Philips, I took a different line from my father. Philips absorbed him almost entirely. He did start many initiatives in Eindhoven not strictly related to the company, including the Eindhoven Telephone Company, the Philips Co-operative, the schools and the housing associations. But he usually avoided wider activities, such as joining the executives of employers' associations. I on the other hand, took an active interest in many aspects of industrial life.

After World War II, when the mines were a key to our economic recovery, I became a member of the Coal Board. The miners rated highly in those years. They were well trained and well paid, and the men on the coal face felt they were pillars of the national economy. The mines were operating at full capacity. I regarded as quite unique the teamwork on the coal face, and both the social and the technical aspects used to fascinate me.

The Coal Board advised the Government about fuel supplies in general. Besides coal extraction and the coke plant, the nitrogen compound plant took an increasingly important place. And after the war extraction of oil from our own ground also increased. Then there were big natural gas discoveries in 1960, when I had already resigned. Nowadays the State Mines Company (DSM) has developed into a powerful chemical concern, but its basic materials still come from Mother Earth.

Employers' Associations

After the war the employers' federations had to be overhauled. The Woltersom Organization created by the Germans had, of course, to be scrapped, but something had to take its place.

Two new organizations were created—and I joined the executives of both. This brought me in contact with the Foundation of Labour, in which the presidents of the employers' federations and of the trade unions used to meet every Friday to discuss social problems and to advise the Government about them. In the Foundation there was a basis of trust which enabled us to discuss things very frankly. The needs of our impoverished country and people were given top priority by everyone, so it was usually not too difficult to arrive at agreement. At a conference in Caux the president of the Socialist Trades Union Congress, Evert Kupers, gave high praise to the co-operation in this Foundation.

Advisory Council for Military Production

In the early fifties, when Europe became aware of the threat from the East, Holland began to spend more on defence. Dutch industries, hoping to play a part in this, felt a need for regular contact with the purchasing departments of our armed forces, and the Ministers of Economic Affairs and Defence formed an Advisory Council for Military Production. The chairman of the Council was a man from industry, and further representatives of the Ministries of Defence, Economic Affairs and Foreign Affairs, the latter in connection with NATO, became members. In addition, the directors of the logistics and suppliers departments of the Army, Navy and Air Force, the chairman of the Council for Military Supplies, the presidents of the various Trades Union Congresses and representatives of industry were on the Council. I was a member for ten years, during later years as chairman.

In the beginning it was not easy to win each other's confidence. The primary aim of the armed forces supply departments was to obtain good stuff as cheaply and quickly as possible. As soon as they had achieved this, their work was done. They were not interested in issues like continuity of production which were so important for the industries—although the Navy was an exception since it had to work with shipyards on a long-term basis. Industry's attitude was not always consistent either. In slack times manufacturers were keen to get defence orders, but as soon as their capacity was fully employed their eagerness waned. After some time we managed to understand each other's point of view better. I remained on this Council until my travels began to claim more and more of my time.

Supervisory Board of Ford Netherlands

I was frequently invited to join the boards of different companies. In our Board of Management we had a general rule to stay away from that kind of outside activity, but when in 1948 Henry Ford II asked me whether I would become a member of the Board of Ford Netherlands, I submitted this to our own Board. Ford, after all, was a rather special case.

Now many of the Philips establishments abroad need outside Board members, and for that office we look for capable and influential people in the country concerned. So there was point in one of our own top management being a member of the local board of another world concern. He might discover whether he was able to make a worthwhile contribution, whether his opinion counted at all and what it felt like if this was not the case—something apt to happen with the members of our own overseas boards, as some of them had no industrial background and the local management would consult them only rarely. Besides, I was quite interested in car manufacturing. So we decided that I should accept the Ford invitation.

I think that I was able to exercise some influence. I soon discovered that the Dutch Ford organization was a mere extension of their British establishment, which owned most of the stock. So, if we made constructive suggestions, they got stuck somewhere on the way. As I frequently visited America and was in personal contact with Henry Ford there, I managed to get Amsterdam switched to the jurisdiction of the Detroit head office. After this, things moved noticeably faster. My visits to Detroit were always highly interesting. There I familiarized myself with head office thinking, and was able to tell them how we looked at things in Amsterdam. In this case, too, my increasing Philips duties finally forced me to resign, but my personal contact with Dearborn has since been renewed, through the collaboration with Ford over the Stirling engine.

Interaction with Education

Education has always been a genuine interest of mine. After the war we had a long struggle to get a technical university erected in our region, and spent a lot of time on numerous conferences, committees and discussions with government departments and parliamentary bodies. Now, however, we have a first-rate modern Technical University with more than four thousand students. Dr. Holst, who chaired the government committee, and Dr. Henk Dorgelo, its first Chancellor, did a remarkable job in creating it. This Technical University fortunately did not become an extension of Philips, although there is a natural interaction between an institution which trains engineers and a concern which needs them.

I have often remarked that if schools of technology produce the engineers, we will supply them with professors. As early as the 1930s people from our physics and other laboratories were becoming professors. This meant an initial loss for Philips, but was a natural contribution to higher education from which we hoped to reap fruits later. For example, one of our research aces, Rathenau, came to me after the war and said that he had been asked to become a professor in Amsterdam. I replied, 'My dear Rathenau, we can't really spare you, but should we prevent Amsterdam from getting a good professor?' He did go to Amsterdam, but later returned and became director of our physics laboratory. And he is not the only one who found his way back into industry.

There are reasons for this. A professor who has come from industry may be very fresh in relation to his subject, but if he does a serious job as a professor, which takes a lot of time and effort, it is hard to stay in living contact with practical reality. Moreover, our scientific men were more spoiled than they realized. If they needed equipment and assistance for research, it would usually be provided at once. As long as they remained within the budget, there was never too much talk about expenses. In scientific education it is different. There every request has to travel a lengthy administrative road before it is fulfilled.

It seems to me useful from the educational viewpoint that a professor should remain in contact with an industry, possibly in an advisory capacity. And for industry it is beneficial to tackle its problems in a scientific way.

I have also been concerned with the training of technical skills for practical life, not only through the Trades School but also through the medium-range technical school in our city, for which the first preparations were made, in 1939, on my father's initiative. In 1940 it was still possible to begin construction. So this school got off the ground during the war, and I became Chairman of the Board of Trustees. When the 1942 bombardment of Eindhoven damaged the building, we succeeded in spreading its different sections over a number of other buildings. After the war this school developed rapidly and today it is an institution for higher professional training in which more than 2,500 students are enrolled, of whom 2,100 follow day courses and 400 night courses.

So far I have been writing about educational activities in Holland. But at one point I got myself involved in education in, of all places, Ethiopia! And this was not scientific education but teaching people the three Rs.

In 1963 I was visiting Ethiopia and met the Minister of Education. I told him about the results which had been achieved in a Latin American country in teaching people to read and write by radio. The Minister said he could not believe this. I answered,

'Excellency, if anyone had told me this some time back, I would not have believed it either. But within two months I will send you a man who knows all about it. He will be able to discuss everything with your educational experts.'

He liked the idea, and after my return to Eindhoven I tried to find a man who was knowledgeable about this. But he did not seem to exist! So we sent a keen man to Latin America to find out everything about these radio courses. After his return, he wrote a good report and then we sent him to Ethiopia. It was only a month later than I had promised, which was not too late in Ethiopian eyes.

He had to overcome a great difficulty—that he naturally did not know the Amharic language. Luckily, he obtained the co-operation of two teachers who were fluent in English, and with these men he created the course. The pupils were to gather in a room or small local hall in their village to listen to the radio. There was a primer which dovetailed with the radio lessons. Then a new difficulty arose. These people were unable to look. They had never possessed a book, never read a newspaper, never learned how to look at a picture, a thing our children learn while playing. So they had to get used to looking at pictures, by first seeing simple drawings of, for instance, a peasant and a ploughing ox. Afterwards they would continue by learning letters. The letter A is the same everywhere: it was explained as a gateway closed by a cross-beam. Then the Amharic alphabet, which contains over 120 letters, followed.

After a year I visited Ethiopia again, and, with the Minister of Education, attended the second lesson of the course. The courses were given in three age groups—children of 8 to 12, of 13 to 18, and older. They were held in a school, where, in order to demonstrate the radio method, the teacher sat in a room with a microphone, while the pupils listened in another room over a loudspeaker. Besides the primer, everyone had a pencil and a copy book, which were provided by a man supervising the lessons. In all the villages where the radio course was used this pattern was followed.

The plan, as I later learned, ended in failure. The boys preferred to go and play football. And among the older ones many could already read and write a bit, and they had enrolled in the course hoping they would get a better job, which did not prove a sufficient motivation. So the students gave up.

The authorities then tried to think up something which would compel people to follow the courses. Eventually they arrived at a simple solution: the courses were to be given in the prisons! To take the course, the prisoners had to go to the class room, and this they liked. When they were released, they were able to read and write. So that plan did work. UNESCO later took over the project from us.

My wife has also been deeply interested in education. After the war she felt impelled to start a secondary girls' school on the basis of Christian principles but not tied to any particular denomination. This school came into being within a year, and as president of the governing body, she has for twenty-five years contributed a great deal to it.

Airports

In the sixties I was asked to become the chairman of a committee set up by the Chambers of Commerce of Brabant to go into the question of a possible second national airport in the southern part of the Netherlands. It was obviously of great importance to pick the right spot and we soon came to the conclusion that, if the new airport was to make sense, we had to examine the need for air transport in the entire Rhine, Maas and Scheldt delta area including the Liège region, the Ruhr, Brabant, Flanders, Zeeland and the urban agglomeration in the triangle of Rotterdam, The Hague and Amsterdam.

We are satisfied that the airport will have to be sited on the line between Rotterdam and Antwerp, and that we must tackle the problem with the Belgians, our neighbours to the South. It is now 1977. When will the decision be made? Even if the airport is only to materialize in ten years' time, it is essential to decide where it should be now. Otherwise, all the possible sites will get built up in the meantime.

These discussions showed me very clearly that the siting of airports is often approached too much from the environmental viewpoint, while the economic factor is ignored. You find many town-planning and regional planning experts on most airport committees, but few representatives of airlines or of groups requiring transport, like travel agencies, the big companies whose staff often have to fly, and air transport brokers. This is odd. For, in everyday life, anyone planning to open a shop tries first of all to find the place where he can expect most customers.

A related issue, which has demanded a lot of time and sometimes made me angry, is the struggle to obtain a limited civil airport for Eindhoven. At present we have a military air base which civil aviation is allowed to use, but the one runway in operation points to the heart of Woensel, the most populous Eindhoven township. This runway will have to be moved, and the way this is to be done is subject to a tug of war between various ecology champions—who would prefer to have the airfield eliminated altogether—and those of us who regard a good air connection as indispensable for the South-East Brabant industrial region. I hope that the final decision will soon be made.

ADELA

I count my work with ADELA—the Atlantic Development Company for Latin America—an important international commitment. The purpose of this association is to assist the social and economic development of Latin America by improving the industrial climate for free enterprise there. We do this by giving technological and financial help and by taking minority interests in existing companies as well as in new projects.

ADELA was started in 1964. Among the founding members were the provides help for a textile factory. In Ecuador a bottle manufacturing plant has been started with ADELA assistance. In Costa Rica it is a cement factory. In Nicaragua a paint factory. And I could continue the list for a long time. ADELA is also in a position to raise sizeable loans on the capital market, enabling it to provide credit on favourable terms to new ventures in the difficult initial stages.

ADELA was started in 1964. Among the founding members was the Swedish banker Dr. Marcus Wallenberg, whom I have already mentioned, George Moore, at the time President of the First National City Bank of New York, and Emilio G. Collado of the Exxon Corporation. Today ADELA has about 200 shareholders, among them many world concerns and big banks. The chairman is elected for a three-year term and is alternately an American and a European. When in 1971 the time came for the American banker, Howard Petersen, to hand over the chairmanship to a European, I was asked to succeed him. I had by then retired as President of Philips, so I gladly accepted.

As I had travelled a great deal in Latin America, I knew something about the feel of that vast continent and also about its potentialities. The President of ADELA, Dr. Ernst Keller, a Swiss who had lived seventeen years in Peru, was an exceptionally energetic person who gave himself day and night with amazing enthusiasm, sometimes even at the peril of his health. He was the kind of man I liked to work with.

We were not handing our charity, but were working to make our ventures pay. We wanted to demonstrate that providing aid and investing money in projects involving risks could, in the long run, produce positive results. This meant we had to keep a watchful eye on our costs. As an industrialist I have been more ready to wait for returns than those of my colleagues who are bankers. All the same we have managed to pay some dividends.

I also felt a special interest in the social advancement of these countries. And one added reason which made me enjoy this job was that, if I visited a country, it was natural that I should also make contact with the Philips establishments. This enabled me to see the progress made in projects started during my presidency.

After completing my three-year term as Chairman of ADELA, I stayed on as a board member. This involvement has given me a great deal of satisfaction, and has taught me that many leading industrialists and bankers look beyond the immediate interests of their enterprises and countries, and think of the world as a whole. I have observed the same quality in others not connected with ADELA, men like G. A. Wagner, who was President of Royal Dutch Shell, René Boël of the Belgian Solvay Concern, and David Rockefeller of the Chase Manhattan Bank, who have all travelled extensively throughout the world, as well as Albert Plesman of KLM, and Robert Carmichael of the French jute industry.

Looking back, I realize how valuable it has been for me to be allowed to work with so many capable people. And what a pity it is that overloaded schedules leave so little chance to continue the friendships after the immediate reason for association has come to an end!

With President Chiang Kai-shek in Taiwan.

My wife and I visiting Hirozo Tanimura, executive Vice-President of the Matsushita Concern, Osaka.

Sitting with Konosuke Matsushita, founder and President of the Matsushita Electric Industrial Company Ltd., in front of a monument portraying pioneers in electro-technology, including my father.

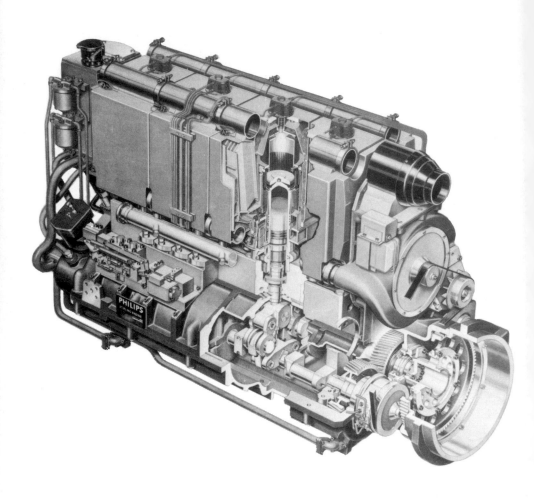

A model of one of the ten pilot engines built by Philips in 1970 using the Stirling principle.

Dr. Roelof Kruisinga, then Dutch Under-Minister of Social Affairs and National Health, inspected the first DAF bus equipped with this Stirling engine, which does not produce pollution or noise.

L. G. Kalff's initial sketch during our first talk about a permanent exhibition building.

The Evoluon, the realization of those first thoughts, three years afterwards at the 75th anniversary of Philips (1966).

Inside the Evoluon. Note the unique roof construction, consisting of segments.

Prince Bernhard questions young researchers at the opening of a laboratory specially for their use (November 1969).

With this combination of radio receiver, rectifier and loudspeaker Philips, in 1926, moved into the Dutch market, an event which led to the establishment of radio factories all over the world.

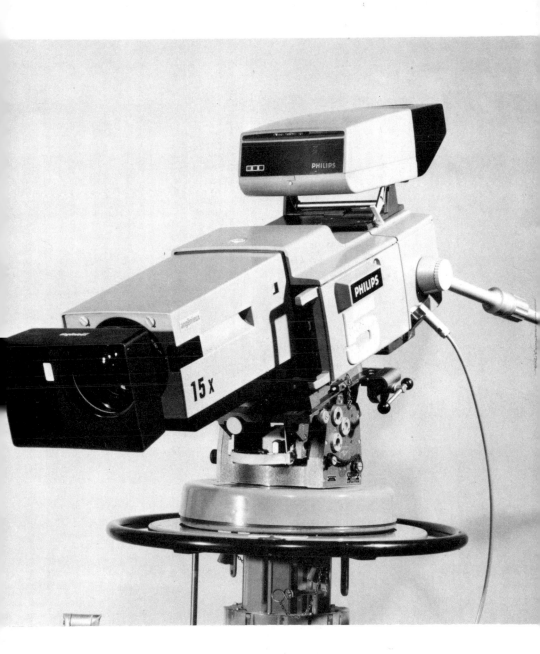

The Philips TV camera equipped with the plumbicon tube. This tube, which brought a great improvement to colour television, is now used all over the world.

Aerial view of our recently opened Telecommunication and Light Factory in Recife (1970). In 1976 this factory was three times larger.

Sylvia, our eldest son Anton, and I arriving in Recife in Brazil, 1970.

The carillon given to us by the managers of all Philips factories on the occasion of the 75th Philips anniversary.

'Earrebarre' (Stork), the gift of the Philips personnel in Holland, on my 40th anniversary of joining Philips.

On 2 February 1967, on the occasion of the 550th anniversary of the founding of Louvain University, the Vice-Chancellor, Professor P. de Somer, conferred twelve honorary degrees. From right to left: Prof. R. L. Mössbauer of Munich; Dr. A. H. Boerma, former Director-General of the FAO; Prof. T. A. Lambo, University of Ibadan, Nigeria, and Assistant Director-General of the WHO; the Vice-Chancellor; and Dr. F. J. Philips.

Chapter 22

Experience and Vision

Looking back on my forty-five years in Philips, my over-riding feeling is deep gratitude. It has been a matchless privilege to be allowed to work and provide leadership in such a dynamic concern during such a dynamic period. As the boss's son, my route did seem to be mapped out in advance; but the fact that I have managed to travel it fills me with thankfulness.

As I draw up a balance at the end of these memoirs—and committing it all to paper has turned out to be more difficult than I had anticipated— I think of the vast number of people with whom I have worked. And this, perhaps, is the greatest source of the pleasure which I have found in my work. Of these people I shall mention only those who have helped me personally in the last years: Han Planje, Theo Hermens, Henk van Essen, Willem van Stratum, Teun de Leeuw, Rin de Groot and Bob Verheeke; and Corrie, Gerda, Ellen, Clari, Jo and Thea. They have worked very hard, and often on matters of a confidential nature.

It is my experience that in the second generation the link between the founder's family and the people in the company can still have a special significance. My parents had passed on to me a love for the company, but above all their intense concern for the people working in it. And as I had from childhood heard important company problems discussed, and met the people in responsible positions almost from the start of my life, I received a lot of information and insight which helped to train my mind. In that respect sons of families which have borne responsibilities are privileged in having a heritage, even if they may often not be aware of it. In later years this became increasingly clear to me.

In other continents, certainly in Latin America, it is very common for sons to succeed fathers in a business, but in Europe it has become less usual, especially in large companies. So much is demanded from the leaders of these companies that it is almost a coincidence if descendants of a firm's founder reach the top. Yet such a 'dynastic' succession has its advantages. To have the familiar name at the top can impart a sense of stability, particularly in an enterprise which has establishments all over the world. In such a company, ties develop between the managers in the outposts and the top men in the head office and if a family tradition plays a part in this, it enhances the feeling of security. The people in distant lands can then say to themselves, 'There is somebody in head office who will never leave us in the lurch to improve his position elsewhere.' Moreover, the man bearing the concern's name enjoys easy access everywhere at home and abroad. My father made use of this asset, and I followed his example.

Such a position inevitably means added responsibilities. At home and abroad people expect a high standard of performance. Physical endurance is also demanded, and that in turn requires a rather strict discipline. I gave up smoking many years ago, and I am in the habit of refusing all cocktails and spirits. I believe that this has been one of the reasons I have been able to work efficiently until the end, and perhaps this example may also have been helpful to younger people in the company, who often have to work under tremendous stress.

I have always highly valued the personal ties with our people. For about twelve years I have driven the same good old Bentley, which can easily be identified. Whenever I overtake one of those big Philips trucks, I honk my horn and wave my hand. The sweep of the driver's arm in reply gives me a brief contact. Similarly I have passing contacts when going through our factories. I like to be there when someone explains the functioning of a piece of equipment or a machine, and often glances of understanding pass between us. These may be small gestures, but they count for me and perhaps for the other person as well.

Readers may wonder what the third generation of the founding Philips family is up to. Do they also have growing ties with the company? I will not conceal my delight that my father's grandsons, among my own three sons, are enthusiastically working in the company. Where they eventually end up depends on themselves. But I dare say that I have noticed that they are more interested in the nature of their job than in the height of their positions. And that is a good mentality to have!

Chairman of the Supervisory Board

Upon my retirement as President I was nominated Chairman of the Supervisory Board, especially charged with keeping in regular touch with the management of the company. This changed my relationship with the Concern. And it was all the more necessary to find the correct conception of the duties of this new office because, just at the time of my nomination, new ideas arose on the function of this Supervisory Board, and the legal position was altered. This Board had been seen merely as the guardian of the shareholders' interests. The new law, however, entrusted it with more duties, because ideas about the position of industrial enterprises in society were changing. According to these ideas, the aim of an enterprise should no longer be exclusively to produce goods and make a profit. But, as I have already told, these new notions had become common currency in Philips much earlier, so after I had become Chairman I was faced with social changes, including modifications in the Companies Act, which gave concrete form to our own ideas.

In particular the relation between Supervisory Boards and Works Councils was given a different character. Supervisory Board members are no longer nominated by the shareholders, but are co-opted after offering a chance to the Works Council and shareholders to recommend or object. This has required the Supervisory Board to create a small committee of its members for consultation with the Works Council. I tried to let this new co-operation flourish, and I believe that we have made considerable progress. The members of our Central Works Council have a great sense of responsibility, and are also very critical, which is their right. And on both sides, there is the desire to solve problems in a constructive manner.

The Supervisory Board has to see that the Board of Management acts correctly, but the latter manages the enterprise and carries the responsibility. I have to take this basic rule into account. But as I have lived all my life in Philips, am living in Eindhoven and have an office in our headquarters building, I am still deeply interested in all that happens in the company. Many problems naturally continue to have my fullest attention. If I notice something, I pass it on to the member of the Board of Management concerned and then it is up to him if he wants to do something about it. And as for my journeys abroad, people would be offended if I did not look in on our establishments there.

Questions About the Future

I am often asked, 'What about the future? Can Philips continue to expand?'

Nobody can give a definite answer to that question. Had someone asked me in 1948, when we had a turn-over of 650 million guilders, whether we would ever achieve a 30-billion turn-over, I would probably have said, 'I

don't know!' And if someone wanted to know now whether we were going
to grow to 100 billion, I would have to say the same thing, because the
future poses many questions, especially for large enterprises.

The first question is whether the area of activity provides enough scope
for growth. Does the range of products now being manufactured offer
adequate opportunities for larger sales? Can the new products being
planned be made at reasonable cost, or are the investments so enormous
as to be impractical? If growth is economically feasible, can the existing
organization cope? Can the management cope?

The answer to the last question, of course, depends on people. Are the
leaders capable of inspiring others to do a job with zest? Do they want to
delegate responsibility and are they able to do so? And here character is
more important than brains, although brains have to be present in
sufficient quantity as well.

Then there is another important question: Will the community, the
parliament, public opinion, permit the unlimited growth of companies?
If the big companies carry on in the right way and stick to some 'basic
considerations', so that they act with the necessary responsibility towards
society, I believe things may be all right. But if managements indulge in
stupid or wrong actions, it will become difficult.

As regards the range of our products, I view Philips' future with
optimism. Of course everything depends on the measure to which personal
prosperity increases, and with it an enhanced demand for the products
we make. In this context I am thinking first of electronic and electric
household articles, but equally, for instance, of hospitals. These are increasing in number all over the world, and if that increase continues at a
rapid pace we will have our hands full. Traffic will also keep us occupied.
If the developing areas attain the same intensive levels of car use as the
West, we still have thousands of kilometres of road lighting ahead of us
and, in addition, automatic traffic controls. Air communications will increase and airports will be improved, certainly in developing countries
which have to cope with such enormous distances that road transport
hardly suffices.

Other means of communication, such as television straight from satel-
lites to people's homes, and telephony from person to person, will also be
in growing demand. Electronic circuits, which are continually being
reduced in size, will play an ever more important part in measuring and
controlling pollution, for instance, as well as in the Stirling engine. We
will also find work in unexpected areas. Road transport, in Holland at any
rate, requires bridges. This involves the use of welding rods, which in

turn need to be checked by X-ray equipment. In the same way, there are these days thousands of kilometres of pipe-line which need to be welded.

Then there is the important question of the people who have to do the job. Up till now our people have mostly come from Europe and the United States, but we will increasingly have to look for them in other countries, wherever people want to work and to accept responsibility. The Dutch contribution in Philips will continue to get priority. The Dutch have always been hard-working people. They like to delve deeply into problems, and have for centuries produced businessmen who were not afraid of venturing out. It may appear now that this spirit is waning, but we still manage to find good men willing to do a pioneer's job even in places with few comforts. And of course, their wives go along with them. I have the highest regard for these women who manage under difficult circumstances in distant lands and who, in addition, exert themselves to do something for the people among whom they live. In that respect I have the fullest confidence in Philips' future.

People often fail to see the part which multi-national enterprises like Philips have to play in bringing prosperity to countries outside Europe, and in increasing world trade. But once developing countries have gained political independence, the next step is to become economically less dependent upon help from outside, and that means developing their industries. They need factories to make the products which the population want and which also, if possible, are exportable. They need market research, technical aid to design factories and plan production, and the machines and tools to make the products. It is essential that the whole set-up be self-sufficient, so that it can continue to function and not become bankrupt after a few years. It is also important that continued technical assistance be guaranteed, so that new techniques and designs for improved products flow in as time goes on.

Usually only big multi-national companies can supply all these elements. They can risk the capital necessary, for there will generally be losses in the first years and local capital will not be available. They can also provide men with experience in setting up new enterprises and who know how to work in far away countries, often under primitive conditions.

Philips has set up a pilot plant in Utrecht where we adapt production to the circumstances in developing countries. Instead of using the most sophisticated and expensive machines and the minimum of man power, we study how we can make parts for radios or TV sets, for example, in the simplest way with small hand presses and cheap tools, thus giving work to more people. Then we train men from the country itself to work with this equipment.

This way of adapting manufacturing methods to local needs is successful and our Utrecht plant has, for more than a decade, initiated many activities all over the world. The experience gained in one country can be used in others. It will take a lot of work, for generations to come, to meet the needs of the Third World, and enterprises like Philips have an important part to play.

A Surprise

In the autumn of 1975 a Philips plane fetched me from London and, as usual, I sat in the right-hand pilot's seat. In the cabin my wife was looking through some mail which had been brought from Eindhoven. She handed me a letter from the University of Louvain, and suspecting nothing, I began to read it. The Dean of the Faculty of Applied Sciences, Professor P. de Meester, wrote that on the occasion of the 550th anniversary of the Catholic University of Louvain, I would be proposed, with other candidates, for an honorary doctor's degree. I had never expected to be accorded such an honour.

Four months later I took part in a unique ceremony. A long procession of professors, preceded by four heralds, went on foot through the streets of the ancient centre of Louvain to St. Peter's Church for a solemn mass, sung by a student choir. The Vice-Chancellors of all universities older than Louvain had been invited, as well as those of all Dutch universities. In their many-coloured gowns, they formed a picturesque company. Then in the great hall of the university the twelve *doctores honoris causa* were handed their diplomas.

This elegant academic occasion was attended by friends from the Board of Management and by most of my children. I was continuing a family tradition, for like my uncle and my father I could now be called 'Dr.' Philips. The citation said that Mr. F. J. Philips had been proposed as *doctor honoris causa*:

> — 'because of the way in which
> he had fully carried out the
> responsibilities of an engineer
> and, as engineer-manager, had
> developed and led a world concern;
> — because of his social concern

and his effective initiation,
support and encouragement of
university and tertiary education
and of technical-scientific
research in the broadest sense;
because his name is a symbol for
the many inventions by engineers
all over the world.'

This experience was out of the ordinary for a non-Catholic Dutch industrialist. I had earlier, too, been honoured by being made a Commander of the Papal Order of St. Gregory the Great, but the greatest privilege has been to be received with my wife in private audience by each of the last three Popes: Pius XII, John XXIII and Paul VI.

My Vision

What is, or rather what should be, an industrialist's purpose? Before I answer that question, let me state my basic attitude towards life.

I firmly believe that a man can change. That does not mean that he becomes a superman or a saint. But after facing where he has been wrong, he can find an entirely new motive. Of course he needs help to experience such an 'inner revolution'. And that help is available. If we are ready to make the first move, God will do the rest.

As I have tried to make clear throughout this book, this conviction of mine is not just a theory. It is an experience. If the fact that when man listens, God speaks, and when he obeys, God acts, were not a very concrete experience in my life, I do not think I would have been able to live life the way I have been allowed to live it.

Further, I am convinced that the conflicts in the world are clashes between people rather than between organizations. In our age there is a lot of talk about structures. There are people who believe that as soon as you have designed the right structure, everything will be fine. My belief is that, however important organizations and structures may be, man is the decisive factor. The best structures and organizations will only work to the extent that men have the right attitudes.

To me, therefore, the postwar development is the story of men rather than of the onward march of impersonal historical forces—men like Schuman, Adenauer, De Gasperi, De Gaulle, Churchill, Stalin, Mao,

Eisenhower, Sadat and Schmidt. And the decisive influence of individuals operates not only in politics, but also in industry. The motives which drive men determine the future of countries and organizations.

I believe—and this again is based on my own day to day experiences—that the Creator of the world has a plan. This plan means that there is enough in the world for all people, and everyone can have a part in carrying it out.

In that plan industry has its place. Therefore people engaged in it must be able to work in teamwork and without endless tensions. This is possible, and I can cite countless examples. But it is also necessary that we agree on industry's purpose in the world. I believe it to be a duty to serve. Industry, like individuals and organizations, is meant to serve the community of which it is a part.

For years I felt the need to spell out this task in more specific terms. In 1969 I sat around a table with some of our social affairs people, including Piet Dronkers, the head of the department, and we drafted a definition. Then at a conference in Caux, we sought the opinion of some British trade union men about what we had formulated. For even if we in management think we have produced a good document, it is worthless if men from the labour side think it nonsense. During the International Industrial Conference at San Francisco in September 1970 I submitted these ideas to 500 leading personalities of world industry, and in 1972, I distributed this document, then called 'Basic Considerations', on a large scale. It is included as an appendix to this book.

In 1975 the Philips Board of Management formulated its guide-lines of the company's aims, which bear great resemblance to the original thoughts which we had put on paper in 1969. In that final version, one element had to be stressed more than in the first draft: the element of ecology and the environment, which had begun to occupy a much more central place in public discussion.

One of the motives behind drafting the document was to make a contribution towards better co-operation between industry and trade unions, management and labour. Co-determination in industry has become a burning issue in many Western countries. The present debate about this issue could lead to a fruitless struggle for control, with devastating results.

I feel that we in management need to discard our defensive attitude. We can moan and gripe about what is wrong in general, but there is one place where we *can* do something: in our own companies. There we can create the right consultation, the right teamwork, the right atmosphere. If we set our own house in order, that is bound to have its effect.

I believe participation is not so much a matter of structures as of attitudes. We can start where we are. Do we include people in our own decisions? Participation has to start from the top, but it also has to percolate right through from top to bottom. And we need to work hard to make this a reality. For what good does it do to brandish slogans about co-partnership while our workers are frustrated by foremen and supervisors still saying, 'Your boss may be wrong, but he is still your boss!'?

For generations it was believed that a man in authority should never show his weaker side and should never admit being wrong. But if we want a new, participatory atmosphere in our companies, this has got to change at every level. And it takes a lot for any man in a position of authority to say, 'This is what has to be done. Can we discuss how to go about it?' rather than, 'This is what has to be done, and this is the way you've got to do it!' It is not easy to ask people under your command for their advice, but it does create a new climate.

Participation without responsibility, however, leads to an unbearable waste of words and time. If people ask me how far co-partnership should go, my answer is: to the limits of the responsibility which people are ready to take and are capable of taking. It is essential that everybody should be given maximum responsibility at the place where he works. And in order to be responsible, he must be given as much information as possible. So regular consultation should be a universal practice. The ultimate decisions, however, must be left in the hands of management. If mistakes are made, it is then clear who is to blame; and conversely, if things go well, they should get the credit.

I believe in free enterprise, for I am convinced that this system throws up the best leadership. There are exceptions, of course, but on the whole the most able people do distinguish themselves and advance into the most responsible positions.

Modern management likes to use computers, and no doubt they can be of great help in decision-making, since they make the relevant data more rapidly available. But just as a man's character, when it comes to giving him a job, is more important than his diploma, so decisions are more than computer data. The ultimate choice is based on more than facts. Experience and vision have a part to play. In the last resort the man in charge has to follow an inner prompting, a voice deep down telling him what is right and what is wrong.

That does not mean that management is a kind of magic. But I believe that there is a system in our world. There are laws of nature like the force of gravity, which we disobey only at the peril of our lives and health. The man who disregards a red traffic light is likely to end up in hospital. In the same way, there is a kind of moral universe in which moral and spiritual standards operate. We can disregard those standards too, but it will do us no good. When a man is confronted in his private life with choices of right or wrong, he finds himself at a crossroad. If he decides wrongly, he will go in the wrong direction. This may not be immediately apparent, but it will become clear before long.

It is no different in industrial management. Of course a manager has to consider whether this or that activity will be profitable or not. But he cannot leave his duty towards his personnel, his country and the world, out of consideration.

Standards of right and wrong? They are linked with our Christian heritage and the cultural pattern of the West. Would these standards survive the destruction of this heritage? For it is at present under heavy attack from materialism on the right and from Marxism on the left. Even the churches and education are affected. Communist forces are gaining territory in continents like Africa. Yet at the same time the Communist system seems to be undergoing a deep crisis: dissidents are raising their voices all over Russia and Eastern Europe.

At any rate, the threat to our values system, from within and without, is a challenge for us. It demands a deep change in our mentality and philosophy, and a commitment to fight here and now and not to drift and to allow circumstances to decide for us. The West has succeeded many times before in averting attacks on its spiritual foundations. And it is my belief that the Creator did intend, as Frank Buchman put it, that hands be filled with work, stomachs with food and empty hearts with a militant faith which really satisfies. That should also be our purpose as industrialists.

In concluding this review of my forty-five years with a large international company, I should like to address myself especially to young people. In large enterprises there are fascinating jobs, inside Europe and on the other continents. A world is waiting for you. But you must know what you are working for and what you want the results of your efforts to be.

My wish for Philips is that it may continue to play the part it deserves and for which I and a great many others have worked. Once again the sentence which I wrote in the introduction of this book comes to mind: Philips must be part of the cure, and not of the disease, of the world.

Postscript

At the author's request his eldest daughter, Digna Hintzen, and his youngest son, Frits, have added personal contributions.

Looking at My Father

The eldest daughter has a special bond with her father. From mine came my love and knowledge of birds—something that never quite rubbed off on any of his other children! One spring evening, when I was about ten, we left by bicycle for a friend's cottage to go birdwatching early next morning, and there we saw the only bittern I have ever come across in its natural surroundings. My father also knew a lot about history and architecture, and these we learned about while bicycling through the villages of Brabant. But the rainy Sunday afternoons when he tried to explain to his daughters how an engine works were less successful, I am afraid.

After the war, when there were seven of us plus a foster-sister at the table, meals were terribly noisy. There was rarely any conversation at all, which was probably why my father never told us anything serious about his work, but only, at times, some of the funny things. One day we cut out a cartoon from the *Saturday Evening Post* with the caption, 'Don't shoot Daddy, save him for the laughs!' Perhaps this attitude helped him to keep a balance in life, as more and more people in the outside world looked up to him. We used to tease him about his hobbies, his love of pewter and other antiques, and the outlandish clothes which were often presented to him on his journeys and which he loved to dress up in for acts at parties. His other specialities were—and are—his performance as a cartoonist, and a sometimes quite brilliant kind of cabaret when he dresses up in the typical outfit of a Brabant peasant—blue shirt, red kerchief and black cap. He surprised all the guests by doing this at the end of a variety show given by Philips people in honour of his fortieth anniversary with the firm.

As a father he had always been most caring, but it was only when I was with him abroad that I started to appreciate him in his capacity as a devoted Philips man. During the years I spent working with Moral Re-Armament in Latin America, I went with him on several of his visits to Philips companies in various countries, and more recently also I have joined my parents on some of these trips, sometimes acting as interpreter in Spanish and Portuguese. For it is often hard for a local interpreter to catch the exact meaning of what my father says, or to translate his jokes!

On these trips I was impressed by several things. First of all was the way he entered into the local situation. I remember a dinner in Iquitos, a town on the Amazon in the eastern jungles of Peru. His hosts were the mayor and the district commanders of the Army and the Navy. He told them how many more miles of waterway they had than we have in Holland, and how amazed he was at the way they were tackling the task of building roads and bridges in that vast area.

I was also struck by his knowledge of the history of different countries, and his vision for their future. Once he had an interview with the President of a Latin American republic, a man of Marxist orientation. Drawing on the history of that nation, he told the President his vision for the country and the dangers he saw. The interview far exceeded its allotted time, and the young Philips manager who was there told me afterwards, 'I never thought I would be present at such a conversation, man to man, with this President. Mr. Philips talked to him as though he was his father. I learned a lot.'

But during these visits my father's heart goes out most of all to 'his own people', the Philips staff, whether they are Dutch or from the country itself. He always insists on having an occasion where he can meet|them with their wives. And, when he makes a speech, it is more like a father talking to his emigrant children. We once had a lunch in the countryside near Bogotà in Colombia, where he tackled over-eager Philips employees who were letting their jobs take priority over their family life. 'If you are not happy at home you won't do your job well, no matter how much you want to impress your boss,' he said, and added, 'And when you have long forgotten this visit of ol' man Philips, I hope you will remember these words.'

Of course he fights hard for the Philips cause during these visits. If one more conversation with a cabinet minister can help, he is always game. But he does not talk much about it. When there is any spare time, he likes to use it to learn more about the country he is visiting. For instance, if he sees a group of workers digging Inca ruins he will say, 'That man over there is wearing a gold watch, although he is dressed like the others. I'm sure he can tell us about what they are doing. Go and ask him.' And then there will be an interesting and informed conversation.

Thanks to his excellent health, maintained by a dive into a swimming pool or a game of tennis whenever there is a chance, my father manages a hectic programme with very late nights remarkably well.

On a trip like this the phrase, 'It'll just be us,' never means only the family. It always includes the local Philips manager and his wife, and the man from Eindhoven who is responsible for liaison with that particular region. And this man's wife, back in Holland, is never forgotten. There is a postcard or a greetings telegram and a sample of local handicrafts as consolation for her husband's absence. In this way a bond of friendship, almost a family tie, is created. One of these men once told us how he was in São Paulo with my parents when the news reached him that his mother had died. They asked him into their room early in the mornmg, talked with him about his mother and whether or not he should return. 'At the end they prayed with me. I'll never forget such personal care,' he said.

I must mention one of my father's characteristics, perhaps an enviable one, although it can be exasperating for those responsible for his programme. This is his amazing freedom from the dictatorship of time, and with it his ability to gauge which things are of long-term value. Once I stayed with him in London with a retired army colonel and his wife, charming elderly people. We were there only for one night, and had to leave early in the morning. Some people in British industry wanted to talk to my father, and we had arranged for them to meet him for half an hour before he left for the office. This only left fifteen minutes for breakfast, and English breakfast at that! I had suspected that it might last a little longer, but when the colonel embarked upon a long story to which my father listened with great interest, prodding him with questions, I really got uneasy. When finally we left the table for his meeting he said to me, 'You know, they are such nice people. I thought I should really take time for them.' I don't remember what happened to the rest of his programme, but I have never forgotten this remark.

It is the same quality which makes him say to the people in his office on a winter morning, 'The De Wielewaal woods are so beautiful, with the sun on the frosty trees. You must come with me in the car and see them. In years to come no one will know how many letters we got through this morning, but a drive like this stays with you for the rest of your life.'

His vision for the Evoluon, the permanent exhibition on humanity and technology, was originally shared by few, but the crowds of all ages who pour in daily have proved he was right.

This sense of what will count most over the years also lay behind his conviction that all the Philips managers from around the world should be at the celebrations of the 75th anniversary of the company: 'To have lived through an occasion like that together is a tremendous inspiration when you are on a lonely outpost, sweating your heart out for the company.' And how true this proved to be, for they were unforgettable days.

The same is true of family celebrations, when he likes to gather his children and grandchildren from all corners of the earth: 'Life is so short, and if you don't make a point of it you see so little of each other . . .' And if possible a good number of cousins are included.

My father is not the kind of man who goes around advertizing his faith. Yet you can tell immediately whether he is relying on his own gifts and charm or whether, aware of his limitations, he is searching for guidance and inspiration 'from above'. To this he is extraordinarily receptive; perhaps he is less troubled by preconceived ideas than most people. I believe this inspiration, whatever it is, has shown him the way to the heart in countless conversations, as well as how to hit the right note when he has been talking to a larger number of people.

Wassenaar, 1975   *Digna Hintzen-Philips*

A Son About His Father

When my father asked me to add a son's perspective to his autobiography and told me that it would mean a lot to him, I felt so flattered that I said 'yes' before I realized what was involved. It is one thing to have a chat with him, and to talk about him with friends and acquaintances is no real problem to me. In both cases I know whom I am talking to and can check how my message comes across. I can clarify and correct, if necessary. But in communicating to you, a complete stranger, I am in a quandary. For who are you? What would you be interested to know about the author from a son's viewpoint? And, on the other hand, what do I want to communicate to you? How open do I want to be—and dare to be—with you about something as essentially personal and private as my relationship with my father? Simple questions, hard to answer!

I decided to go ahead, after six months' hesitation, for two reasons. First, I just did not have the heart to let my father down. Second, I have some true missionary zeal when it comes to getting my message across to an audience. And in this context my message is that, at various stages of my life, I benefited from my father's clear insights and practical philosophy, and I wish that others had had the same wisdom at their disposal. So I would like to reproduce some of those insights, using his language when I remember it, my own when I cannot trace them back to any statements he made but where it was his attitude that influenced me.

Fights

'It's all right with me if you hit each other over the head when you quarrel, as long as you talk it over immediately afterwards.' In practical terms this meant that the warring parties among us seven children would bring the following procedure into effect:

   each party offers his apologies to the 'opposition' for the (clearly negligible!) extent to which he was responsible for the conflict;
   both parties try to find the best solution on the basis of 'what's right, not who's right';
   if that does not work, the conflicting parties join my mother in a 'quiet time' of listening to find a solution to the problem.

Of course, our conflicts were fierce and frequent enough—no angels in our family!—but, thanks to this immediate and systematic approach, the air was cleared fairly quickly. There were no lasting or embittering wars between us. I cannot remember ever having gone to bed with a conflict still unresolved.

Learning and development

'The cleverness you need to succeed in school is valued much too highly by most people. Of course, you need to be reasonably knowledgeable in life, but I think that it is much more important that you turn out to be a pleasant and reliable person whom others want to co-operate with. That's why I think it is such a good experience for you to play sports in a team. You can only understand through practical experience what it means to work as a team.'

'If teachers would exchange their remote teaching positions for practical assignments every so many years, they would have a much clearer understanding of the qualities in young people that society is crying out for.'

'Sometimes you run into people whose development as human beings with a sense of balance and integrity has not kept up with their intellectual development. They've become so clever, they outreason themselves, as well as the people around them, with terrible consequences for everyone. Beware!'

When I was wondering if I should study law at Leiden University, he told me emphatically: 'Of course you should go. You'll learn a lot. Surely, the knowledge you'll pick up is the least important part of it. What's more important is that you'll develop as a person and make friends from all over the country. You'll be able to discover what kind of problems you're really interested in, and to study those problems at your leisure. It will not always be an easy time, but you'll benefit from it, and I'm sure you'll also have a lot of fun in the process. I'm sure you're clever enough to pass your exams.' (Which I did, in reasonable time.)

'What's more, when you're a graduate yourself, you're not likely to be over-impressed by others with academic credentials. You won't even be surprised when they occasionally make incredibly silly statements, particularly when you find you're capable of producing them yourself!'

On work

"How are you? What are you doing these days? Is it fun?' These are the questions he likes to ask when he runs into someone he has not seen for some time.

'You have to invest so much time and energy in your work, the only way to keep going is to enjoy what you're doing.' What does he mean when he refers to work as fun, as something you should be able to enjoy? What follows is what I have distilled from the many talks we had on the subject. Some of the ideas expressed here are clearly his. Others are mine, but reflect his influence, by example, on my thinking about work. They have fused into a unity that has made it impossible for me to make the distinction.

To be 'fun', work must meet a number of requirements. First, the job content must appeal to you. The problems you have to tackle must be important enough to deserve your commitment and interesting enough to spark your curiosity and provoke your inventiveness. That is why it is important to figure out beforehand what you find important in life and what kinds of problems stimulate you.

Second, as you are working your way into the job, you should try to develop a 'vision': a clear view of the direction in which you want to move and an understanding of how you will get there. Such a vision helps you to translate your general sense of direction into a daily course of priorities. It provides a perspective that makes the difficult and plainly boring parts of your job more acceptable. You know they are part and parcel of the job and by dealing with them you will have made some practical progress.

Third, moving in that direction should be both important and fun. Try and find people you enjoy working with: pleasant, with a good sense of humour, who do not take themselves too seriously and who dare, and know how, to be playful. My father: 'Usually if you enjoy your job, you will soon learn how to do it well.' And on another occasion: 'Many people view their work purely as a liability, a burden. What a pity! Work is there to be done, but also to be thoroughly enjoyed! You must take the time to enjoy life, on and off the job.'

Finally, by means of your work you should seek and exploit opportunities to develop those qualities that are uniquely yours. You should do this for your own satisfaction, but you also have a responsibility towards your family, your organization and society to do so. Your work should be a stimulus to and a reflection of your creativity. That is why it is important to care about what you are doing, for you can only be creative in work you care about.

Fighting for what is right

'When you have looked thoroughly into a problem and have come to certain conclusions, you must have the courage to stand up and fight for them. You shouldn't be influenced by whether your point of view is popular or not. But if you have to fight, make sure you don't take issue with people but only with their misconceptions. You should be able to disagree vigorously with a person and yet maintain a relationship with him. Later on when the business requires it, either of you should be able to turn to the other for help or co-operation. You can't afford to let your relationship with someone be strained simply because you disagree with him. If you consistently took that attitude, you would end up talking to nobody.'

When you find yourself in such a confrontation with my father, you find that his engagingly cordial behaviour makes it very hard to reject his reasoning. He paternally confirms you as a younger person; at the same time his amiable tone of voice urges you to accept—in your own interest, of course!—the suggestion that he, as your elder, more experienced and thus wiser counsellor, knows what is best for you.

You get to know him as the amiable leader who is used to being followed and as the astute bargainer who loves getting his way: the benevolent patriarch! When you insist on claiming your own responsibility for a decision and on setting your own course, he sends out the hurt signals of someone who has been personally rejected: 'All right, it's up to you. If you want to be so damned obstinate about it!' Clearly, you are the 'wise guy' in this situation. However, such an incident does not unsettle our relationship. After all, in this respect, we both practise what he preaches!

Eindhoven, March 1977   *Frits Philips*

Appendix

Some basic considerations on industrial policy

The industrial enterprise fulfils an important economic and social role in society. Its primary function consists in the production of goods and the provision of services. It thereby creates employment and income and opportunity for personal development for many people in and outside the enterprise. The market economy in which it operates is a stimulus to the development of new products and techniques and new forms of organization. Its research, geared to possibilities in the future, contributes to the scientific potential of society. All these factors have enabled industrial enterprise to have a positive influence on the growth of prosperity and well-being.

Private enterprise, essentially characterised by initiative, adaptability, resourcefulness and the willingness to take risks, must have sufficient freedom of action if it is to be able to adjust to constantly changing circumstances. In turn, private enterprise is expected to understand its position and role in society.

The increase in the mutual involvement of enterprise and society has led Philips to formulate for itself some basic considerations for the policy of enterprise.

Basic considerations

● In fulfilling its function, Philips aims at the continuity of its enterprise. This continuity, for which profitability is indispensable, is vital to the interests of employees as well as of the providers of capital, of directly involved third parties and of society at large.
● Philips must therefore ensure a sufficiently strong financial position, which entails seeking a return on capital that is adequate for the reasonable remuneration of shareholders and others who provide the financial or capital resources and that enables necessary self-financing of operations and investments.

- Philips considers it to be its task towards its employees:
—to aim at an organization and at work that enable each employee to make optimal use of his talents and skills and to have appropriate responsibility;
—to provide safe and satisfactory working conditions;
—to give adequate information and to promote two-way communication at all levels of the organization;
—to encourage the development of representative internal consultation.
- Terms and conditions of employment must meet the reasonable needs of all employees and must enable the company to attract and retain qualified personnel. Philips is prepared to negotiate on these matters with the representative associations in which employees are organised.
- Philips has relations with many groups in society—its employees, those who provide the financial and capital resources, its suppliers and customers, the local community and a wide variety of other groups—and recognises the interest of each of these groups.
- Because of the ever-growing interaction between the various groups in in society, Philips must extend its contacts beyond those groups that make up its business relations. Philips will have to maintain contacts with social institutions such as educational bodies and religious and cultural organizations and is open to the views and stimuli resulting from such contacts.
- Philips pays great attention to the utility, soundness and safety of its products and to the requirements imposed on its services. In a broader context, too, it wishes its products and services to respond to the needs of society.
- Philips is alive to the necessity of making responsible and economic use of natural resources such as water, living space, air and raw materials.
- Philips endeavours to contribute towards economic and social development in countries of settlement, working in harmony with local circumstances and cultural patterns. Within the structures of the social and legal order it will work towards improvements in social and other areas where this is compatible with its tasks.

The future of private enterprise will be partially determined by the manner in which it is experienced by groups in society. It is of the utmost importance therefore that the policy of enterprise should be clear and unambiguous.

Board of Management
N.V. Philips' Gloeilampenfabrieken   May 1975

Index